MW01141863

ON PILGRIMAGE
WITH
MAGNIFICAT

Publisher: Pierre-Marie Dumont

Editor: Peter John Cameron, O.P.

Copy editor: Susan Barnes

Proofreader: Janet Chevrier

Assistant to the Editorial Staff: Romain Lizé

Iconography: Isabelle Mascaras

Cover and inset: Anaïs Acker

Production: Annie-Laurie Clément

Concept and Design: MAGNIFICAT

Cover: *Mother and Child*, Franz Dvorak (1862-1927), Private collection.
© Whitford & Hughes, London, UK / Bridgeman Giraudon.

Inset: *The Triumph of Religion in the Arts* (1840), Johann Friedrich
Overbeck (1789-1869), Städel Museum, Frankfurt, Germany.
© Ursula Edelmann / Artothek.

ISBN: 978-0-9798086-3-0

First edition: September 2008

© MAGNIFICAT USA LLC

ON PILGRIMAGE
WITH
MAGNIFICAT

MAGNIFICAT®

TABLE OF CONTENTS

AN INTRODUCTION TO THE MAGNIFICAT WAY OF LIFE
ROMANUS CESSARIO, O.P.

Mara: "Violaine, I am not worthy to read this Book! Violaine, I know that my heart is too hard, and I am sorry for it: I wish I could be different."
Violaine: "Read on, Mara. You do not know who chants the responses."

[Silence...]

Mara (with an effort takes up the Book, and reads in a trembling voice):
"The Holy Gospel according to Saint Luke." [1]

Paul Claudel

---

1. Paul Claudel, *The Tidings Brought to Mary: A Mystery*, trans. Louise Morgan Sill (New Haven: Yale University Press, 1916), act three, scene three, p. 117.

SACRAMENTAL MEDIATION IN THE CHURCH

Among the excerpts from Sacred Scripture that have found their way into the life and liturgy of the Church, the Canticle of Mary written in the first chapter of Saint Luke's Gospel holds a preeminent place. The *Magnificat* (Lk 1: 46-55) records the divinely inspired words that the Blessed Virgin Mary spoke to her relative, Saint Elizabeth, on the occasion of visiting the house of the latter's husband, the prophet-priest Zechariah. This celebrated visit occurred immediately after Mary had received the message from the angel Gabriel that she would become the Mother of God. When he describes what the Church now calls the Visitation of the Blessed Virgin Mary, Saint Luke reminds his readers that both women, Mary and Elizabeth, were with child. Mary carried in her womb the incarnate Son of God. Elizabeth, though advanced in years, was pregnant with Christ's precursor, Saint John the Baptist.

Place yourself for a moment at the scene of the Visitation. Mary brings the embryonic Christ to her cousin Elizabeth, and thereby puts him in personal contact with the child that Elizabeth carries in her own womb. This encounter foreshadows the pattern of sacramental life that today flourishes in the Church of Christ. Why this foreshadowing? Why attach a sacramental interpretation to the Visitation? The answer is simple: something parallel to what occurs at the Visitation happens to Catholics when they receive one of the seven sacraments. Each of the seven sacraments of the Church brings us into personal contact with Jesus Christ.

For a number of years now, we have become accustomed to think of the sacraments as symbols or signs. The mystery of the Visitation reminds us that these sacred signs further supply, to those who receive them in a proper manner, effective instruments of God's healing forgiveness and upbuilding love. In a word, the sacraments do something. Through a visible, external action, God accomplishes an interior, invisible effect. We call this sacramental effect "grace" or "favor." "Grace" means that we share in God's life and friendship. The Church gets to the heart of all sacramental mediation when she explains trenchantly that "the sacraments confer the grace that they signify." [2] Even as she affirms that this principle of Catholic faith applies preeminently to each of the seven sacraments, Catholics may by analogy extend the principle to include every genuine instrument of invisible grace. Some saints recognize a sacramental character in the whole of creation. To adapt the words of one philosopher: "It is as if one plunged into the ocean, to find on its floor a magic mirror in which the sky were reflected." [3]

Does evidence exist that some form of proto-sacramental mediation or causality occurs at the moment Mary greets Elizabeth? Yes. Elizabeth supplies her own witness to what occurred. She tells Mary and the world that upon her arrival and at her greeting, "the infant in my womb leaped for joy" (Lk 1: 44). The child of course is John the Baptist. It is commonly accepted that this leaping for joy provided the external sign of John's cleansing from original sin. In other words, Marys greeting effected the hidden baptism of the man who would himself baptize Christ. [4] Through the maternal mediation of the Mother of God, John the Baptist first met the Savior of the world. So also today, Catholics meet Christ in the sacraments, and in those things that help them celebrate worthily the sacraments of the Church. The intuition that we meet Christ in the sacraments enjoys a long history in Catholic thought, many saints having remarked that, while Christ no longer

---

2. See CCC 1127: The sacraments "are efficacious because in them Christ himself is at work."

3. Jacques Maritain, *La philosophie de la nature* (Paris: Tequi, 1935), p. 29.

4. See the treatment of this question by Saint Thomas Aquinas in his *Summa theologiae* IIIa q. 27, art. 6, where the author however reports the hesitancy that Saint Augustine expressed in his Letter to Dardanus (Letter 187, PL 33: 840-41) about the uterine sanctification of John the Baptist.

remains physically present among us, Catholics still meet him in the sacraments.

The Visitation of the Blessed Virgin Mary comprises many mysteries of faith. Catholics cherish the encounter of Mary with Elizabeth, the aged wife of Zechariah, the man struck dumb for failing to believe what had been spoken to him by an angel. They recognize in the Visitation an icon of the personal contact with Christ that Catholics enjoy each time they receive, especially from the hands of a priest, one of these seven sacraments. They also discover a more general pattern of mediation that exists in the Church. We behold Mary bringing Jesus to Elizabeth, and we gradually realize that God has provided the Church with many forms of mediation. At the center of this pattern of sacred persons and sacred things, stands for ever and excellently the Blessed Virgin Mary. In contrast to Zechariah, she believed the word that the angel spoke to her. For she had "found favor with God" (Lk 1: 30). Above all, the MAGNIFICAT way of life, which configures the life of faith and sacraments to the personal requirements of each one who follows this way, aims to draw those who repeat Mary's prayer into the same divine grace and favor that is hers in super-abundance. The *Magnificat* transforms each day into a day of divine visitation.

MARY'S *MAGNIFICAT* AND CHRISTIAN LIFE

From the instant that the Eternal Son of God becomes man, his mission of sanctifying love and onerous redemption proceeds through a set of concrete relationships that involve in one way or another the cooperation of his mother. In an important piece of Marian instruction, Pope John Paul II enunciated a key principle that governs the MAGNIFICAT way of life. "The Church," wrote the pope, "which from the beginning has modeled her earthly journey on that of the Mother of God, constantly repeats after her the words of the *Magnificat*." [5] The pope went on to encourage Catholics to join the company of the Blessed Virgin Mary, and to sustain the Canticle of Mary, her *Magnificat*, as a perpetual hymn of praise and thanksgiving.

The counsel to repeat the *Magnificat* follows a centuries-long tradition of Catholic liturgical and devotional practice. In fact, the Church daily provides an occasion when Catholics together sing Mary's hymn of praise and thanksgiving. In the Liturgy of the Hours, the official prayer of the Church, Evening Prayer always concludes with the *Magnificat*. For generations, Catholics, both extraordinary saints and everyday believers, have brought their days to a close echoing the *Magnificat* of Mary. They have made her prayer their own. They have joined the poverty of their own hearts to the abundance of graces that God infused into what the French priest Saint John Eudes named the Most Pure Heart of the Blessed Virgin Mary. This self-committal to a mother brings a serene peace to the world, when the bustle of the day's obligations and the distractions of the day's business are left behind, and Catholics everywhere turn to Mary as they anticipate the repose that night brings. We come to the conclusion that when they recite the *Magnificat*, Catholics sacramentally bless the nightly repose and prepare themselves to welcome the dawn.

When Pope John Paul II reminded the Church that we should repeat again and again Mary's *Magnificat*, he also followed a tradition well documented in the lives of the saints. Take one example. A great lover of Our Lady in the seventeenth century, another French priest, Saint Louis-Marie Grignon de Montfort, explains why this prayer remains so important for the Church. The *Magnificat*, he says, "is the only prayer, the only work, which the Holy Virgin composed, or rather, which Jesus composed in her; for He spoke by her mouth." To give some indication of the

---

5. Encyclical Letter of Pope John Paul II, "Mother of the Redeemer" (*Mater Redemptoris*), no. 37.

importance of repeating the *Magnificat*, the saint goes on to suggest that Mary's prayer, her canticle, represents "the greatest sacrifice of praise which God ever received from a pure creature in the law of grace." In this prayer, Mary sums up all the expectations of Israel, and expresses once and for all the confidence that the Church, the new Israel, maintains before God: "He has mercy on those who fear him in every generation" (Lk 1: 50). No wonder de Montfort concludes about the *Magnificat*, "There are in that song mysteries so great and hidden that the angels do not know them." [6]

EUCHARISTIC LITURGY AND DIVINE WORSHIP

It is not easy to uncover mysteries that remain hidden even from the angels. MAGNIFICAT, however, takes on the task. Those persons responsible for composing MAGNIFICAT aspire to provide its readers a glimpse of "things into which angels longed to look" (1 Pt 1: 12). The features that appear regularly in the monthly MAGNIFICAT supply discreet markers of grace that, like surveyors' measurements, establish the contours of the MAGNIFICAT way of life. Of course in the final analysis, the MAGNIFICAT way of life embodies the biblically warranted life of faith and sacraments lived out in full communion with the Catholic Church. MAGNIFICAT does not provide a forum for an alternative practice of the Catholic faith. It supplies only what is helpful to enter deeply into the mysteries of the Catholic faith. At the center of these mysteries and the communion they generate stands the Eucharist, source and apex of the Church's worship.

MAGNIFICAT manifests integrally the Church's liturgical life, which itself constitutes the summit toward which the activity of

---

6. Louis-Marie Grignon de Montfort, quoted in *Virgin Wholly Marvelous*, ed. David Supple, O.S.B. (Cambridge, MA: The Ravensgate Press, 1981), p. 41.

the Church is directed.[7] No wonder that the Church instructs her priests that they should encourage Mass-goers with the words: "Lift up your hearts" [Hofer]. Each Mass affords the opportunity for Catholics to pray exquisitely and full-heartedly to God. Above all, the Mass remains an act of worship of God. Through this act of worship the Mass creates the communion of believers who, because of Christ's once-and-for-all sacrifice, find themselves united in the same religion. Philosophers like to point out that Christianity exhibits the characteristic of being a transnational religion. Catholics throughout the world form a worldwide communion of friends. Those who use MAGNIFICAT likewise constitute within the Church a worldwide family of readers and subscribers.

The act of Eucharistic worship also provides our Holy Communion. It is the Bread of Life, our Bread from Heaven [Esolen]. Only those who are ready to receive so great a gift do so fruitfully. There is a venerable Catholic hymn that captures with delicacy the dynamics of the Eucharist when this unsurpassable Gift is introduced into the world of sinners.

> *Both the wicked and the good*
> *Eat of this celestial Food;*
> *But with ends how opposite!*
> *Here 'tis life; and there 'tis death;*
> *The same, yet issuing to each*
> *In a difference infinite.*[8]

---

7. See "Constitution on the Sacred Liturgy," *Sacrosanctum Concilium*, no. 10 in *The Documents of Vatican II*, trans. W. M. Abbott (New York: Herder & Herder, 1966), p. 142.

8. Saint Thomas Aquinas, *Officium de festo Corporis Christi ad mandatum Urbani Papae*: Sequence for the Mass, *Lauda Sion*, strophe 9: "Sumunt boni, sumunt mali:/ Sorte tamen inaequali,/ Vitae vel interitus./ Mors est malis, vita bonis:/ Vide, paris sumptionis/ Quam sit dispar exitus." See David Hiley, *Western Plainchant: A Handbook* (Oxford: OUP, 1993), II.22, pp. 172-95.

The Eucharist neither traps unsuspecting sinners nor sets up a game of chance where the outcome remains uncertain until the last day. According to the plan of divine mercy, God has provided for imparting forgiveness to sinners. God makes it possible for us to return to this celestial Food with most pure hearts. We receive new hope – a new "end" – through the sacrament of penance.

MAGNIFICAT devotes considerable space to preparing Catholics to receive the sacrament of penance and reconciliation. The examinations of conscience are especially helpful. We use them to move us away from what is old. The saints always look at things with a fresh outlook. One of them, Venerable Pio Bruno Lanteri, liked to remark: "Now I begin!" [9] [Carzon]. Penance offers the forgiven Catholic an opportunity to start over, to begin afresh. Now! We are fortunate to meet Christ in this sacrament where, through the ministry of his ordained priests, the Lord himself pronounces the words that untie and loosen: "And I absolve you."

When we have sinned grievously, penance and reconciliation admit us back into Eucharistic communion. To receive Holy Communion is a great gift; however, everyone, including sinners, may place themselves in the saving presence of the Lamb of God. It is characteristic of Christian believers that they want to dwell with the Eucharist, and when possible to seek the opportunity to come before the Blessed Sacrament for adoration and praise. We are reminded of this invitation each time the priest at Mass holds up the host and says, "This is the Lamb of God" [Bushman].

The high place that Christ accords to his priests who dispense the sacraments of new life compels those who exercise the priestly office and, what is more important, those young men who are

---

9. Pio Bruno Lanteri, "Pertanto se verrò a mancare anche mille volte al giorno, mille volte pacificamente compunto dirò subito: Nunc coepi, mio Dio, mio Dio!" English translation: "Even if I should fall a thousand times a day, a thousand times peacefully repentant I will say immediately: Nunc coepi (Now I begin), my God, my God!" (See the notes in Father Carzon's essay in this volume for reference to the works of Pio Bruno Lanteri).

being drawn to become priests, to seek spiritual support. They especially appreciate the words that Saint Thérèse of Lisieux, after her retreat in 1897, addressed to the Blessed Virgin Mary:

> *"When I'm struggling, O my dear Mother,*
> *You strengthen my heart in the fight.*
> *For you know, at the evening of this life*
> *I want to offer Priests to the Lord!"* [10]

What a great consolation comes to priests and to the Church from this expression of sisterly solicitude!

SAVING INSTRUCTION FOUND IN THE CHURCH

The Catholic tradition compares the seven sacraments to the canonical – that is, the authentic – Scriptures. As Saint Thomas Aquinas teaches us, in order to describe spiritual realities to us, Scripture employs corresponding sensible realities. [11] MAGNIFICAT appears among us as an especially efficacious instrument of the divine word, of God's Word. No Christian life develops without prayerful exposure to the revealed word of God that is contained within the Bible. Many persons are unable to attend Mass each day, but the Church encourages the salutary practice of reading the scriptural texts assigned to each day of the Church's liturgical calendar. These readings present, as it were, the foundation for everything else which transpires in the Church that day. Why should we read the Scriptures every day? There are many reasons. One is suggested by the image of the two-edged sword found in Hebrews, chapter 4. This text reminds us of our need for personal enlightenment, for illumination: "Indeed, the word of God is living and effective, sharper than any two-edged sword, penetrating even

---

10. "To Our Lady of Perpetual Help," 4th couplet in *The Poetry of Saint Thérèse of Lisieux*, trans. Donald Kinney, O.C.D. (Washington, D.C.: ICS Publications, 1996), p. 198.
11. See, for example, Saint Thomas Aquinas, *Summa theologiae* IIIa q. 60, a. 4.

between soul and spirit, joints and marrow, and able to discern reflections and thoughts of the heart" (Heb 4: 12) [Turro]. This passage from Scripture reminds us that darkness envelops those who remain alienated from the light of Jesus Christ. We need to receive light so that we can discover the truth about ourselves, so that we can discern the thoughts of our hearts. One source of light emanates from the daily Scripture readings that are found in every issue of MAGNIFICAT. Catholics appreciate the illumination that the Sacred Scriptures bring into their minds. They know, moreover, that they require such illumination as a means for obtaining their salvation, for "everything is naked and exposed to the eyes of him to whom we must render an account" (Heb 4: 13).

While the Scriptures are easy to read, they are not always easy to understand. Everybody needs to take a step back, and to look for some help. Making sense of Scripture falls to those who have been deputed officially with the task of unlocking the mysteries of the faith contained in the revealed word of God. The Scriptures first of all belong to the Church. Only in the Church do Christian believers discover the authentic meaning of Sacred Scripture [Girard]. Christ himself initiated and thereby gave warrant for all time to this ecclesial norm and practice. We read about his doing this in the Gospels. Again it is Saint Luke who reports that the risen Christ met two disciples while they were on the road to Emmaus: "Then beginning with Moses and all the prophets, he interpreted to them what referred to him in all the scriptures" (Lk 24: 27).

The hidden richness of the biblical texts today awaits us. To discover these riches, we can turn to saints and spiritual authors, who themselves have learned from the Church what the Scriptures instruct us about God's love. When we pay close attention to the whole body of revealed truth contained in the canon of Scripture, that is, the books of the Bible recognized by the Church, our minds are opened. When we turn to those who have engaged in this saving exercise in the past, those who have already discovered the hidden richness of the biblical texts and have left us records of their reflections, our lives become enriched. It is not a sign of weakness that we need help making sense of the Scriptures. Rather, the instinct to try to obtain help shows that we understand another variation of the mediation that God has established within the Church. God willed that we rely on others so that both saving grace and saving instruction will extend throughout the world and proceed for all generations. Our Lady predicted that this divine activity would center on her when she proclaimed: "From now on will all ages call me blessed" (Lk 1: 48).

Throughout the course of a given year, MAGNIFICAT supplies excerpts from recognized authors who interpret for us the Word of God. By reading these texts, we discover little by little the dimensions of God's love in the world. We discover "what is the breadth and length and height and depth" of Christ's love (see Eph 3: 18, 19). In a word, those who observe the MAGNIFICAT way of life seek to discover daily the hidden mysteries of God's love that unfold in the Scriptures, as well as in everything that transpires in our lives. They make this discovery not so much by way of intellectual operation as by affective beholding. The MAGNIFICAT way of life grows when Catholics become accustomed to praying, not just using, their MAGNIFICAT [Cameron].

READING AND PRAYING WITH MAGNIFICAT

The *Magnificat* is the song both of the Mother of God and of the Church: so affirms the *Catechism of the Catholic Church*.[12] Catholic believers pray in imitation of Mary and in union with the whole Church. Their daily prayer observes the rhythms of the twenty-four hour day. In monasteries and religious houses, specific times are prescribed for personal or private prayer as well as for the liturgical offices that punctuate the daily routines of

---

12. CCC 2619.

monks and religious. Monasteries practice the Catholic life in a way that exceeds all other models. We witness in the lives of contemplative men and women an exemplary expression of the MAGNIFICAT way of life. [13] Monks and nuns were not the only early Christians who worshiped according to a daily rhythm of prayer. When the laity use MAGNIFICAT, they are also following the practices of early Church assemblies that date back at least to the third century.

The *Catechism of the Catholic Church* stipulates vocal prayer, meditation, and contemplative prayer as the specific forms of prayer recognized in the Church. [14] MAGNIFICAT mainly supplies an assortment of vocal prayers that suit the various requirements of the Catholic believer. The daily offices – Prayer in the Morning, Prayer in the Evening, and Prayer at Night – may be used by individuals or in groups. These offices in fact provide samples of "the form of prayer most readily accessible to groups." [15] They allow the laity, whose legitimate vocation in life keeps them in the world, the opportunity to establish their own rhythms of prayer. Lay men and women do not pray the daily MAGNIFICAT offices in order to achieve a second-best form of Christian living. On the contrary, when laymen and laywomen use these daily offices, they embrace the best expression of prayer, but in a form adapted to the needs of those who live in the world, who raise families, and who by their own proper activities are charged to transform the world. When it is possible for persons together to use MAGNIFICAT, whether within the intimacy of the family or within the circles of religious fraternity or within ordinary parish prayer groups, one finds the comforting promise of the Lord realized: "For where two

---

13. Pope John Paul II, Post-Synodal Apostolic Exhortation, *Vita Consecrata*, no. 32.
14. See CCC 2700-2724.
15. CCC 2704.

or three are gathered together in my name, there am I in the midst of them" (Mt 18: 20).

MAGNIFICAT supplies hymns and the tunes to sing them so that the Christian people can pray twice, as an ancient proverb expresses it.[16] Singing sacred music makes gathering together in the Lord's name a joyful experience. When they lift up their voices in singing God's praises, Catholics also imitate Mary's canticle or hymn of praise and thanksgiving [Glen]. Words without thoughts rarely to heaven go. To make the best of vocal prayer, the practitioners of the MAGNIFICAT way of life accustom themselves to attach the longings of their hearts to their spoken or sung prayers. The psalms that appear in each of the daily offices express timeless prayers of the human heart that we can make our own. When we pray these ancient prayers, especially when our own hearts appear dry and weary, we join generations of Christians who have made the Psalter of David the basis for their personal exchanges with God [Elliott].

Praying with MAGNIFICAT begins with the meditations that each day capture one or another indispensable truth for Christian living. These texts are selected from the approved writings of ancient Christian writers, but also from recognized spiritual authors of later periods as well as those who are writing today. In short, the meditations expose the richness of the Church's treasury of spiritual wisdom. For example, we discover the much-valued testimonies of our Fathers in faith [Orlando]. This instruction occurs not so much by reading in order to become informed as it does by reading in order to become transformed. Meditation realizes a specific form of prayer, one that is generated with the help of spiritual texts that fill our minds with holy thoughts.

---

16. See *General Instruction of the Roman Missal*, no. 39: "There is... the ancient proverb: 'One who sings well prays twice.'" This ancient adage has been attributed incorrectly to Saint Augustine, but it does capture his thought on the relationship between song and prayer.

Those who adhere to the MAGNIFICAT way of life develop the habit of praying outside of the times allotted for prayer, whether they be public and communal or private and individual. Gradually, prayer moves away from being an activity; it emerges as a habit of the heart. Catholics need to form this habit of the heart in order to develop the life of recollection. Only the recollected life ensures that whatever we do is done in the name of the Lord Jesus. We receive this imperative from Saint Paul: "And whatever you do, in word or in deed, do everything in the name of the Lord Jesus, giving thanks to God the Father through him" (Col 3: 17). The recollected life provides the indispensable background for contemplative prayer that the Catechism describes in the words of Teresa of Ávila as "a close sharing between friends." [17]

There exists an ancient practice in the Church called *lectio divina*. So much does the Church value the right kind of instruction given to her members that she refers to this *lectio*, this reading, as "divine" or "sacred." From this sacred reading, friendship emerges. The more that we become absorbed in the holy thoughts that have been set down by Christians throughout the ages, the more we find ourselves growing steady in the MAGNIFICAT way of life. The movements of the heart experienced while engaged in *lectio divina* represent touches of divine grace that invite us to renewed communion with the Lord. So we discover a new source of constancy in our lives. Things no longer seem haphazard and willy-nilly. The daily flow of events that mark the passage of our weeks, and of our years, and of our lives, no longer strikes us as random and unforeseen. Instead, we come to view the things that happen one by one as transpiring under the watchful gaze of a providence that, whatever sufferings may befall us, we cannot help but recognize as a loving providence. In a word, we discover the reasons for Mary's canticle of praise and thanksgiving. Our prayer spills over into gratitude. We find ourselves

---

17. See CCC 2709.

observing, with Mary, what Saint Paul advised the people of ancient Thessalonica: "Continue steadfastly in prayer, being watchful in it with thanksgiving" (1 Thes 5: 18). To sum up, those who cultivate the practices of prayer, whether spoken prayer or contemplative prayer, develop a grateful, Magnificat heart. Their constant refrain becomes the words that the Church proclaims each time the Scriptures are read: "Thanks be to God" [Quirk].

Learning from Personal Examples and Exemplar Images

Mary stands at the center of the mediation of divine love that enters the world at the conception of her Son, our Lord Jesus Christ. "And the Word became flesh." She stands at the center, but she does not stand alone. Around her in heaven rejoice those holy men and women who have done the will of God throughout the ages. These are the saints, both those who are formally recognized and those who contribute to the building up of the Church but remain unknown, such as the countless Catholic martyrs whose names and witness are known only to God. The saints serve as spiritual guides for daily living [Martin]. Each Sunday at Mass, we profess with the whole Church that we believe in the communion of saints. Like all of the mysteries of the faith, we need help to penetrate the complete meaning of this article of Catholic and divine faith. The communion of saints, of course, means the Church, those members who have gone before us, those now living, and those still to be born – all those united together in Jesus and Mary.

One way to enter into the mysteries of the saints is to read their lives. We learn as it were to navigate by the stars through the variegated challenges life poses. One hymn to Our Lady, "'Tis the Month of Our Mother," includes this salutary exclamation: "How dark life's journey without Mary would be!" Mary and the saints point us in the right direction. They also help us escape the shoals.

They guide us to safe harbor. The Little Flower of Lisieux,
Thérèse Martin, liked to compare herself to a little boat sailing
toward the eternal shore. Her resolve was never to take her eyes
off Jesus, the Star of stars. [18] MAGNIFICAT offers daily accounts of
the lives and the witness of the saints of today and yesterday. The
overall impression that we take away from reading these accounts
should surpass our wildest imaginations. Who would have thought
of the thousands of different ways that men and women have
succeeded in realizing the Christian life. The Church has always
understood that the best way to discover the mysteries of the
Christian life is to draw close to the saints. So she keeps a list of
saints in a book called the *Martyrology*, the official calendar of
saints celebrated in the Church's liturgy. Many of these saints and
their stories appear in the pages of MAGNIFICAT.

The saints present themselves as so many personal illustrations
of the MAGNIFICAT way of life. The Church has always authorized
the veneration of their images along with the veneration of images
of Christ and the Blessed Virgin Mary. No one who has held a
MAGNIFICAT in his or her hand remains ignorant of the role that
sacred art – the Beautiful – plays in the sacramentalization of our
daily lives. We meet Christ in the sacraments. We also meet him
in sacred images. So much does the tradition of the Church recognize this form of encounter with Christ that she accords special
reverence to the most sacred images or icons of Christ, of Mary,
and of the saints. They become sacramentals. Sacred art opens up
the mysteries of the faith in a way that remains altogether unique.
The uniqueness springs from the fact that great works of art find
their basic structure in the incarnation of the Son of God. "And the
Word became flesh and made his dwelling among us" (Jn 1: 14).

---

18. "O Divine Pilot! whose hand guides me,/ I'm soon to see you on the eternal
shore./ Guide my little boat over the stormy waves in peace/ Just for today."
From "My Song for Today (1 June 1894)," in *The Poetry of Saint Thérèse of
Lisieux*, p. 52.

Artists draw out from their materials a form that is supra-intelligible, a form that surpasses the usual categories of interpretations. This form results from the word that the artist incarnates in paint or plaster or words or music, and this artistic form makes the difference between a work of art and an exercise in graphic design. Good art reflects the divine. We are drawn into the beauty of God and there discover the traces of his divine being: integrity or completeness, right proportions or harmony, and brightness or illumination. As *The Triumph of Religion in the Arts* [Morris] makes clear, there exists an affinity between art and divine truth. This painting, whose alternative title is *The Magnificat of Art*, depicts Mary with the child Jesus surrounded by certain key saints in heaven, and they are looking down on an assembly of artists and poets whose relationships to each other and the whole depict the relationship of Church to art and of truth to beauty. "Sacred art is true and beautiful when its form corresponds to its particular vocation: evoking and glorifying, in faith and adoration, the transcendent mystery of God." [19] Over and above the individual examples of beauty that come with each issue of MAGNIFICAT, there is the beautiful thing that MAGNIFICAT itself embodies. Like the form of life that it seeks to foster and develop, MAGNIFICAT itself possesses integrity, displays harmony, and radiates brightness. No wonder we all become accustomed to keeping it close at hand. We flee the ugly and the obscene. We are drawn to the beautiful and the chaste as to a friend.

THE "DOMESTIC CHURCH" AND LITURGICAL SEASONS

MAGNIFICAT belongs to the laity. It was, in fact, a Catholic husband and father of a large family who conceived and produced the first MAGNIFICAT and who continues as its chief support and guide. The majority of persons who work to make MAGNIFICAT

---

19. CCC 2502.

appear each month are members of Christ's lay faithful. MAGNI-FICAT, then, first of all belongs in the home. It above all purports to serve the needs of the domestic church. [20] One of the most difficult challenges that faces the Church today, at least in the Western world, emerges in the mandate to preserve Christian marriages. Ideological assaults on marriage and family appear in many disguises, some of which masquerade as progress [Franks]. No task weighs more heavily on Christian parents than that of introducing their children into the sacramental life of the Church. While there are outstanding examples of late-in-life converts to the MAGNIFICAT way of life, the surest way to make Christian life flourish remains the education and rearing of children in the Catholic faith. The Blessed Virgin Mary inspires Catholic parenting. Mary encourages Catholic parents lest they lose heart, lest they become tempted to think that other, more applauded ways of life exceed the MAGNIFICAT way of life.

The celebration of liturgical seasons does not belong only in churches. One of the best examples of liturgical renewal appears in the customs that families develop to introduce their children to the various liturgical seasons and the graces that are specific to them: Advent wreaths; lenten foods and practices: Easter eggs; feast day celebrations with special desserts. The list goes on. MAGNIFICAT frequently has suggestions for observance of the liturgical seasons with children in the home. In thus surpassing its didactic purpose, in offering practical instruction, MAGNIFICAT shows us how to live [Lickona]. Family members who use the many prayers, litanies, blessings, spiritual exercises, and other pious activities found in each month's MAGNIFICAT discover that their lives have become sacramentalized. The mystery of the Visitation has taken over.

---

20. The term "domestic church" comes from the Second Vatican Council, Dogmatic Constitution on the Church, *Lumen gentium*, no. 11. See also CCC 1655-1658.

When parents and children follow the MAGNIFICAT way of life, the domestic church comes alive, and gives new life to the Church. In the mystery of God's providence, families give way to new families and to new vocations in life. Some are blessed to maintain family ties long into the autumn of their lives, whereas others are left alone because of death or other causes of separation within the family. MAGNIFICAT provides consolation and help for spiritual growth in whatever circumstance of life one finds oneself. But as the Visitation of the Blessed Virgin Mary reminds us, special care is required to provide for each succeeding generation. Introduced to it by their parents, grandparents, godparents, or other guardians, children should become the first beneficiaries of the MAGNIFICAT way of life.

CONCLUSION

We began with the Visitation. Let us end with Easter. It is the great Saint Augustine who impressed on the Christian imagination the view that the Christian life forms a pilgrimage. "You are walking now by faith," he says to some newly baptized Catholics, "still on pilgrimage in a mortal body away from the Lord; but he to whom your steps are directed is himself the sure and certain way for you: Jesus Christ, who for our sake became man." [21] Then this great Doctor of the Church expresses the consoling thought that Christ himself provides already what we need to reach successfully the completion of the pilgrimage that constitutes Christian life. "For all who fear Jesus Christ," the Doctor of Grace tells us, "[Christ himself] has stored up abundant happiness, which he will reveal to those who hope in him, bringing it to completion when we have attained the reality which even now we possess in

---

21. Saint Augustine, *Sermo 8 in octava Paschae* 1, 4 (PL 46: 838, 841) cited in the *Liturgy of the Hours*, Office of Readings for the Sunday within the Octave of Easter, vol. II, p. 636.

hope." [22] The mention of fearing Jesus Christ should not cause us alarm. He is repeating Mary's *Magnificat*: "He has mercy on those who fear him in every generation" (Lk 1: 50). Like the Blessed Virgin Mary, Saint Augustine wants us to reverence Christ, to take the Lord and his life-giving mysteries seriously. Catholics are inducted into this life of reverent fear and sacramentalized hope by the Easter sacrament, baptism. Saint Augustine concludes his catechesis by assuring newly baptized Catholics and each member of the Church that "your own hope of resurrection, though not yet realized, is sure and certain, because you have received the sacrament or sign of this reality, and have been given the pledge of the Spirit." [23] This is the same Spirit that Gabriel announced would come upon Mary: "The holy Spirit will come upon you, and the power of the Most High will overshadow you. Therefore the child to be born will be called holy, the Son of God" (Lk 1: 35). Then the Gospel writer reports the words that continue to bring comfort to all practitioners of the MAGNIFICAT way of life: "And behold, Elizabeth, your relative, has also conceived a son in her old age, and this is the sixth month for her who was called barren; for nothing will be impossible for God" (Lk 1: 36-37).

---

22. Ibid.
23. Ibid., p. 637.

"LIFT UP YOUR HEARTS"

Praying the Parts of the Mass

ANDREW HOFER, O.P.

"Lift up your hearts!" These words of the priest celebrant to the faithful translate the ancient Christian call of *Sursum corda*. The joyful command directs our attention to the heavenly goal of the sacrifice of the Mass. In an Easter homily, Saint Augustine preaches the fittingness of this liturgical call for the members of Christ. Christ our Head is in heaven! On this account, Christians have their hearts lifted up to the Lord. This raising of hearts is not due to the people's own merits, but is a gift of God. Augustine explains that the priest bids the faithful to give thanks, because without God's grace our hearts would be earthbound. He concludes the homily by showing how this dialogue between the priest and the people comes before the sanctification of God's sacrifice and the reception of the body and blood of Christ. "So receive the sacrament in such a way," the North African Doctor preaches, "that you think about yourselves, that you retain unity in your hearts, that you always fix your hearts on high. Don't let your hope be placed on earth, but in heaven. Let your faith be firm in God; let it be acceptable to God. Because what here you don't see now, but believe, you are going to see there, where you will rejoice without end." [1]

Saint Augustine's preaching on "Lift up your hearts" can indeed help us see the importance of praying the parts of the Mass for daily life, that we on earth may fix our hearts always on high. In fact, one of the simplest definitions of prayers is precisely raising the heart to God (cf. CCC 2559). All of the various prayers, readings, hymns, antiphons, dialogues, gestures, and other actions of the Mass can be a ceaseless font of prayer to have our hearts raised. Throughout the Mass, the Lord comes to us where we are. He knows our weaknesses, fears, struggles, and sins. He knows them better than we ourselves do. Christ comes to us where we are – so that we will not stay there for ever! He leads us from a confession of our sinfulness at the beginning of the Mass to receiving his body, blood, soul, and divinity in Holy Communion. He directs our whole lives from earth to his home in heaven's endless joy. Praying the parts of the Mass thus traces the movements of the Lord who calls us to pick up our cross *daily* (cf. Lk 9: 23) and follow him to the heavenly Jerusalem. Thus, when we pray the parts of the Mass, we receive form and direction for the way we live daily life in a pilgrimage of hope.

PREPARATION TO PRAY THE MASS

Vatican II calls the eucharistic sacrifice "the source and summit of the Christian life." [2] As source, the Eucharist propels us to live the life of Christ. As summit, the Eucharist beckons us to be raised above what has gone before. All in our life that precedes the Mass

---

1. St. Augustine, Sermon 227 in *The Works of Saint Augustine: A Translation for the 21ˢᵗ Century*, Part III, Sermons, vol. 6: Sermons 184-229Z, trans. Edmund Hill, O.P. (New Rochelle, NY: New City Press, 1993), p. 256 (slightly revised).
2. Vatican II, *Lumen Gentium* 11.

can be seen as a preparation, as steps leading to "the altar of God, the God of my joy" (Ps 43: 4).

In order to pray the parts of the Mass properly, some preparations are absolutely needed. Saint Justin Martyr, in the middle of the second century, noted three requirements for reception of the Eucharist: faith in the teachings taught, baptism for the remission of sins, and conduct of life as Christ has commanded.[3] These are the basics that the Church has consistently emphasized when making restrictions about eucharistic reception. Also, the Church may teach further details about our readiness. For example, the simple discipline of the one-hour eucharistic fast can direct our attention to living the spiritual hunger that Christ called his disciples to practice (cf. Mk 2: 20). It is a fast that prepares us for the wedding feast of the Lamb, the bridegroom of the Church. I sometimes think of the Eucharist in terms of a most delicious all-you-can-eat buffet. This is not in the sense of picking and choosing, but in the sense that you want to bring a big appetite to receive the abundant spiritual food that God gives to hungry souls.

Out of our hunger for the Lord, we may have different habits of good preparation. Many will use MAGNIFICAT to read and pray over the Mass readings and prayers before the Mass begins. Many will also prepare themselves with a sense of entering the Mass with particular intentions and needs. Saint Catherine of Siena gives a key to right preparation: holy desire. She uses the image of candles of different sizes for us to imagine holy desires. All of us come with candles to be lighted in Holy Communion. Everyone's candle bears the whole light with its heat, color, and brightness. However, those with the greatest candles, i.e., those with the strongest of burning desires, receive in proportion to their

---

3. St. Justin Martyr, *1 Apology* 66.

greater love and can share after reception of the Eucharist even more of the light with others. [4]

Indeed, with the right preparations before Mass, we can more fully enter Vatican II's renewal in the active, full, and fruitful participation in the liturgy. [5] Such participation is first of all a transformation of the heart. In *Sacramentum Caritatis*, Pope Benedict instructs: "It should be made clear that the word 'participation' does not refer to mere external activity during the celebration. In fact, the active participation called for by the Council must be understood in more substantial terms, on the basis of a greater awareness of the mystery being celebrated and its relationship to daily life." [6] With attention then to the mystery celebrated and its connection to our life, we consider how to pray the various parts of the Mass.

INTRODUCTORY RITES

Preparation done before Mass intensifies and takes a new form at the opening of Mass. The purpose of the introductory rites is "to ensure that the faithful who come together as one establish communion and dispose themselves to listen properly to God's word and celebrate the Eucharist worthily." [7] I can remember the time I really learned the importance of the Mass's beginning. When I was in high school my saintly parish priest, Monsignor Vincent Hogan, taught Wednesday evening religion class to the seniors. Monsignor Hogan told us what he thought was the most important part of Sunday Mass: the entrance hymn! Monsignor knew that he was on somewhat shaky theological ground, strictly speaking, but his point was this: If you are there for the opening

---

4. Cf. St. Catherine of Siena, *The Dialogue*, trans. Suzanne Noffke, O.P., Classics of Western Spirituality (New York: Paulist Press, 1980), pp. 207-8.
5. Cf. Vatican II, *Sacrosanctum Concilium* 14-20; 30ff.; and 48ff.
6. Pope Benedict XVI, *Sacramentum Caritatis* 52.
7. *General Instruction of the Roman Missal* 46.

hymn, you are there for the Mass. You are present for the Lord. Much of life is simply showing up.

In the sign of the cross and the greeting, we recall that our communion takes place in the communion of the Father, Son, and Holy Spirit. The Triune God has summoned us to worship, and it is only in God's name that we gather. The priest and the people mutually offer each other properly Christian greetings in the Lord. We are not at Mass because of political affiliation, our line of work, or entertainment tastes. We are there because God has formed a priestly people to offer worship.

Calling to mind then that we come into the presence of God in the sacred mysteries, we confess our sinfulness. If the penitential rite takes the form of the Confiteor, we not only admit that we have sinned in thought, word, deed, and omission, we also beg the help of the Church in heaven and the Church on earth for prayers. This means that we are both saying the Confiteor and also hearing it on the lips of our brothers and sisters who are asking for *our* prayers. From that consciousness of our great need, we then call upon the mercy of the Lord Jesus. As the angel Gabriel said to Saint Joseph before the Lord's birth, Jesus "will save his people from their sins" (Mt 1: 21).

On Sundays outside of Advent and Lent as well on other festive occasions, the Church sings the Gloria, echoing the multitude of the heavenly host on Christmas night. An ancient prayer, the Gloria leads us to pray first to God the Father, then to God the Son, before concluding in a Trinitarian doxology. It empowers our souls to be doxological, proclaiming the greatness of the Lord (cf. Lk 1: 46). Like Blessed Elizabeth of the Trinity, we can strive not only to give, but also to be "a praise of glory." [8]

The introductory rites close with the prayer called the collect.

---

8. Cf. Letter 250 in Elizabeth of the Trinity, *I Have Found God*, Complete Works, vol. 2, *Letters from Carmel* (Washington, DC: Institute of Carmelite Studies, 1995), p. 233. Cf. Eph 1: 12.

After the priest celebrant calls the people to pray, "all, together with the priest, observe a brief silence so that they may be conscious of the fact that they are in God's presence and may formulate their petitions mentally."[9] By this instruction, we pray better when we do precisely that: call to mind our entrance into the awesome presence and the petitions that we bring to God. The Trinitarian prayer that follows focuses on some specific praise of God and petition to God for the Church to live the mysteries of faith. After the collect, we are ready to pray the Liturgy of the Word.

LITURGY OF THE WORD

The Mass is made up of the Liturgy of the Word and the Liturgy of the Eucharist, which are "so closely interconnected that they form but one single act of worship."[10] In beginning to consider the Liturgy of the Word, we can reflect on the words of the third-century Alexandrian teacher Origen. He preached how the faithful receive the body of the Lord in the divine mysteries with all caution and reverence so that nothing of the consecrated gift should slip away. He then says, "But if you employ such caution, quite properly, in keeping the body of Christ, how can you think that it is less of a sin to have treated the Word of God with negligence than to treat his body with negligence?"[11]

Scriptural Readings and Chants

Here, we do well to heed a reflection about silence and word by Pope Benedict before he assumed the Chair of Saint Peter. In *The*

---

9. *General Instruction of the Roman Missal* 54.
10. *General Instruction of the Roman Missal* 28; cf. *Sacrosanctum Concilium* 56.
11. Origen, *Homilies on Exodus* 13.3, in Daniel J. Sheerin, *The Eucharist*, Message of the Fathers of the Church, vol. 7 (Wilmington, DE: Michael Glazier, 1986), p. 178.

Feast of Faith, the then Cardinal Ratzinger said, "The only way we can be saved from succumbing to the inflation of words is if we have the courage to face silence and in it to listen afresh to the Word. Otherwise we shall be overwhelmed by 'mere words' at the very point where we should be encountering *the Word*, the Logos, the Word of love, crucified and risen, who brings us life and joy." [12] The Liturgy of the Word presupposes a listening heart, a heart of fertile silence where the Word can be planted.

Besides the attentive silence required of us in the Liturgy of the Word, we also speak various responses at times. One such response with great theological meaning is "Thanks be to God." This acclamation signals our gratitude for the proclamation of the Word for our souls. The phrase was sometimes found on the lips of early martyrs who had been sentenced to death. For example, in the earliest text of Christian Latin extant, we read the account of the condemnation from July 17, 180, of the martyrs of Scilli in North Africa. They were carrying the letters of Saint Paul, professing the Christian faith, and not offering pagan sacrifice. When they heard their condemnation, they exclaimed, *"Deo gratias"* – "Thanks be to God!" Perhaps in connecting the Liturgy of the Word with our daily life, we too can say "Thanks be to God" not only for the Word proclaimed in the liturgy, but also in the moments we feel the burden of the cross in our lives. Such was the attitude of Saint Gianna Molla, the Italian physician, wife, and mother. Saint Gianna, who knew how to express a grateful heart in good times and in bad, is quoted as saying: "Also in suffering, let us say: Thanks be to God." [13]

The high point of the Liturgy of the Word comes in the

---

12. Joseph Cardinal Ratzinger, *The Feast of Faith: Approaches to a Theology of the Liturgy*, trans. Graham Harrison (San Francisco: Ignatius Press, 1986), p. 73.
13. Pietro Molla and Elio Guerriero, *Saint Gianna Molla: Wife, Mother, Doctor*, trans. James G. Colbert (San Francisco: Ignatius Press, 2004), p. 150.

proclamation of the Gospel.[14] Various gestures, such as the assembly standing, set the Gospel off from the rest of the Liturgy of the Word. The added reverence at Mass for the Gospel reading can influence how we treasure the Gospel accounts in our daily life. Saint Thérèse of Lisieux knew their incomparable power and wrote: "It is especially the *Gospels* which sustain me during my hours of prayer, for in them I find what is necessary for my poor little soul. I am constantly discovering in them new lights, hidden and mysterious meanings."[15]

Homily

The homily, based on the Sacred Scriptures and/or the Mass of the day, "should take into account both the mystery being celebrated and the particular needs of the listeners."[16] Here again, we see explicitly the union of mystery and daily life in the Mass. However, if you think you are not getting from the homily what the Church expects, know that you are not alone. Pope Benedict did not hesitate in *Sacramentum Caritatis* to note that the state of the homily must be improved.[17]

An important aspect of praying this part of the Mass is to pray for the preacher. Whether you consider the preaching to be spiritually nourishing or a spiritual wasteland, pray for the one called to speak to you words of life. Christ our priest always has a message for us in the Liturgy of the Word. Listen to Christ, who uses humble instruments, in the homily.

---

14. Cf. *General Instruction of the Roman Missal* 60.
15. *Story of a Soul: The Autobiography of St. Thérèse of Lisieux*, trans. John Clarke, O.C.D. (Washington, DC: Institute of Carmelite Studies, 1976), p. 179.
16. *General Instruction of the Roman Missal* 65.
17. *Sacramentum Caritatis* 46.

Profession of Faith

In the fourth century under the crisis of the Arian heresy, which denied the full divinity and co-eternity of the Son with the Father, the Church composed the Niceno-Constantinopolitan Creed. This is the Creed we usually recite on Sundays and solemnities. Here, it would be especially helpful for prayer to study the articles of the Creed and see how the rule of faith gives light to our journey to heaven. For example, consider how wonderful it is that we profess faith in the "maker of heaven and earth, of all that is seen and unseen." God is the Lord of everything! This can have great ramifications for our daily lives.

At Easter, the Church renews the profession of baptismal faith with questions that call for the response "I do." Our profession of faith at Mass points us back to our first sacrament of faith, baptism, and also can prepare us for the goal of faith. According to the rites of Viaticum, it is desirable for a dying person to renew the baptismal profession of faith before receiving the Eucharist as food for the final steps of the journey on earth. Knowing where we have come from and where we are going, we can profess our faith with confidence in God. This is the faith handed on through generations of the faithful, the faith that martyrs died for, the faith we hand on to the next generation. Profess the faith boldly!

General Intercessions

We pray for the needs of the Church, for public authorities and the salvation of the whole world, for those burdened by difficulties, and for the local community. It is noteworthy that from the earliest times the Christian faithful prayed for those beyond the Church. For example, the first Letter to Timothy (1 Tm 2: 1-2) has: "First of all, then, I ask that supplications, prayers, petitions, and thanksgivings be offered for everyone, for kings and for all in authority, that we may lead a quiet and tranquil life in all devotion and dignity."

Intercessory prayer has tremendous power. When treating the

biblical mystery of predestination, Saint Thomas Aquinas says that prayers can affect the salvation of our souls and others' due to God's providence. [18] In other words, from all eternity God plans and takes into account our intercessions as secondary causes for what he wills. This includes our ultimate goal, which is nothing less than everlasting happiness with God. Such an attitude toward prayer is quite different from simply thinking that prayer changes only the one who prays.

LITURGY OF THE EUCHARIST

When the risen Lord came to the two disciples on the road to Emmaus, their hearts were burning within them as he opened the Scriptures for them. They then recognized Jesus in the breaking of the bread. We too have Christ as a most mysterious companion on our pilgrimage. In the transition from the Liturgy of the Word to the Liturgy of the Eucharist, our hearts, having been set on fire by the Word, now come to know Jesus in the Eucharist. The two disciples asked Jesus, "Stay with us" (Lk 24: 29). Here, we find that the risen Lord remains with us his people, even until the end of the world (cf. Mt 28: 20).

Preparation of the Gifts

The Liturgy of the Eucharist begins with the preparation of the gifts. Because we know that God has given to us, we can give in return. Indeed, giving takes on special significance in our faith. After the birth of Christ, the wise men came from afar with gifts. They saw the child with Mary his mother, whereupon they fell down and worshiped him (cf. Mt 2: 11). We who are likewise from the nations also approach the King of the Jews with gifts. The bread and wine brought to the altar come from the goodness of God's creation, but are also of human fashioning, our

---

18. *Summa theologiae* I, q. 23, a. 8.

stewardship over creation. Moreover, it is customary to have the collection at this time. The money offered to the Lord represents our life, our work, and our desire to render to the Lord who has been good to us. We may not be rich as kings, but we count our blessings and give.

In offering our gifts we can remember the story of the multiplication of the loaves from chapter 6 of John's Gospel. Jesus saw the vast crowd coming to him and turned to Philip to test his response about where they could buy enough food for all of them. Philip seemed exasperated by the sheer magnitude of the task. But Andrew saw that a boy was offering what little he had – five barley loaves and two fish. What good was that? That was enough! Jesus worked his great miracle, a sign that points us to the miraculous feeding of the Eucharist in which Jesus gives himself body, blood, soul, and divinity – but only when we offer a little bread and wine.

Eucharistic Prayer

The eucharistic prayer stands as "the center and summit of the entire celebration." [19] This most holy of times in our life can be considered under its various elements: thanksgiving, acclamation, epiclesis, institution narrative and consecration, anamnesis, offering, intercessions, and final doxology. [20]

Eucharist comes from a Greek word meaning **thanksgiving**. The priest especially gives thanks in the preface that falls between the dialogue beginning "The Lord be with you" and the *Sanctus*. The preface glorifies God in gratitude for the mysteries of salvation and corresponds to a particular mystery celebrated in the Eucharist. It concludes by joining the praise of the Church on earth with heaven's song.

---

19. *General Instruction of the Roman Missal* 78.
20. Cf. *General Instruction of the Roman Missal* 79.

The Church on earth's **acclamation** of the *Sanctus* blends with the "Holy, Holy, Holy" sung by the seraphim of whom we are told in Isaiah (6: 3). In addition, it recalls the Lord's triumphant entrance into Jerusalem, when the children of Israel repeatedly cried out hosannas and exclaimed, "Blessed is he who comes in the name of the Lord" (Mt 21: 9). The joyful exclamation of "hosanna" means "grant salvation." How appropriate it is that we pray for Christ our Savior to grant us salvation in the Eucharist!

The **epiclesis**, or invocation, implores the sending of the Holy Spirit upon the gifts offered on the altar. It also asks that the spotless Victim be received in communion for the salvation of those who partake. In the eucharistic prayer, we can behold the "profound unity between the invocation of the Holy Spirit and the institution narrative." [21] The mission of the Son and the mission of the Holy Spirit are intimately united in salvation history, and more particularly in the Mass, for the glory of God the Father. Knowing this, we can, in our prayer, be ever more attentive to the work of the Holy Spirit in the sacrament of the body of Christ, which was formed in the Virgin Mary's womb when the Holy Spirit came upon her (cf. Lk 1: 35). In commenting on John, chapter 6, Saint Thomas Aquinas says, "The one who eats and drinks in a spiritual way becomes a sharer in the Holy Spirit, through whom we are united to Christ by a union of faith and love, and through whom we become members of the Church." [22]

By means of the very words and actions of Christ, **the institution narrative and consecration** make present Christ's sacrifice. Expressing this central mystery, the Fourth Lateran Council (1215) beautifully stated that Christ's "body and blood are truly contained in the sacrament of the altar under the forms of bread and wine, the bread and wine having been changed in substance

---

21. *Sacramentum Caritatis* 48.
22. St. Thomas Aquinas, *Commentary on the Gospel of John* 6, lect. 7.

(*transsubstantiatis*), by God's power, into his body and blood so that in order to achieve the mystery of unity we receive from him what he received from us." [23]

Anamnesis is a Greek word for remembrance. In this part of the eucharistic prayer, the Church recalls the passion, resurrection, and ascension of the Son. To ignite our eucharistic amazement, the great Pope John Paul II writes in *Ecclesia de Eucharistia*: "At every celebration of the Eucharist, we are spiritually brought back to the paschal Triduum: to the events of the evening of Holy Thursday, to the Last Supper and to what followed it." [24] We remember that Christ "was handed over for our transgressions and was raised for our justification" (Rom 4: 25).

The **offering** during the eucharistic prayer is of course different from the offering of the preparation of the gifts because now Christ himself is offered. United as members of Christ's Body, we are taught to offer also our whole lives in Christ to God the Father. By doing so, we heed Saint Paul's exhortation "to offer your bodies as a living sacrifice, holy and pleasing to God, your spiritual worship" (Rom 12: 1).

The eucharistic prayer always has **intercessions**, prayers for the living and the dead. Here we can think how the Church is so much more than the particular assembly gathered around the altar. It is the universal Church – the Church of the Virgin Mother of God and all the saints, the Church of the faithful departed awaiting their final glory, the Church found throughout the earth, led by the Pope and by the local bishops in union with him.

In the **final doxology**, the priest with the Eucharist raised high gives glory to God the Father through, with, and in Christ, in the

---

23. Fourth Lateran Council, Constitution on the Catholic Faith. In *Decrees of the Ecumenical Councils*, vol. 1, *Nicaea I – Lateran V*, ed. Norman P. Tanner, S.J. (Washington, DC: Georgetown University Press, 1990), p. 230 (slightly revised).
24. Pope John Paul II, *Ecclesia de Eucharistia* 3.

unity of the Holy Spirit. All the faithful with hearts raised high cry out praise to God in the great Amen. Let this communal Amen resound throughout the earth!

Communion Rite

The Lord's Prayer begins the communion rite. Christ taught us to pray this most perfect prayer to God the Father in the midst of our difficulties and needs, and so we dare to say it. It is a matter of courage! In commenting on the Lord's Prayer, Saint Teresa of Ávila treats the petition "Give us this day our daily bread" in a beautiful eucharistic interpretation. She says, "Let us ask the Eternal Father that we might merit to receive our heavenly bread in such a way that the Lord may reveal himself to the eyes of our soul and make himself thereby known since our bodily eyes cannot delight in beholding him, because he is so hidden." [25]

After the embolism, in which the priest prays for the Lord's protection from evil, sin, and anxiety, the people give an acclamation of praise. Some Christians typically give this acclamation immediately after the Lord's Prayer. It is of course not a part of the prayer itself, but it most admirably expresses our praise that all things belong to God.

The next element of the communion rite is the sign of peace. Contrary to some misperception, the sign of peace begins with the words of the priest celebrant to Christ: "Lord Jesus Christ, you said to your apostles…" Indeed, in the Gospel of John (14: 27), we read that on the night before Christ died, he said, "Peace I leave with you; my peace I give to you." This peace recalled in the priest's prayer to Christ then radiates from the altar to the

---

25. St. Teresa of Ávila, *The Way of Perfection* 34.5. In *The Collected Works of St. Teresa of Ávila*, vol. 2, trans. Kieran Kavanaugh, O.C.D., and Otilio Rodriguez, O.C.D. (Washington, DC: Institute of Carmelite Studies, 1980), p. 170 (slightly revised).

assembly. This is not some worldly peace, but the peace of Christ himself.

During the breaking of the bread, the Church prays to Christ in the repetitions of "The Lamb of God." We can remember that Christ himself is our new Passover, the Lamb whose blood was shed for the protection of Israel from the evil of slavery. This prayer can also point us to the Book of Revelation, the last book of the New Testament, so filled with details about the heavenly liturgy. There, the Lamb receives the ceaseless prayer of the countless multitudes of angels and humans.

Finally, communion begins after the priest genuflects and repeats the words of John the Baptist (cf. Jn 1: 29). The priest and the people together consider their own unworthiness, imitating the centurion's words found in the Gospel of Matthew (8: 8). Although we are to celebrate the sacraments worthily, nobody counts oneself worthy before receiving sacramental gifts. In the rite of ordination, the deacon about to be ordained a priest is not asked if he is worthy, but the bishop does inquire of another if the ordinand is worthy. After the bishop formally chooses the candidate, relying on the Lord's help, the people give their acclaim – typically with deafening applause. An Eastern tradition is to shout, "*Axios, Axios, Axios!*" "Worthy, worthy, worthy!" In the midst of the people's fervent support, the ordinand remains silent, perhaps even more conscious of his unworthiness. I imagine that in some similar way the angels cry out the worthiness of silent, graced communicants before the throne of the Lamb. The Lord does heal the soul by his word!

When Holy Communion is given, the communicant has one simple response to the minister's statement "The body of Christ" or "The blood of Christ." Saint Ambrose explains the significance of our eucharistic Amen: "And you say, 'Amen', that is, 'It is true'. What the mouth speaks, let the mind within confess; what words utter, let the heart feel." [26]

Immediately after communion may be a time of fervent prayer, perhaps assisted by song. We treasure the reception of our Lord, who has chosen to dwell with us. The prayerful silence of our hearts leads finally to the conclusion of the communion rite in the prayer after communion. This prayer considers the effects of the Eucharist for our lives upon earth and our preparation for heavenly joy.

CONCLUDING RITE

Following the prayer after communion, there may be some announcements about events and other information needed for the gathered community. Immediately after the Trinitarian blessing, the dismissal marks the time for the faithful to go in peace – an action of great consequence. In fact, this sacrament is called Holy Mass (*Missa*), "because the liturgy in which the mystery of salvation is accomplished concludes with the sending forth (*missio*) of the faithful, so that they may fulfill God's will in their daily lives" (CCC 1332). Here, yet again, we see the explicit connection between the Mass and daily life. If Mass is not transforming our day-to-day living, then the Mass will not lead us up to the heavenly home.

LIVING THE EUCHARISTIC LIFE

The eucharistic liturgy is itself the Church's greatest act of thanksgiving. After Mass, "it is good to give thanks to the Lord" (Ps 92: 2), who graciously allows us to give thanks. This is not a redundancy, but a continuation and implementation in life of the

---

26. *On the Mysteries* 9.54 in *Saint Ambrose: Theological and Dogmatic Works*, trans. Roy J. Deferrari, The Fathers of the Church, vol. 44 (Washington, DC: The Catholic University of America Press, 1963), p. 26.

mysteries celebrated. As one eucharistic preface prays: "You have no need of our praise, yet our desire to thank you is itself your gift. Our prayer of thanksgiving adds nothing to your greatness, but makes us grow in your grace, through Jesus Christ our Lord." To have a heart full of thanks after Mass, throughout the day, and every day truly shows forth the eucharistic transformation of our life. Our gratitude carries us along what is assuredly a difficult path to the glory of heaven.

"Lift up your hearts!" *Sursum corda!* When we hear these words at Mass, we can experience something of the mystery of God's grace at work to lead us in our daily pilgrimage. Christ, whose home is in heaven, comes to travel with us. This is our MAGNIFICAT way of life. In conclusion, we ponder this mystery with the help of the final reflection of Pope Benedict's *Sacramentum Caritatis*:

> *True joy is found in recognizing that the Lord is still with us, our faithful companion along the way. The Eucharist makes us discover that Christ, risen from the dead, is our contemporary in the mystery of the Church, his body. Of this mystery of love we have become witnesses. Let us encourage one another to walk joyfully, our hearts filled with wonder, towards our encounter with the Holy Eucharist, so that we may experience and proclaim to others the truth of the words with which Jesus took leave of his disciples: "Lo, I am with you always, until the end of the world" (Mt 28: 20).* [27]

---

27. *Sacramentum Caritatis* 97.

MAN, THE INSENSIBLE

ANTHONY ESOLEN

G. K. Chesterton once complained about the way journalists had of talking about the ordinary man. "You have never in your life met an *ordinary man*!" he thundered. That is because every man and woman and child you meet has been made in the image of God, and has been redeemed by Christ.

We Christians know that. It says so in the Catechism, after all. But is that all it is for us, a piece of theological information? Imagine someone racing up to us to say, "Have you heard? The prophet has raised his friend from the dead in Bethany! He has raised a man from the dead!" Would you then reply, "Yes, I have the reports right here. They seem to be quite accurate. It looks like rain outside, doesn't it?"

In this sense, the old pagans of Greece and Rome and the Northlands were onto something. While they were yet young at heart, they looked upon man with wonder. Maybe now and then a child of our own might do so too. The old janitor trudging from the furnace with his tools clanking from his belt is a god of fire and ironwork. The little boy rolling a ball along the grass might well have rolled a planet down the Milky Way. The golden-haired woman with her arms flouring the dough and kneading it into a loaf might be herself the corn goddess working in the sun.

But it is the object of the modern school to rub all this nonsense out of the soul of a child. That loss of childlike wonder is part of growing up. It might better be called part of growing down, into flatness and insensibility. The old Germanic warriors, fighting and singing and falling in love and dying in the shadows of the towering firs of the Black Forest, thought there was a divinity in trees, and worshiped them. Then Saint Boniface came among them to preach the good news. He did not call them fools for worshiping trees. He told them they had got the wrong Tree. The modern educator comes among them to tell them that a tree is *only* a tree, or a man is *only* a man, or love is *only* the instinct for self-preservation and the propagation of the species. *Only* is almost the only word the modern educator understands. Then the pagans set about to worship far sillier and more dangerous things than trees – "choice," for instance, or "self-fulfillment," or "my dreams," and other idols you can't even hang a tire-swing from.

So I believe, in our current state, the Eucharist can teach us as much about our own too-familiar world as about the world to come. The fashionable agnostic will say, "That wafer of bread is *only* bread, and that cup of wine is *only* wine." Many of our brethren in the Protestant faiths, alas, will agree. We must reply, "My friend, you are quite wrong about that – but what do you mean when you say *'only'* bread? Don't you know that bread is the staff of life? Have you never *really* tasted the wine that gladdens the heart? Your problem is not just that you deny the Eucharist. You don't really know about bread and wine to begin with. Perhaps we ought to talk about those, first."

And that's because, though we so seldom see it or even consider it, our world is a eucharistic world. To show you how that is so, I'd like to take you to one sacred place in Catholic

literature. I'll begin not with an ordinary man, but a *typical* man
– I mean, an insensible man, who cannot understand the reality
transpiring a few feet in front of him. The work is the medieval
Quest of the Holy Grail.[1] The man's name is Lancelot.

Like all the knights of Arthur's Round Table, Lancelot has
sworn to undertake, for a year and a day, the quest of the Grail,
which is nothing other than to "see revealed what tongue could not
relate nor heart conceive" (283), not simply the reality of Christ's
presence in the bread and wine of the sacrament, but the reality
of his presence simply. It is a quest to behold the Incarnate Word
through whom all things were made. Now that is a mighty quest.
If the Grail, the platter upon which Jesus served the bread, his
body, to the apostles at the last supper, were in a church in Cleveland, the good questing knight would simply buy a railroad ticket
to Cleveland, take a cab to the church, give the platter a good
lookover, and pick up a postcard on his way out. But in our tale
of the quest, the Grail seems to be anywhere or everywhere; like
the Spirit, it blows where it will. Had the Grail not suddenly come
to the court of the Round Table, the knights would still be hanging
about Camelot, feasting, fighting, seducing young ladies, going to
church, and performing other necessary duties of the equestrian
life. But on the feast of Pentecost,

> *there came a clap of thunder so loud and terrible that
> they thought the palace must fall. Suddenly the hall
> was lit by a sunbeam which shed a radiance through
> the palace seven times brighter than had been
> before. (43)*

That sunbeam that does not break wall or window is an image
both of the incarnation of Christ in the womb of the Virgin,

---

1. *Quest of the Holy Grail*, trans. P. M. Matarasso (London: Penguin, 1969). All
quotations in this essay are taken from this prose edition of the work. Page
numbers for quotations appear throughout the text within parentheses.

leaving her intact, and of the silent and penetrating working of the Holy Spirit. Meanwhile, as the knights and ladies gaze upon one another in stupefied wonder,

> *the Holy Grail appeared, covered with a cloth of white samite; and yet no mortal hand was seen to bear it. It entered through the great door, and at once the palace was filled with fragrance as though all the spices of the earth had been spilled abroad. It circled the hall along the great tables and each place was furnished in its wake with the food its occupants desired. When all were served, the Holy Grail vanished, they knew not how nor whither. (43)*

One would think, at this point, that there would be no need for a quest. If the Grail suddenly were to appear at your parish picnic, to give each owner of the correct raffle ticket the food he most desired, you might think yourselves sufficiently blessed already. But the knights understand at least this much. As the Eucharist is a taste of the heavenly banquet to come, so this miracle at Pentecost still veils infinitely more than it unveils. Anyone who has been given so much must crave more and more, for the Eucharist is that strange food that most whets the appetite when it most satisfies. Therefore the knights pledge to undertake the quest.

Lancelot is among their number, though, and that poses a problem, because for twenty-four years he has been breaking faith with God and with his king and friend, Arthur. That is how long he has been *keeping faith* – a treacherous faith – with Arthur's wife Guenevere, the object of his adulterous love. As he will later confess to a holy hermit:

> *"It is she who gave me abundance of gold and silver and such rich gifts as I have distributed from time to time among poor knights. It is she who exalted me and set me in the luxury I now enjoy. For her love alone I*

accomplished the exploits with which the whole world rings." (89)

"Fall down in homage to me," says Satan to our Lord, "and all these kingdoms will be yours." Lancelot has fallen down in homage, and behold what has happened. He is no tyrant. He is no monster of cruelty. Except in the matter of Guenevere, he holds to his duty as a knight, and fights valiantly in Arthur's cause, though for love of Guenevere rather than for love of Arthur. He gains riches from the queen, and does not seem to care greatly for them, but uses them to assist the poor, and perhaps to win their affection and admiration. On her account he strains every fiber when the fight is fierce, the warfare long. All of that wins him glory by the world's standards; and there is absolutely no one at Arthur's court who does not esteem him and enjoy his gentle company. Even Arthur will say of him, I believe with only a slight and sad irony, "I know you without a doubt for the best knight in the world" (35).

What happens, early in the quest, to this best knight in the world should sound a stern warning to all of us who may lack Lancelot's natural gifts but who share his divided love. One evening Lancelot comes to what looks like – and, let me stress that in a eucharistic universe if you judge by appearances you must expect to be deceived – a ruined chapel, grim and desolate, near a stone cross. He unhitches his horse to let him forage, hangs up his shield, and wanders over to the building, peering between the bars of an iron grille at a window. What he sees there should startle him into vigilance: there is "an altar richly hung with silken cloths and other trappings, and illumined by the radiance of six candles which burned before it in a massive silver candlestick" (82). But when he can find no way in, and no one to explain what is going on, he seems to give up. He returns to the stone cross, without so much as a prayer, idly unlacing his helmet and laying his cross upon the ground. Then he lies down to sleep. Why should he not? The ruined chapel is only a ruined chapel.

Consider it a fine example of the sinner who does not know in what peril he lies, disarmed, seeking a momentary comfort; nor what grace waits for him to surrender to it, to strengthen him and make him new. It is no extraordinary example. Consider how many Masses Lancelot must have attended these twenty-four years. Consider how many nights he has taken the bridle off his steed to let him forage. Would you fall asleep on the brink of a precipice? But that is what we do all the time. Would you fall asleep in the vicinity of the miraculous? We do that all the time too. Lancelot lies there, "between sleeping and waking," says the author, gaining from his sleep neither the natural refreshment of rest nor the supernatural visions God sends at times to his saints. He is held fast in a spiritual torpor. Meanwhile, a sick knight comes to the chapel on a litter slung between two horses, crying out, "Ah, God, shall my suffering never be abated? God, when shall I see the Holy Vessel which is to ease my smart? God, ah! God, did ever man endure such agony and for so venial an offense?"

Let us pause to note the irony. We never do learn what sin the sick knight has committed, but if we take his word for it, and he does seem credible, it was a pardonable sin; yet such is God's hatred of sin, even those pardonable sins that we smile at, that the knight has been reduced to a cripple, crying out to be healed. Lancelot, meanwhile, is afflicted by a sin unto death, though to all appearances he is sturdy and whole. The sick knight, whose cries of torment are also cries of love, follows Christ's command to knock and knock again, and Paul's advice to pray without ceasing, and yet, says the author, "all this while Lancelot lay without speech or movement, as though in a trance, yet he saw him clearly and heard his words" (83).

To him who knocks, it shall be opened. So finally, as if moved by an unseen hand, the silver candlestick comes forth from the chapel, along with a silver table holding the Holy Grail. The sick knight pleads to be healed of his infirmity, not so that he may return to his fellows and say that he had seen the mysteries of the Grail, but precisely so that he may too "undertake the Quest wherein all worthy men are entered." In other words, he longs for the Eucharist to heal him so that he may return with all the greater ardor to the Eucharist itself. His quest will not end but begin; the Eucharist is the bread for the wayfaring Christian, but also the feast to which he sets his steps. And everything about this unnamed knight suggests love, passionate love. The Grail does not deign simply to come to him. He drags himself by main force up to it, pulls himself to the silver table, kisses it, and gazes upon the vessel. At which point his sufferings are relieved. "Ah! God," he cries, "I am healed" – and he falls back, in a sweet sleep. But all this while Lancelot, "whether from exhaustion or from the weight of some sin that lay on him," never stirred.

Consider that: he never stirred, even though, in a kind of extrinsic and ineffectual way, he knew that a miracle was occurring not twenty feet away from him. He saw, and did not see. In a seminar on the *Quest of the Holy Grail* I asked my students if any of them had been nearby while a miracle was taking place. I did not mean simply the wonders of this natural existence, what you might call the miracles of ordinary time, wherein things follow their ordered train of cause and effect. I meant those wonders whose immediate cause could only be attributed to the transcendent will of God. None of them replied; and they were a talkative group, many of them churchgoing Catholics. It did not occur to them that miracles are, so to speak, rather mundane things in Christ's Church – that they are in fact regularly scheduled in the chapel within sight of our classroom. "Then you have never been at what is called a 'Mass'" I said, teasing them. "Or a baptism, or a wedding? You have never received absolution of your sins in a confessional? You have never attended a confirmation?"

They smiled – they knew they had been caught unawares. Yet I don't believe that they had taken the miracle of the Eucharist for granted. Even with their mostly spotty catechesis, they knew that the bread and wine became the body and blood of our Lord, or at least they knew that that was what they were supposed to believe. But, like Lancelot, they saw it as something outside of themselves, almost like something occurring in a parallel universe, without any contact with the heart of our lives here. They are functional Zwinglians. The world has been desacralized. Nothing is a sacrament; not even a sacrament. A mile or so farther down that road lie skepticism and, finally, atheism. And then nothing is left to rouse the heart of man to wonder: only the empty shake of the head at the childish wonder of others.

Let us return again to Lancelot, and see whether even now we understand what has transpired. Recall the scene in the Gospels when the friends of a paralytic man had to lower him on a pallet through the thatch of a house so that he might see Jesus, as the crowds were too thick to let them gain entry by the normal means. It is an ironic study in contrasts. Outside, all is yearning, jostling, waiting, praying – or muscling the way round back and, perhaps, tearing a hole in someone else's roof. Inside are the Pharisees, believing themselves to be holy already and awfully perspicacious, rhetorically circling around Jesus, watching him intently, and not understanding what he says or who he is. Then comes the great miracle. Jesus, seeing the cripple on the pallet, says to him, "Your sins are forgiven."

Had that been the end of it, would the man have been disappointed? Would his friends have gone home, muttering, "We thought we would see a wonder"? How strange our blindness is! Do we really believe that, by his own power alone, without the grace of God, any man can turn from a single sin, let alone from the overmastering sins that come to define our existence? As if an Ebenezer Scrooge could at last reject his enslavement to avarice only by looking at a couple of poor people and making a reasonable conclusion regarding their welfare? Every day of our lives we witness the silent action of God, as he performs that most radical of cardiac surgeries, the removal of our hearts of stone and their replacement with hearts of flesh, upon which he has engraved his laws. Yet that is not enough for us. It was not enough for the Pharisees, who grumbled that only God can forgive sins, and did not trouble to ask themselves whether the man's sins indeed had been forgiven. So Jesus condescends to work the lesser miracle. "Which is easier to say," he asks the Pharisees – and notice that he does not say that it is therefore a lesser thing to perform – "your sins are forgiven, or rise and walk?" No reply. "That you may know that the Son of Man has power on earth to forgive sins," says Jesus, who does not trouble to finish his sentence, but turns to the paralytic to say, "take up your pallet, and walk."

In other words, Jesus works the signs that even blind men might see, to bring us faith in the miracles that we cannot see because we are blind. So it is with the cripple at the chapel. We will not meet him again in the *Quest for the Holy Grail*; his sole purpose is to open our eyes to our position. We are all, the author suggests, either that cripple crying out for mercy, or, far more likely, Lancelot, who does not cry out, because he is too deeply wounded to feel his wounds. The sick knight rises up refreshed from sleep and eager to ride forth on the journey. But he looks upon Lancelot with some surprise. Why did the man not move? His squire replies that it must have been because of some unshriven sin, and gives to his master Lancelot's sword and horse. "Mount, my lord," he says. "I have certainly given you nothing that you will not put to better use than the worthless knight who lies there sleeping" (84).

And this moment, too, should strike us with a shock. How, in the light of a full moon, can anyone not recognize the features of Lancelot? But the good squire and his lord have begun, by the power of the Eucharist, to see as God sees, not as man sees. For they *do see what Lancelot is*. They are not, out there on the moor, dazzled by the glare of worldly honor, the high feasts at Camelot, the genteel manners and ermine-tipped gowns. Their eyes have beheld realities on this night, and that is why they overlook the deceptive surface of a noble knight, the accidents, if you will, of flesh and bone, and look instead upon the man in his heart. He is in fact a worthless knight, and their apparent mistake, which is instead a flash of genuine insight, will help to heal Lancelot, who is still suspended in that state of seeing and not seeing, waking and not waking. For when Lancelot finally sits up and returns to the iron grille, wondering whether what he saw was real or a dream, he is granted no vision at all, but a voice that calls out to him in these words:

> *"Lancelot, harder than stone, more bitter than wood, more barren and bare than the fig tree, how durst thou presume to venture there where the Holy Grail abides? Get thee hence, for the stench of thy presence fouls this place."* (85)

At which the knight, as if pierced through the heart, cries the terrible cry of Job and curses the day that he was ever born.

That is not, however, the end of the quest for Lancelot. In a way, it is a preparation for the beginning. He does not understand the words spoken to him, but, groaning beneath his bad conscience, he does at least understand that he does not understand them, and so he seeks counsel from a holy hermit. After a long and wise interpretation, the hermit, fairly weeping for the gifts that Lancelot has squandered, points the knight's attention to a symbol which is no mere symbol. "Sir, do you see that cross?" he asks. When Lancelot replies that he does, the hermit observes that the arms of Christ are thrown wide to welcome all who would come to him in repentance, no matter the gravity or the duration of the sin. It is, to all appearances, a quiet and ordinary moment in a little cell in the middle of nowhere, with a shabby old man speaking to a weary traveler. Yet something more precious, and worthier of our wonder, than all the stars and planets hangs in the balance – a human soul. To Lancelot it will seem as if the object of his dearest love lay dead at his feet; yet it is a false love, and he must slay it to gain the true. He utters words he had uttered to no man before. He admits that he has sinned with the queen for twenty-four years. He repents.

Now sometimes when a paralytic is healed, he slings that pallet under his arm and marches home, whole and new. Saint Paul seems to have undergone a searing moment of conversion, that struck him blind with excess of light and vision. But most of us must undergo the quiet working-out, in time, of God's stinging grace, washing us with vinegar and disappointment, that we may be white as snow. So it will be with Lancelot. Wonder after wonder is in store for him, though the worldly eye will see little more than barrenness, frustration, and pain. He leaves the hermit and comes upon a man who asks him his name. Upon hearing it, the man reviles him:

> *"Are you not he who saw the Holy Grail appear and work an undoubted miracle before his eyes, and lay as wooden at its coming as might an unbeliever?" (135)*

No one should dare talk to Lancelot of the Lake, greatest knight in the world, with such scorn. Poor Lancelot, relying on the weak reed of the knightly code, does not know what to do. It is beneath his dignity to attack the mere squire, and beneath his dignity to listen. At least, that is what he thinks, and that is how he replies. But the squire will have none of it. "There is nothing left you but to listen," he says, "for no other good will ever come of you" (136). That is what happens when you give your heart over to one who does not consider your genuine good, and who there-fore does not really love you. It is not true that Lancelot has lost his chance to see the mysteries of the Grail because of love. It is rather true that he has first lost his love, that is, his love for the God who is Love himself. To say that Lancelot has been in love all these years is to speak in the worldly way of people who only see the glare and glamor, and not their empty promises.

But Lancelot hears; the lesson is not lost. He finds another holy man, to whom again he tells his name and his quest, and again he hears such hard words as Jesus spoke to the blind and self-righteous Pharisees: "Seek them you may," says the priest, referring to the mysteries of the Grail, "but find them you will not" (140). And yet, he continues, "many people have dwelt long in darkness and in the murk of sin, whom our Lord has recalled to the true light, as soon as He saw they willed it in their hearts." That, of course, is what is happening here – not in a lightning-flash, but in the slow leavening of grace. Lancelot is being brought to will to see. Do we really believe that the blind want to see? Not at the cost of looking upon that most dilapidated temple, their own heart. Lancelot will hear from this hermit an account of all the special graces God had granted to him, and what miserable use he had made of them; it is a soul-sifting that none of us should like to undergo. Then the hermit will compare the knight to the man in Jesus' parable who came to the banquet poorly dressed – though no doubt *he* thought his tuxedo was good enough – and who was cast into the outer darkness. To assist Lancelot in his seeing, to help him to better clothing and better feasting, the hermit enjoins upon him a penitential life, which is the medicine that prepares us for the medicine, the Eucharist. He is to wear a hair shirt, and to abstain from meat and wine all while he is on the quest, and to attend Mass every day, if circumstance permits. Then Lancelot "accepted this command in penance's name, and stripping in the good man's sight, he received the discipline with a willing spirit. Then he took the hair-shirt with its rasping bristles and donned it first beneath his tunic" (146). So he leaves, with the hermit urging him to seek confession every week. In this sense Lancelot is himself now a mystery: under the appearance of a comfortable knight we now find a soul in hard training for battle with the enemy. The hair shirt and the confession are a part of his spiritual exercises; his table is but bread and water; no more does he seek his ease at night, but he prays, and pillows his head on a stone; he does sleep, and is granted a dream, both terrible and comforting, wherein he is driven out of the king's mansion, but then addressed at last in these words, "It is for thee to choose whether I love or hate thee" (148).

I don't have the leisure here to recount all of Lancelot's subsequent adventures. He will make plenty of mistakes still; but for the first time in his life, he is a Christian knight. One morning finds him stranded in a wild and lonely place, hemmed in by a deep and dangerous river before him, cliff walls to right and left, and a terrible forest behind. It is, to all appearances, a place to flee. But instead of taking matters into his own hands, and judging what to do according to what little his mind might comprehend, Lancelot does something else, something unusual for him. He engages in another one of those miraculous actions which we cannot see as miracles. He prays, "beseeching Our Lord to come in His mercy to comfort and visit him with his counsel, lest through the devil's wiles he fall into temptation or be dragged down into despair" (161). Set aside for the moment the miracle of an answered prayer. Is it not a wonder that man can pray at all? That the heart of man longs for what he cannot see? And that God, the creator of all this universe, who powdered the sky with stars, should lend an ear to the cry of dust? But God, the God who became Man, and who every day in the sacrament of bread and wine comes to feed Man, he it is who united himself with that same dust, and reunites himself with it in the Eucharist. So when Lancelot awakes, he sees before him near the rocks a boat with neither tiller nor pilot nor oar. He embarks, as he has been commanded to do. On that boat, Lancelot will be fed, sustained by "the Almighty Lord who fed the Israelites with manna in the desert and brought water out of the rock for them to drink" (257), not now with earthly food that corrupts, but with the food of the

Holy Spirit, so that "it seemed to him that he had partaken of every delicacy earth could offer."

Finally, the knight will come to a chapel, as he had before. He is still foolish, but his heart is kindled with love, and it is that love that allows him to see – not wholly, not clearly, but a little. He stands at the threshold, commanded by a voice to keep away from the sanctuary. Within he sees the Holy Vessel on a silver table; it is the sacrifice of the Mass as it exists in reality, with ministering angels all about the altar, bearing incense and candles and crosses. The old priest is about to consecrate the host, and, at the elevation, "Lancelot thought he saw, above his outstretched hands, three men, two of whom were placing the youngest in the hands of the priest who raised him aloft as though he were showing him to the people" (262). It is a stunning moment. What indeed do we think is going on when the priest says, "*Hoc est enim corpus meus*"? Is it not the act of the Father, making the Son present to us by the working of the Holy Spirit? Lancelot thus glimpses the great mystery of the Trinity, a mystery of God's life of love, and does what any half-blind and muddleheaded knight would do, moved by a real love, but still self-willed and impatient. He bursts in upon the scene to help the old man, who seemed to him to be trembling under the weight of the body of Christ. He is still, alas, a man of flesh, seeing only the flesh.

But he is also a man of faith. For his presumptuousness he is flung from the chapel, scorched by a blazing wind and left half-dead, "powerless to speak or utter a word" (263). Yet this is not the listlessness that seized him when the cripple came to be healed. Lancelot himself has been the cripple, and now he falls, apparently insensible, but in reality asleep, slowly being healed within. Some people of the nearby castle discover him and bring him in, and, just like the squire at the ruined chapel, they do not recognize who he is. But they do not treat him with scorn, for now he deserves none. Says a holy man to the rest, "This man has been one of the foremost knights in the world, and shall be again one day, so it please Our Lord." So Lancelot lay in the castle for twenty-four days neither eating nor drinking, one day for every year of his sin with Guenevere.

Finally the man awakes, and cries out, in the same accents and with the same fervor as had that other knight who had been healed at the ruined chapel: "Ah! God, why didst Thou waken me so soon? I was far happier now than ever I shall be again!" (264). When his watchers, rejoicing to see that he has wakened from his coma, ask him what he has seen, he replies: "Such glories and felicity that my tongue could never reveal their magnitude, nor could my heart conceive it. For this was no earthly but a spiritual vision." And yet it was happening, silently, unexpectedly, right there in an ordinary chamber, to a sick man whose name his nurses do not even know.

And we can rest assured that the penitence has marked a real change in Lancelot. It is not appearance. He has been born again, and as a sign of this, he refuses to be within merely what he appears to be without. That is, when he at last rises to dress again, he takes up the hair shirt that had been his penitential garment. But the good and compassionate people of the castle, whose vision in this case is limited, urge him not to do so, because Lancelot will see no more of the Grail now. They wish to spare him further pain. But their words "could not sway Lancelot's resolve: he took the hair shirt and put it on, slipping on next the linen gown, and finally a gown of scarlet cloth that was brought him" (265). Only then are the eyes of the onlookers opened. "What," they exclaim, "my lord Lancelot, is it you?" They see the man with the outer robes of the world, and know him for the knight they had often seen before. Yet in another sense, only now is it really Lancelot, for only now has that knight been made new, made more himself than he had ever been. He stands before us now as Lancelot in truth, the man who seems glorious in the world's eyes, but who knows he is a sinner; yet with each prick of the hair shirt he wears hidden beneath, he joins his sufferings to those of his savior,

Christ. The grace of the Eucharist is working within him now, too, and he becomes in his own person an emblem of what the accidents of the world reveal and conceal, and the mysteries of God's providence within that world. He is slowly being conformed to the One who also, long ago, was not recognized by his friends, as in the typical half-sleep of man they accompanied him on that dusty road one afternoon, till they stopped at an inn, a hermitage, a castle, the small church at the village corner, and they knew Him in the breaking of the bread.

"Now I Begin"

New Hope through the Sacrament of Confession

Thomas Carzon, o.m.v.

"Father, I hope God forgives me." It is not uncommon to hear someone say this in confession, especially one whose heart is heavily burdened.

"Excuse me," I will ask, "did you just say that you *hope* God forgives you?"

"Yes, Father, I hope God forgives me."

While this sounds like a straightforward expression of hope, it hides a desperation born of the fear that my sin is greater than God's ability or desire to forgive.

I don't hope *that* God forgives me. On the contrary, I hope *because* God has forgiven me. Jesus Christ offered himself once and for all (Heb 10: 10), giving his life on the cross for the forgiveness of sin. The sacrament of confession is the first gift of the risen Lord, who said to the apostles, "Peace be with you… Receive the Holy Spirit. Whose sins you forgive are forgiven them" (cf. Jn 20: 21-23). "I hope God forgives me" is an expression of my struggle to forgive myself rather than a profession of unshakeable confidence in God's boundless mercy.

The journey from desperation to hope is one we take up each day in our Christian life. Father Bruno Lanteri, O.M.V. (1759-1830), a devoted apostle of mercy and promoter of the sacrament of confession, summed up this daily pilgrimage in a letter of spiritual direction:

> *Say with courage:* Nunc coepi – *Now I begin, and walk always in the service of God. Do not keep stopping to look back, because he who looks back cannot hasten forward. Do not content yourself with beginning this year; begin every day, because for each day and for each hour of the day the Lord taught us to say in the Our Father: Forgive us our trespasses. Give us this day our daily bread. And do you not yet see that the enemy seeks to take away your tranquility and confidence in God, two dispositions so necessary for praying well? Take therefore the counsel of Saint Teresa: Let nothing disturb you, not even your spiritual miseries, because these are the object and the starting point of the infinite mercy of God, which infinitely surpasses the malice of all the sins of the world.* [1]

Only in the light of God's infinite mercy do we see the full extent of our sin, and the Lord gently calls us forth from the dark night of fear and shame into the new day of his saving love. In the

---

1. Pio Bruno Lanteri, "Lanteri a suor Leopolda Mortigliengo; 10 gennaio 1813." Scritti e Documenti d'Archivio / Pio Bruno Lanteri, vol. 1 (Fossano, Italy: Editrice Esperienze, 2002), p. 154; my translation from French original. The writings of Pio Bruno Lanteri are published in a four-volume edition prepared by the Benedictine monks at Maredsous. The entire work is also available in a searchable format online at www.lanteriwww.net.

sacrament of confession, we open our hearts to Jesus Christ as the rising sun of justice with healing rays (Mal 3: 20).

While the entire journey of conversion is the work of God, the Lord invites us – and his grace empowers us – to respond in freedom. Sin obscures our dignity, the sacrament of confession restores it as we acknowledge our freedom and responsibility for what we have done or failed to do. Freely acknowledging our sin is the beginning of the free response of love we make to God, and each day by God's grace we can grow in the freedom from sin and the freedom to love.

Drawn by grace, we come before God as we are. We come to touch God and be healed. God's power in us accomplishes "far more than all we ask or imagine" (cf. Eph 3: 20). The Lord brings us to a true repentance, a deep love that becomes a pleasing fragrance by which God can draw others to life (cf. 2 Cor 2: 14-16). The Lord leads us to a deeper sorrow unto "repentance without regret" (2 Cor 7: 10). And the Spirit of the Lord who restores our freedom makes us new, transforming us into God's own image, "from glory to glory" (2 Cor 3: 18).

REVEALED TO THE CHILDLIKE

In the sacrament of confession, we come before God as we are. After they sinned, Adam and Eve were ashamed and they tried to hide from God. How childish, to think that a fig leaf, or a whole forest of trees, or even the vast expanse of an entire universe could conceal us from the view of the Creator of all. As the Psalmist puts it, "Where can I hide from your spirit? From your presence, where can I flee?" (Ps 139: 7). All of us sinners are familiar with this first wound of sin, and the utter childishness to which it reduces us. This primordial wound begins to heal when in confession we stand before God in childlike simplicity.

When Jesus praised his Father for revealing to the childlike things hidden from the wise and the learned (cf. Mt 11: 25), I wonder if he envisioned the celebration of First Penance. Confession is not child's play, but it is accessible to the merest, the simplest of children. In confession, for the first time, a child stands as a free and responsible individual before God. Here is a place where neither mother nor father nor any other intermediary stands present to explain, excuse, or accuse. Here this child comes before the living God, and here this child begins to learn what it means to trust God in an absolute way.

Shortly after a First Penance service, I was called from "lisping children's humble prayers"[2] to the emergency room, where a woman lay dying. She had been away from the Church for many years, and she asked me to hear her confession. The contrast was striking, and it moved me deeply. I confess that a certain cynicism had entered my heart as I sat hearing those first confessions. How many of these dear children, I wondered, would seldom return to the sacrament after receiving their First Holy Communion? All the care and attention that went into preparing these young ones to meet the merciful Lord could so easily be wasted, sidetracked by the busyness of life and daily concerns.

That emergency room confession changed my perspective. This woman had been away from the Church for many years, but now, in this moment of need, she opened her heart to the long-hidden mystery of God's mercy. When she finished her act of contrition, I asked who had taught her that prayer. "My grandmother," she said. "Imagine how pleased she would be," I answered, "to know that the seed she planted so long ago is bearing this fruit right now."

Far from being a cause for discouragement, this woman's long absence from the Church testified to the power of that simple faith she had learned as a child. Although it had not been nourished by the regular reception of the sacraments, that faith was still intact

---

2. The phrase comes from the hymn "On This Day, O Beautiful Mother," which can be found in Rohr's *Favorite Catholic Melodies*, 1857.

– a gift of the good Lord from beginning to end. Whatever had caused her to hide from the Lord's presence, to flee from his spirit, her final act of trust showed that nothing need ultimately "separate us from the love of God in Christ Jesus our Lord" (Rom 8: 39).

Parents and catechists plant the seed of hope in young hearts, introducing them to Jesus, our merciful Lord. In the words of the simplest prayers they teach children a new language with which to address the living God. Those who carry out this noble vocation should not be discouraged when their efforts seem to be in vain. Remember what Saint Paul wrote, that one plants the seed, another waters it, but it is God who gives the growth (1 Cor 3: 6).

With confidence that God is at work in us, we can come before him in the sacrament of confession with childlike simplicity. We come as we are, and meet God as he is, the gracious and merciful Lord.

"WHO TOUCHED ME?"

In the sacrament of confession, we come to touch God and be healed. But we can be so focused on our wounds that we fail to notice the Healer whose desire is greater than ours that he should touch us with his power.

"Bless me, Father, for I have sinned. It has been thirty-eight years since my last confession." What courage it must take to come back to the sacrament after so long – a courage that can come only from the power of the Holy Spirit at work in a person's heart.

This woman had quite an interesting, though hardly uncommon, story. Raised Catholic, she abandoned the practice of the faith as a young adult. A rather chaotic period ensued, promising happiness, but leaving some profound wounds, the deepest of which was an abortion. After getting married and starting a family, she rediscovered the importance of her faith. Several years ago, she started coming back to Sunday Mass, and became very active in her local parish. She finally felt at home again. But she was ashamed to come to confession.

Undeniably, God's grace was at work in her life. Yet just as surely, something was still missing. In theological terms, the Lord was sustaining her moment by moment by actual graces. But he desired to abide in her as in a welcome home by sanctifying grace. He was calling her to the absolute assurance of that saving grace in the personal encounter of the sacrament.

In the course of our conversation, I asked if she had a favorite Scripture passage. "I love the story in Luke, chapter eight, about the woman who touched the hem of Jesus' garment. For twelve years she suffered from her illness, and now she touched him and was healed." I had been thinking about that very passage (Lk 8: 42b-48), so I took her response as a providential sign.

"You are that woman. For years, you have been carrying a deep, hidden wound. You know about the healing power of the Lord Jesus, and you have again drawn close to him, and you have touched him. But until this moment, you have been cowering, anonymous in the crowd, feeling guilty that you have somehow stolen his grace, and fearful that if he finds out, he will take it back."

In the Gospel story, Jesus stopped in the midst of the crowd that was pressing in on him, he turned around and asked, "Who touched me?" One woman had touched him in faith, and healing power truly went out from him. But Jesus did not want to leave her living in fear. He wanted her to know that her healing was the fruit of a personal encounter in which she was seen and known and loved. God's grace cannot be stolen; it can only be received as a free gift of his love.

God has sovereign freedom to act where and when and as he wills. His saving action is not limited to the sacraments. But in his boundless mercy, he has bound himself to the sacraments, giving to them the absolute assurance of his saving grace by the word of the Lord Jesus and the gift of his Spirit. And so in the sacrament of confession, our hope of touching God and being healed is fulfilled. God meets us, touches and heals us.

A person can find himself afraid of approaching Jesus, yet inextricably drawn to him. If you are such a person, drawn to confession but afraid of confessing to your own priest, go to another parish, to a shrine or chapel, and open your heart to a priest you don't know. But if you can possibly overcome that fear of human regard, do not deny your own pastor the opportunity of sharing in the great "joy in heaven over one sinner who repents" (Lk 15: 7). What a gift you can give, by standing in truth before the truth of God's boundless love.

"Child, Your Sins Are Forgiven"

In the sacrament of confession, God often gives us something different from what we expected, but he never gives us less. His grace is always far more than we can conceive. Mark tells the story of four men who carried a paralytic to Jesus in order for Jesus to heal him. Jesus, seeing their faith, gives far more than they imagined. How surprised they must have been to hear him say "Child, your sins are forgiven" (Mk 2: 5). The Pharisees were scandalized, and perhaps the paralytic himself was disappointed. This was not what anyone expected. Jesus addressed the Pharisees: "Which is easier, to say to the paralytic, 'Your sins are forgiven,' or to say, 'Rise, pick up your mat and walk'? But that you may know that the Son of Man has authority to forgive sins on earth" – he said to the paralytic, "I say to you, rise, pick up your mat, and go home" (Mk 2: 9-11).

When I became a priest, I expected to do important things for important people. I was ready to save the world and do great things for God. Soon, the ordinary routine of daily life set in. I found myself on one of those ordinary days rehearsing the familiar list of people I would see. "Lord, is this really what I've given my life for – to care for these same people day after day?" No sooner had I formulated the question in my mind than a quiet, clear answer came. "Of course. What did you expect?"

It dawned on me that these were the very people whom God put in my path so that I, like the friends of the paralytic, could bring them to the feet of Jesus. He was calling me to share his healing, saving work in their lives. But then I saw something else. I was the one paralyzed by my own expectations that kept me from walking with simplicity the path God opened up for me each day. These people, by their strong and simple faith, were lifting me up and bringing me to the feet of Jesus.

A particularly distressing form of spiritual paralysis is the struggle against compulsive or habitual sin. Some people say they feel like hypocrites when they keep confessing the same things. But to keep walking in trust, even though we stumble, is not hypocrisy. Others promise God never to commit this sin again. If it were truly in our power to keep such a promise, we would have no need of a Savior.

God never wills that we sin, and he never leaves us in a situation where we must sin. But God is supremely patient with us, and as Peter writes, "Consider the patience of the Lord as salvation" (2 Pt 3: 15). Through the regular practice of confession, the Lord keeps us from despair and strengthens us to grow in humility, patience, and above all trust. And God does not ask for our promises; he gives us his promise of faithful, steadfast love, which does not always look like what we expect.

Confession restores our freedom, it gives us courage to get up and begin again. But it does not give us the assurance that we always will use that freedom well. When Jesus forgave the woman caught in adultery, he told her, "Go, [and] from now on do not sin any more" (Jn 8: 11). He did not say, "I will forgive you this sin if you don't sin any more," or, "Promise me you won't do this again." He gave her the freedom to walk a new path. She was not doomed by her past, and she could look to her future with hope, not because she would be invincible, but because she had discovered in Jesus God's unfailing love.

The miracle of forgiveness and healing that takes place in the sacrament of Confession is open to each of us today. By our own practice of the sacrament, we can grow in faith, and like the friends of the paralytic, bring others to Jesus, whose healing power we have experienced in our own lives. We can also pray that the Lord will raise up many new priests, laborers in the vineyard to carry out this ministry of merciful love.

THE HOUSE WAS FILLED WITH THE FRAGRANCE

As the Lord leads us to a true repentance, he produces in us a deep love that becomes a pleasing fragrance that draws others to life (cf. 2 Cor 2: 14-16). But the aroma of Christ which delights the repentant heart is obnoxious to the heart that is hardened (cf. Wis 2: 12).

Mary, the sister of Martha and Lazarus, anoints the feet of Jesus in a tender act of grateful love. Jesus had raised Lazarus, calling him forth from the stench of the tomb by the word of his mouth. Now, the fragrance of Mary's extravagant gesture fills the whole house (cf. Jn 12: 3). Jesus receives this anointing as a preparation for his own burial, but Judas objects at the apparent waste of money. Mary is not trying to make a statement. She is simply expressing her love for the Lord. By opening her heart in this way to Christ, she allows him to touch others through her.

Likewise in the Gospel of Luke, when the penitent woman anoints the feet of Jesus in the house of Simon, she elicits a strong response (cf. Lk 7: 36-50). Her act of love is intimately connected with the forgiveness of her sin. Simon is scandalized that Jesus allows himself to be touched by this woman, but Jesus shows that Simon himself is in need of his healing touch.

Pope Benedict describes the eloquent message of this passage. "God forgives all to those who love much. Those who trust in themselves and in their own merits are, as it were, blinded by their ego and their heart is hardened in sin. Those, on the other hand, who recognize that they are weak and sinful entrust themselves to God and obtain from him grace and forgiveness... In the Sacrament of Reconciliation, whatever the sin committed, if it is humbly recognized and the person involved turns with trust to the priest-confessor, he or she never fails to experience the soothing joy of God's forgiveness."[3]

The "soothing joy of God's forgiveness" is the fragrance that can draw others to Christ. This is a good reminder to parents whose children have left the practice of the Catholic faith. Rather than worrying over lost opportunities or nagging your children to assuage your own sense of guilt, draw close to the Lord yourself. No matter where we are along our path of conversion, he can draw others to repentance and new life by his grace in us if only we let his goodness toward us be seen.

PUT YOUR FINGER HERE

Through the practice of regular confession, the Lord can lead us to a deeper sorrow unto "repentance without regret" (2 Cor 7: 10). It is only in the light of God's infinite goodness that we see the full reality of our sin.

The examination of conscience in preparation for confession is not simply a matter of making a laundry list of sins. Much less is it an exercise in scrupulosity, looking for sin where there is none. The paralyzing fear and anxiety of scruples are a real cross to those who experience them.

In examining our conscience, we open our hearts to God's

---

3. Pope Benedict XVI, "Address to the participants in a course on the internal forum organized by the Tribunal of the Apostolic Penitentiary," Friday, 7 March 2008. Accessed 10 April 2008 (http://www.vatican.va/holy_father/benedict_xvi/speeches/2008/march/documents/hf_ben-xvi_spe_20080307_penitenzieria-apostolica_en.html).

grace and ask him to show us what he wants us to see. And the Lord will show us what we need to see when we are ready to see it. Regular confession helps us grow in friendship with God, making our hearts more sensitive to his love, so that we are saddened when we offend that love. A perfect act of contrition is an exquisite gift of God's grace. It is not a matter of wracking my heart with guilt; rather, I allow him to rend my heart with his love. From beginning to end, the examination and confession of our sins is the work of Christ's love.

When the risen Jesus appeared to the apostles to give them his peace and the gift of the Holy Spirit for the forgiveness of sins, he showed them his wounds. Rather than being stung with remorse at these signs of their cowardice and betrayal, they are filled with joy at these proofs of his love (cf. Jn 20: 20-23).

The same is true when we meet the risen Lord in confession. Pope Benedict reminds us that "what is central [in the Sacrament of Reconciliation]... is... the personal encounter with God, the Father of goodness and mercy. It is not sin which is at the heart of the sacramental celebration but rather God's mercy, which is infinitely greater than any guilt of ours." [4]

If you find difficulty in examining your conscience, in showing your wounds to our wounded Lord, still come to the sacrament and, with the help of your confessor, let the Lord lead you. Father Lanteri expressed the sentiment that resides in the heart of every confessor: "If I knew that there might be someone among you who still had not surrendered himself to God's forgiveness, I would like to throw myself on his neck, and not leave him until he was converted. I would like to make myself certain of the assurance of his forgiveness, I would like to assure him that the vengeance of God consists in transforming those wounds, renewed through sin, into so many sources of blessings. I would like to assure him that the heart of God is ready to die at his feet in order to give him life,

---

4. Ibid.

if necessary. And if he should still struggle with the difficulty of the examination and contrition, I would tell him that rather than not coming, come without examination: I will examine his conscience. Come without contrition: we will weep together over his sins; and he will return content, in the grace of God." [5]

Until we touch the wound of our sin, we cannot open it to God's mercy to be healed. The Lord brings to mind what he wants us to see when he wants us to see it, when we are ready to let him touch and heal us.

BEHOLD, I MAKE ALL THINGS NEW

The Spirit of the Lord who restores our freedom makes us new, transforming us into God's own image, "from glory to glory" (2 Cor 3: 18). We would like to think that God is glorified in us despite our weakness. But he delights to show his power in mercy, which continually renews us. God, who says, "Behold, I make all things new" (Rv 21: 5), makes not only new heavens, a new earth, and a new Jerusalem, but also a new heart, a new spirit (Ez 36: 26) and the new self which we have put on in Christ (cf. Col 3: 10). The lives of Peter and Paul give us striking examples of the transforming power of God's love.

It is amazing to see how boldly Peter preaches after being filled with the Spirit on Pentecost. The hearts of his hearers are stung when they hear his words: "God has made... both Lord and Messiah, this Jesus whom you crucified" (Acts 2: 36). Has Peter forgotten his own role in the crucifixion of the Lord? He had vowed to go to prison and to die with Christ if necessary (cf. Lk 22: 33), but in his weakness and fear, he denied Jesus three times.

---

5. Pio Bruno Lanteri, "Meditazione del Figliuol prodigo." Scritti e Documenti d'Archivio / Pio Bruno Lanteri, vol. 4 (Fossano, Italy: Editrice Esperienze, 2002), pp. 3000-3001; my translation from the Italian original.

Peter's weakness was no surprise to Jesus. At the Last Supper, Jesus foretold Peter's turning away: "Simon, Simon, behold Satan has demanded to sift all of you like wheat, but I have prayed that your own faith may not fail; and once you have turned back, you must strengthen your brothers" (Lk 22: 31-32). At one and the same time, Luke shows Jesus both foretelling Peter's fall and confirming his call to leadership. In the Gospel of John, the risen Jesus appears to Peter on the seashore, gently calling him to repentance for his threefold denial. "Simon, son of John, do you love me?" (cf. Jn 21: 15-17). Again, the Lord calls Peter to repentance and, at the very same time, strengthens him to carry out his appointed mission.

Peter was able to speak with such conviction, to stir hearts to conversion, not in spite of his weakness but precisely because he knew the transforming power of God's love in his own life. Peter's very life became the story of God's mercy in action. He invited his hearers to experience this same mercy in their own lives.

Paul, too, knew the transforming power of God's grace. He never forgot his encounter with the risen Lord Jesus on the road to Damascus. "Saul, Saul, why are you persecuting me?... I am Jesus, whom you are persecuting. Now get up and go into the city and you will be told what you must do" (cf. Acts 9: 4-6). This transformation was so profound that Paul would later write, "yet I live, no longer I, but Christ lives in me; insofar as I now live in the flesh, I live by faith in the Son of God who has loved me and given himself up for me" (Gal 2: 20). Paul knew the power of God's love, and so with courage and conviction he could call others to that love.

We too meet the risen Lord Jesus in the sacrament of confession. There is nothing we bring before God that is not healed, transformed, and made new by his saving grace. Even the memory of our sins, seen in the light of Christ's love, can become a witness to his power. We can encourage one another in hope because we know in our own lives that our sin is not greater than God's mercy in Christ Jesus.

This path of mercy, this way of hope, is open to us at every moment, every day. No matter where we are or what we have done, Jesus gives us the grace to begin anew with tranquility and utter confidence. Drawn by his love, we can come before God as we are. Jesus is eager to touch and heal us, to accomplish far more than we could ever ask for or imagine. The soothing joy of his forgiveness in our own lives can draw others to life through sincere repentance, to daily transformation in his love.

God has forgiven us in Christ, and so we have hope.

BEHOLD THE LAMB OF GOD

The Saving Presence of the Eucharist

DOUGLAS G. BUSHMAN

INTRODUCTION

The *Catechism of the Catholic Church* gives us the proper context in which to take up a consideration of Jesus as "the Lamb of God who takes away the sins of the world." In a section entitled "Our communion in the mysteries of Jesus," it quotes Saint John Eudes:

> *We must continue to accomplish in ourselves the stages of Jesus' life and his mysteries and often to beg him to perfect and realize them in us and in his whole Church... For it is the plan of the Son of God to make us and the whole Church partake in his mysteries and to extend them to and continue them in us and in his whole Church. This is his plan for fulfilling his mysteries in us.*

The Catechism gives its own succinct summary: "Christ enables us *to live in him* all that he himself lived, and *he lives it in us.*" [1] The liturgy is the means by which Christ imparts to us a participation in his mysteries, since "the mysteries of Christ's life are the foundations of what he would henceforth dispense in the sacraments." [2]

It is significant that among the numerous names and titles for Jesus, the one taken from John the Baptist has such a prominent place in the Mass: "Behold, the Lamb of God, who takes away the sin of the world" (Jn 1: 29). Appearing in the Gloria, it is also repeated three times in the *Agnus Dei* as the assembly of the faithful addresses its eucharistic Lord. A final time, it precedes the celebrant's acclamation of blessing for all who are called to the Supper of the Lamb.

The Mass not only communicates the benefits of Christ's mission as the Lamb of God to those who receive the Lamb in faith. It also brings about a participation in the mission that must be lived in daily life. Reception of the Lamb of God in Holy Communion, then, calls for the development of what Pope John Paul II called a "liturgical attitude," so that we may receive the Lamb of God in faith, and for a genuine "spirituality of the Lamb of God" that is this fruit of the liturgical encounter in our daily lives.

THE WORDS OF JOHN THE BAPTIST

"Behold the Lamb of God, who takes away the sin of the world" (Jn 1: 29). We hear these words shortly before receiving Holy Communion. Two of John's disciples, Andrew and John the Evangelist, were the first to hear these words, which they interpreted as a signal from the Baptist to follow Jesus. This is one of those "great events of salvation history" that the Church "re-reads

---

1. CCC 521.
2. CCC 1115.

and re-lives… in the 'today' of her liturgy." [3] John the Baptist continues to send to Jesus all who have embraced his call for repentance.

> *The fundamental content of the Old Testament is summarized in the message by John the Baptist:* meta-noeìte – *Convert! There is no access to Jesus without the Baptist; there is no possibility of reaching Jesus without answering the call of the precursor, rather: Jesus took up the message of John in the synthesis of his own preaching:… Convert and believe in the Gospel (Mark 1: 15).* [4]

John's mission was to announce, prepare, and dispose God's people to cooperate with the Holy Spirit in creating a "people of the 'poor' – those who, humble and meek, rely solely on their God's mysterious plans, who await the justice, not of men but of the Messiah." The Catechism calls this "the great achievement of the Holy Spirit's hidden mission during the time of the promises that prepare for Christ's coming." [5]

To become a disciple of the Lamb of God one must recognize sin and embrace the call to do penance. From this vantage point alone is it possible to discover in Jesus the fulfillment of a life of conversion. In Jesus the Lamb of God, all of mankind's struggles to overcome evil and suffering and sin find their definitive answer. Let us turn to consider, then, how God prepared his people to discover the fulfillment of their faith in the mission of Jesus, the Lamb of God.

---

3. CCC 1095.
4. Joseph Cardinal Ratzinger, Address to Catechists and Religion Teachers On the Occasion of the Jubilee of Catechists, December 10, 2000.
5. CCC 716.

THE SACRIFICE OF ISAAC

Three important passages from the Old Testament shed light on what the apostles understood by calling Jesus the Lamb of God: the account of Abraham's sacrifice of Isaac, and the lamb provided by God; the account of the Passover lamb; and Isaiah's account of God's suffering servant. The most obvious element common to them is the association of the sacrificial death of a lamb with an event of salvation. Isaac is saved from being a sacrificial victim, Israel is saved from slavery in Egypt, and the chosen people and even the nations will be saved by the suffering servant from the consequences of sin.

When John the Baptist identified Jesus as "the Lamb of God," his followers could quite naturally have understood him to be referring to the lamb that Abraham had predicted God would provide. "'Father!' he said. 'Yes, son,' he replied. Isaac continued, 'Here are the fire and the wood, but where is the sheep for the holocaust?' 'Son' Abraham answered, 'God himself will provide the sheep for the holocaust'" (Gn 22: 7-8).

The key is the link between Abraham's faith and God's provision of the lamb for sacrifice. [6] The test of faith was a confrontation with what appeared as the complete negation of God's promise. God cannot contradict himself, yet two things seem certain. On the one hand, Isaac is God's gracious gift and God has promised that through him the blessing of Abraham would continue for unending generations. On the other hand, God has spoken just as surely in requiring the sacrifice of Isaac, and neither

---

6. For a discussion of Abraham's offering of Isaac, see Léopold Sabourin in Stanislaus Lyonnet and Léopold Sabourin, *Sin, Redemption, and Sacrifice: A Biblical and Patristic Study* (Rome: Biblical Institute Press, 1970), p. 264. See also Jean Daniélou, *From Shadows to Reality: Studies in the Biblical Typology of the Fathers*, trans. W. Hibberd (Westminster, MD: Newman Press, 1960), pp. 118-19.

Abraham nor Isaac questions his prerogative to do so.[7] If God is the source of both, then either he is not God or there exists a wisdom unique to him that is alone able to resolve the contradiction. Abraham's faith resolutely opts for the latter, and this is the significance of his words: "God himself will provide the sheep for the holocaust."

Israel would find itself in similar situations of contradiction throughout its history. Moses experienced it most intensely when God made known his intention to obliterate the very people he had just liberated from slavery in Egypt. God's mercy resolves the contradiction between man's God-given aspirations and the reality of the suffering and death that seem to threaten them.

The drama of Isaac's sacrifice is the human drama of deciding whether the hopes that the Creator has inscribed in our being are real or illusory, to be taken seriously or ignored. Dare we hope for peace on earth? Do our hearts deceive us when we intuit that death should not simply be the end? Is it dreaming to envision self-mastery and perfection in virtue? God has placed within us the aspirations that give rise to them. Is it all simply a game, or even worse, a display of cruelty, an existential tease of a malign divinity?

Throughout Israel's history, in the midst of the apparent non-fulfillment of his promises, God provides. There is the lamb. Could God have tested and proved Abraham's faith without having provided the lamb? Abraham demonstrated his faith before he spotted the lamb; what does the sacrifice of the lamb add to the internal disposition of faith?

---

7. There is no return to God without sacrifice, without blood, without death. Barthélemy develops this premise in terms of the disfigured image of God as a result of sin. "In the region of the land of Canaan, the sacrifice of first-born sons to God was a well known custom. Men felt they had no right to be fathers until they had acknowledged the primacy of the divine fatherhood by sacrificing their first-born. It is a case of anxiously disfiguring God's face..." (Dominique Barthélemy, *God and His Image* [New York: Sheed and Ward, 1966], p. 39).

The lamb serves to remind us that there is a price attached to man's return to God. Sin and the overturning of sin are matters of life and death. God's promise of a posterity for Abraham was resolved, but the ultimate conflict of life and death was not. Of this, the lamb caught in the thicket will be a perpetual reminder.

Israel's liturgy of sacrifice will be a constant call to conversion, the very conversion that constituted the mission of John the Baptist and that leads to Jesus, the Lamb of God who takes away the sin of the world.

The God Whose Heart Recoils against Itself

Before we consider the Passover lamb and the suffering servant, the confrontation of Abraham and Moses with the apparent negation of God's promise invites a reflection on a paragraph in the first encyclical of Pope Benedict XVI. It is based on Hosea 11: 8-9.

> *How could I give you up, O Ephraim, or deliver you up, O Israel? How could I treat you as Admah, or make you like Zeboiim? My heart is overwhelmed, my pity is stirred. I will not give vent to my blazing anger, I will not destroy Ephraim again; For I am God and not man, the Holy One present among you; I will not let the flames consume you.*

Pope Benedict commented on this text to show that the demands of God's justice and of his mercy appear to be contradictory. The recoiling of God's heart conveys that his merciful love overrides the justice by which he "should judge and repudiate" Israel for her adulterous infidelity. God's merciful love is "so great that it turns God against himself, his love against his justice." [8]

Pope Benedict was intent on showing that what Hosea wrote

---

8. *Deus caritas est*, 10.

about God's conflicted heart finds in Christ a realization that could never have been imagined. In the recoiling heart of God, "Christians can see a dim prefigurement of the mystery of the Cross: so great is God's love for man that by becoming man he follows him even into death, and so reconciles justice and love."[9]

Many years earlier, Cardinal Ratzinger had meditated on the same passage.

> *He can be angry with the wife of his youth on account of her adultery. He can punish her, but all this is simultaneously directed against himself and pains him, the lover, whose "bowels churn." He cannot repudiate her without rendering judgment against himself. It is on this, on his personal, innermost bewilderment as lover, that the covenant's eternal and irrevocable character is based... God's divinity is no longer revealed in his ability to punish but in the indestructibility and constancy of his love.*[10]

On yet another occasion, the Hosea text led him to write:

> *God takes the destiny of love destroyed upon himself; he takes the place of the sinner and offers the Son's place to men once more, not only to Israel, but to all nations. The pierced Heart of the crucified Son is the literal fulfillment of the prophecy of the Heart of God, which overthrows righteousness by mercy and by that very action remains righteousness.*[11]

---

9. Ibid.
10. Joseph Cardinal Ratzinger, *Daughter Zion* (San Francisco: Ignatius Press, 1983), p. 22.
11. Joseph Cardinal Ratzinger, *Behold the Pierced One* (San Francisco: Ignatius Press, 1983), p. 64.

Jesus is the lamb that God provides to resolve all contradictions between man's hopes and his incapacity to see how they can be fulfilled, between his sense of God's justice and his enfeebled sense of God's mercy. In Jesus, the Lamb of God, the intuition about the debt of death due to sin, kept alive in the tradition of sacrificing lambs, is definitively affirmed. Abraham and Isaac knew that everything must pass over to God. At the same time, faith and hope in God's promises, that death does not have the last word, is also affirmed. Jesus, the Lamb of God, took upon himself the anguish of the ages caused by the experience of these unresolved contradictions.

THE PASSOVER LAMB

"For our paschal lamb, Christ, has been sacrificed" (1 Cor 5: 7). The Gospel of John affirms the same thing, though more subtly, by noting that Jesus was being prepared for his death at the same time that the Paschal lambs were being prepared to be killed (Jn 19: 14), and that Jesus' legs not being broken fulfills the Scripture regarding the Passover lamb (Jn 19: 36; see Ex 12: 46). Jesus' blood is the blood of the Lamb of God for the definitive liberation of God's people, liberation not from Egypt, the land of sin and oppression, but from sin itself.

There is irony in the fact that those who were intent on his destruction, for the sake of protecting the purity of doctrine and of worship, would not enter into the praetorium with Jesus, "in order not to be defiled so that they could eat the Passover" (Jn 18: 28). Two understandings of the Passover collide here. While the Jews who condemned him were concerned with reliving the sacrificial offering of the Passover lamb so as to commemorate the mighty works by which God delivered his people from slavery in Egypt, Jesus is living in himself the deeper reality of the first Passover by fulfilling what it means to be saved as a victim.

To perceive this deeper reality it is necessary to see the blood of the Passover lamb in light of the Old Testament understanding of the blood of the innocent crying out to God. [12] "God cannot leave the crime unpunished: from the ground on which it has been spilt, the blood of the one murdered demands that God should render justice (cf. Gn 37: 26; Is 26: 21; Ez 24: 7-8). From this text the Church has taken the name of the 'sins which cry to God for justice.'" [13] The blood of the innocent, then, is a pledge of God's intervention.

The blood of the Passover lamb signifies that Israel was saved as a victim. [14] God chose this sign in order to reveal himself as the Author and protector of life, and as the One whose promises for a future are not illusory. This was Israel's fundamental catechesis in the justice of God, who hears the cry of the poor. [15] By experiencing God's mercy in the situation of being a victim, Israel was being brought to the realization that God himself is the victim of sin.

This pedagogy is personified in the conversion of David. The prophet Nathan provokes the king's sense of horizontal justice: he brings the cry of blood for justice – the blood of a lamb, a stolen lamb, an only lamb – to David, the Lord's anointed, and the king pronounces his judgment: "As the LORD lives, the man who has done this merits death!" (2 Sm 12: 5). Nathan thereby prepares David for the realization that, because he has arranged Uriah's death, he is the one who deserves this sentence. From that point forward, David perceives in all of his afflictions the just punishment for his sin, and yet he also perceives that his anguish over sin and his bearing of its consequences are pleasing to God and are the occasion for God's mercy. [16] The contrite and repentant heart of the great king makes him a worthy disciple of John the Baptist,

---

12. See Gn 4: 10.
13. *Evangelium vitae*, 9, referring to CCC 1867 and 2268.
14. This is the interpretation of Dominique Barthélemy in *God and His Image*, pp. 166-67.
15. See Dt 24: 15, Ps 72: 12, and Prv 21: 13.
16. See 2 Sm 16: 12 and 19: 1 and Ps 51: 19.

disposed to leave all things in order to follow the Lamb of God who takes away the sin of the world.

THE SUFFERING SERVANT

The text of Isaiah 53: 7 is especially important as background to understand Jesus as "the Lamb of God who takes away the sin of the world," because, only a few verses after the suffering servant is compared to a lamb that makes no complaint and offers no resistance when going to its slaughter, it is said of him: "Because of his affliction/ he shall see the light in fullness of days;/ Through his suffering, my servant shall justify many,/ and their guilt he shall bear./... He surrendered himself to death/ and was counted among the wicked;/ And he shall take away the sins of many,/ and win pardon for their offenses" (Is 53: 11-12). [17]

The great lesson of the prophets, the conscience of Israel, has finally been internalized. Aware of the people's sins, God's servant perceives the rightness of suffering, and even death. If that is the case for God's chosen people, then how great must be the peril of the other nations, which have not benefited from the divine pedagogy to reach this understanding? God will bring about the conversion of the nations through the incontestable sign of the suffering servant. In him, Israel's faith lets go of any residual sense of temporal blessing being the sign of election and the message of the prophets is definitively acquired. True prophecy is distinguished from false prophecy precisely in this, that the blessings of God must be preceded by the purification that comes through suffering.

---

17. The NAB stands out for translating verse 12 as "he shall *take away* the sins of many" while other English translations (NJB, NAS, RVS, DRA) render it in terms of bearing or having borne the sins of many. Pierre Grelot argues that it should be translated as "take away" and asserts: "It is entirely plausible that the formulation of John [1: 29] takes up that of this text by retranslating it from the Hebrew and putting it in relation to the Lamb of verse 7 of the same chapter [of Isaiah]" (*Les Poèmes du Serviteur* [Paris: Cerf, 1981], p. 181).

The suffering servant, as fulfillment of the lamb tradition, brings resolution to the apparent contradictions that men experience in their relationship with God: on the one hand, the sense of just punishment [18] and of the price of turning away from sin in order to return to God, and on the other, the conviction of faith in God's faithful and merciful love. Suffering and death cannot be the last word, but they appear to be exactly that. With the suffering servant, after centuries of divine pedagogy, there is finally someone who reacts to sin as God does, seeing the suffering caused by sin as a privilege of grace [19] and as mission.

Seeing his own image in man, God permits him to participate in the process of passing through darkness in order to come into the light. Man is granted the dignity (which perhaps on occasion he experiences as a burden, and which he would rather renounce) of participating in the convulsions of God's own heart that are caused by sin. Remorse of conscience caused by our own sin is participation in the suffering of the Lamb of God whose suffering was caused by sin. [20] Through him, with him, and in him we can also suffer for the sins of others as though they were our own. In this way, Christ lives his paschal mystery in us and we live it in him.

Several centuries after Isaiah, in another cultural world, Socrates would arrive at the insight that it is preferable to be the victim of an injustice than to be a perpetrator of injustice. This is a meeting point between philosophical wisdom and the wisdom of faith, for faith too holds that acts that inflict injury on humans "do more harm to those who practice them than to those who suffer from the injury." [21] The victimizers are the real victims.

---

18. This is expressed in the First Eucharistic Prayer: "Though we are sinners, we trust in your mercy and love. Do not consider what we truly deserve, but grant us your forgiveness."

19. See CCC 1473.

20. See *Dominum et Vivificantem*, 45.

21. See *Gaudium et spes*, 27.

What is revealed in the suffering servant goes further. His fidelity to God, his martyrdom, has become in God's plan the means of conversion for those who have inflicted unspeakable suffering upon him. He is servant precisely as victim.

THE LAMB WITHOUT BLEMISH

Just as the Passover lamb had to be "without blemish" (Ex 12: 5), [22] so Jesus, "the Lamb of God who takes away the sin of the world," was himself without sin. "You were ransomed... not with perishable things like silver or gold but with the precious blood of Christ as of a spotless unblemished lamb" (1 Pt 1: 18-19). [23] What is the significance of Jesus being an unblemished Lamb offered to God in sacrifice?

The sacrifice of an unblemished lamb is contrary to our way of thinking. First, it goes against the prudent provision for the future. Second, it seems to offend a natural sense of justice. Immolation is an odd reward for lacking imperfection. Both of these considerations may enter into the requirement that the Passover lamb and other lambs offered in sacrifice be "without blemish." [24] Ritual sacrifice expresses man's desire to pass over into the realm of the sacred, that is, into communion with God, so God must come first. There is no room here for a pragmatic calculation such that man could pursue his earthly well-being first and then offer to God what is left over.

More importantly and more profoundly, in the mind of Israel the unblemished lamb was the ideal sacrifice because it corresponded perfectly to God's original intention. Untouched by the consequences of sin, it aptly represented what God had envisioned from the beginning in the order of his wisdom and love. In

---

22. See Lv 22: 20-25.
23. See also 1 Jn 3: 5, 2 Cor 5: 12, and Heb 9: 14.
24. Ex 12: 5. See also Lv 9: 3 and 22: 19.

the unblemished lamb, God could behold creation as pure reflection of his own infinite beauty. This is why Israel could be confident that it would be acceptable to him. [25] "God will not reject a blameless man" (Job 8: 20), but who is blameless?

The spotless lamb symbolizes man's desire to be without blemish, that is, to be rid of the weight of sin in order to be worthy to stand in the presence of the all-holy God.

> *It is in the very gesture of immolation that its meaning is revealed. A member of Adam's race, which is destined for death, slays an animal, in other words a creature that has not fallen under the condemnation that weighs on man himself. Man pours out before God the life-blood of this creature as a substitute for his own life that has been condemned by God. The outpoured innocent blood mysteriously becomes an intercession for him who poured it out. Only the blood of a spotless victim can intercede for guilty man.* [26]

Jesus is the unblemished Lamb. Tested like us in all things though never having sinned, [27] he fully "satisfied the Father's eternal love." [28] He is exactly what God had always wanted men to be. He is the One who alone can elicit from the Father the words: "This is my beloved Son, with whom I am well pleased" (Mt 3: 17). Yet, because "Christ enables us *to live in him* all that

---

25. Roland de Vaux stresses that the fact that the animals sacrificed as sin offerings were considered "most sacred" (Lv 6: 22) "contradicts the theory according to which the sin of the one who offers the sacrifice is placed on the victim so that it would become 'sin'. No, it is a victim pleasing to God that, in consideration of this offering, takes away the sin. It is evidently in this ritual meaning of the word that St. Paul uses it: 'for our sake [God] made him [Christ] to be sin who did not know sin, so that we might become the righteousness of God in him'" (*Les Institutions de L'Ancien Testament*, II [Paris: Cerf, 1967], p. 297).
26. Barthélemy, *God and His Image*, pp. 167-68.
27. See Heb 4: 15.
28. *Redemptor hominis*, 9.

he himself lived, and *he lives it in us*" (CCC 521), Jesus' experience of being the object of his Father's love becomes our own.[29] The certainty that God's favor rests on him and that he lives this mystery in us and we live it in him gives rise to the prayer of the preface for Ordinary Time: "You sent him as one like ourselves, though free from sin, that you might see and love in us what you see and love in Christ."

GOD IS THE FIRST VICTIM OF SIN

The startling reality is that God himself fulfills what the innocent victim-lamb prefigured. All along man thought that he was in search of God, while all along God was in search of him. "The Incarnation of the Son of God attests that God goes in search of man… It is a search which *begins in the heart of God…* God therefore goes in search of man who *is his special possession…* Man is God's possession by virtue of a choice made in love: God seeks man out, moved by his fatherly heart."[30] The lamb seemed a perfect symbol for man's status as a victim, when in reality it is God himself who is the victim – of the rejection of his love.

A common form of the so-called problem of evil runs as a complaint against God. In the words of the Catechism: "If God the Father almighty, the Creator of the ordered and good world, cares for all his creatures, why does evil exist?"[31] If God foresaw all of the suffering, especially of the innocent and of children, why did he go ahead with creation?

The question betrays the incapacity to consider the issue from God's perspective. The first thing God foresaw, in his

---

29. "With Baptism we become *children of God in his only-begotten Son, Jesus Christ*. Rising from the waters of the Baptismal font, every Christian hears again the voice that was once heard on the banks of the Jordan River: 'You are my beloved Son; with you I am well pleased' (Lk 3: 22)" (*Christi fideles laici*, 11).
30. *Tertio millennio adveniente*, 7.
31. CCC 309.

all-embracing plan, was the suffering of Christ on the cross. This was established before God created. Jesus the Lamb was "slain before the foundation of the world" (Rv 13: 8). In this light the question takes on an entirely different meaning. What is it that moved God to become man, to experience himself the contradiction between the promise and hope of life and the destruction and despair of death in order to suffer and die to save us? What does it say about the perfection of his love that the certain knowledge of what it would mean for him to love the creatures he endowed with free will did not deter him from creating them and remaining faithful to his love for them "to the end"?

As the Easter Sequence puts it: "The Lamb has saved the sheep." God has never been indifferent to human suffering. It is possible, however, as Hosea saw, for God's heart to recoil within over his love for the people who reject his love. God saw clearly that the perfection of his love would lead to his being "pierced for our offenses, crushed for our sins" (Is 53: 5). It is as though God held himself accountable for a situation for which in reality he had no responsibility. In human affairs such an extension of responsibility beyond the sphere of one's control is not only discouraged but considered pathological and treated with counseling. With God it is the logic of love.

The revelation of the Lamb of God in Jesus makes any claim to innocence impossible. The refined sense of justice and of being a victim in the horizontal sense now is seen to apply above all to the vertical relationship with God. "Look what you have done, in this man, to your God." [32]

---

32. This is taken from the meditation of Karol Cardinal Wojtyła on the second station of the Cross, given as part of the retreat for the papal household of Pope Paul VI. The text can be found in the book *Sign of Contradiction* (New York: The Seabury Press, 1979), p. 186.

"Lamb of God, who takes away the sins of the world, have mercy on us"

This prayer, the *Agnus Dei*, implores the mercy of God that was fully revealed in the sacrificial death of Jesus. To know Jesus as the Lamb of God is to know the final and definitive revelation of God's mercy. The structure of the *Agnus Dei* is a statement of faith followed by petition based on that doctrine.

This pattern displays a general principle about prayer: doctrine, the truth about God, is the foundation of prayer and dictates its content. The experience of God's compassion that corrects sinners became a part of Israel's creed, an essential element of the content of its faith, and it nourished Israel's prayer. The truth is: God is merciful and he reproves, admonishes, and teaches (see Sir 18: 11-13). The prayer is: "Punish us, O Lord, but with equity,/ not in anger" (Jer 10: 24). The truth is: God is "a merciful and gracious God, slow to anger and rich in kindness and fidelity, continuing his kindness for a thousand generations, and forgiving wickedness and crime and sin" (Ex 34: 6-7). The prayer is: "If I find favor with you, O Lord, do come along in our company. This is indeed a stiff-necked people; yet pardon our wickedness and sins, and receive us as your own" (Ex 34: 9).

All of the prayers for forgiveness and for God to be faithful simply translate doctrine into petition. The one who prays wants to experience God's fidelity and saving power now, in a particular circumstance.[33] The revealed truth is: Jesus is the Lamb of God,

---

33. "When the book of Wisdom, for instance, narrates the 'expiation' of Aaron (Wis 18: 21-25), it not only considers it as an 'entreaty' but that 'entreaty' is nothing else but a word of Aaron by which he recalls God's promises (v. 22: 'recalling the oaths and covenants'; see 18:6). Hence it happens that the intercession fundamentally is reduced to an act of faith in God's fidelity or to fidelity of man answering to the fidelity of God which comes first from every point of view" (Stanislaus Lyonnet, in Lyonnet and Sabourin, *Sin, Redemption, and Sacrifice*, p. 146).

who takes away the sin of the world. The prayer is: Have mercy on us.

BOUND BY LOVE TO PROVE LOVE

The revelation of God's love culminates in the paschal mystery of the Lamb of God. Finally, the meaning of the lamb that has accompanied man's return to God through sacrifices, from Abel to Abraham and Isaac and the annual memorial sacrifice of the Passover lamb, is fully revealed. Now man knows what God has known from the beginning. God, as the first victim of sin, has accompanied man throughout his pilgrimage of faith.

In the Eucharist, the prophetic intuition of Israel is fulfilled in ordinary people of faith who become one with the Lamb of God in offering themselves with him as victims for sin. Here we discover the foundation for the spirituality of being a victim soul. The Church's participation in the priestly office of Christ is a participation in that unique dimension of his priesthood whereby priest and victim are one.

This is the final conclusion of the logic of love. The dignity God sees in us, made in his image, requires that he save us from sin in a way that actualizes to its fullest our capacity to love. We are called to love as he has loved (see Jn 13: 34). Love means "I want what is good for you," but it also means "I want to be completely one with you in truth, love, and life." Such full sharing of life that God desires for us includes his way of reacting to sin. God wants us to suffer over sin, not as a punishment that is inflicted from the outside, because that is not how he suffered, but by entering into the turmoil of his own recoiling heart. He is not content to leave us mere observers and beneficiaries of his love. He draws us into his love.

Israel learned and made its own the lesson that God is especially close to his people in times of suffering. The saving presence of the Lamb of God in the Eucharist is the way in which God's accompaniment of humanity as first victim of sin is perpetuated. The Mystical Body of Christ makes its own the words of Psalm 40, attributed to Christ: "Sacrifice and offering you did not desire,/ but a body you prepared for me;/ holocausts and sin offerings you took no delight in./ Then I said, 'As is written of me in the scroll,/ Behold, I come to do your will, O God'" (Heb 10: 5-7).

God wants men to know how sin affects him, and since it cannot diminish his divine beatitude (see Job 35: 6), he became man in order to fulfill the symbol of the lamb that accompanies man throughout the economy of salvation. Now there is no question about how God reacts to sin. The Lamb without blemish takes sin upon himself in order to remove it.

In the course of our reflections we have asked if the sacrifice of the lamb was necessary for the purification of Abraham's faith and if the Passover lamb was necessary for the deliverance of Israel from slavery in Egypt. Here, too, we need to ask if it was necessary for Christ to be immolated as the Lamb of God in order to save us from sin. The answer is the same. God's power is not limited in any way that would make this sacrifice necessary in an absolute sense. [34] But without it, how would we know how our sins affect God, how he reacts to sin? How, then, would we, as image of God, know the right way to react to sin?

In the garden, Jesus turned to his Father in order to be irrevocably bound to his sacrifice: "My Father, if it is possible, let this cup pass from me; yet, not as I will, but as you will" (Mt 26: 39). He is bound by the logic of divine love that desires to have men know that in this Lamb God himself suffers because of our sins.

------

34. See St. Thomas Aquinas, *Summa theologiae* III q. 46, aa. 1-2.

HOW DOES JESUS TAKE AWAY THE SINS OF THE WORLD?

The answer is twofold. The first part is a straightforward assertion of faith that the sacrifice of Christ is the cause of the gift of the Holy Spirit, who is opposed to all that is sinful (see Rom 8: 5; Gal 5: 16-17). The second part will lead us into an analysis of the very roots of sin as rejection of God's love; that analysis shows that sin is taken away when man becomes newly convinced that God is love.

The Sacrifice of the Lamb Brings the Gift of the Holy Spirit

"Christ came 'to take away the sin of the world' in this sense, that he communicates the Holy Spirit to man... and thus provides him with the necessary strength for avoiding sin." [35] The sacrifice of the Lamb of God is the efficient cause of the gift of the Holy Spirit sent upon the Church at Pentecost and into the hearts of all who believe. "The Holy Spirit will come insofar as Christ will depart through the Cross: he will come not only afterwards, but *because of* the Redemption accomplished by Christ." [36] The Holy Spirit draws from the mystery of redemption in Christ to "convict the world in regard to sin" (Jn 16: 8) and by the power of the Holy Spirit the apostles will forgive sins as Christ did (see Jn 20: 22-23). On Pentecost, Peter's proclamation is: "Repent and be baptized, every one of you, in the name of Jesus Christ for the forgiveness of your sins; and you will receive the gift of the holy Spirit" (Acts 2: 38).

---

35. Stanislaus Lyonnet, *Sin, Redemption, Sacrifice*, p. 40. Kereszty indicates essentially the same thing: "The blood of sacrificial animals, symbolizing the human life of the offerers, is given over to God, the source and Master of life. Thus, symbolically, Israel's sins are expiated; she again belongs to the Holy One of Israel. The integrity of the order that governs creation and covenantal election has been restored" (*Wedding Feast of the Lamb*, p. 10).
36. *Dominum et Vivificantem*, 8. The theme is carried through the encyclical. See *Dominum et Vivificantem*, 3, 11, 13, 61, 63.

Sin as Suspicion of God's Love

Jesus, the Lamb of God, took away the sin of the world by giving a final and definitive testimony to the truth that God is love. To grasp what this means we must have a clear understanding of the nature of sin and the reality of mercy.

Sin is the rejection of God's love. "Sin sets itself against God's love for us and turns our hearts away from it." [37] The interior reality of the sin of Adam and Eve was to doubt God's love, placing him in a "state of suspicion." [38] Despite the abundance of evidence that all God had done in creating them and providing for them was done out of love, our first parents were seduced into thinking that God gave the commandment to prevent them from becoming what they desired to be. "For in spite of all the witness of creation and of the salvific economy inherent in it, the spirit of darkness is capable of showing God as an enemy of his own creature, and in the first place as an enemy of man, as a source of danger and threat to man." [39]

This doubt about God's love led ineluctably to disobedience of the commandment he had given. If the commandments do not come from love, then they must be ordered to some form of utility. Suspicion about God's love leads to viewing the commandments as a threat to what man perceives his real happiness to be. Disobedience follows naturally. The sin of Adam and Eve was repeated in the desert, when Israel put God to the test even though he had demonstrated his love through the great acts that liberated them from slavery in Egypt (see Ps 95: 9).

God's Answer to Sin

The analysis of sin points in the direction of what God's response to it must be. He must provide new evidence of his love

---

37. CCC 1850.
38. *Dominum et Vivificantem*, 37.
39. *Dominum et Vivificantem*, 38.

to convince his people that his love for them is absolute, true, and unfailing. Then they will see his commandments for what they truly are, namely, his wisdom for their fulfillment and happiness.

The Catechism strongly underscores the relation between the truth about God and his commandments. They must be understood in the context of God's self-revelation to his people and the establishment of the covenant. [40] This is seen in the way the ten commandments are introduced in the Bible: "And God spoke all these words, saying, 'I am the LORD your God, who brought you out of the land of Egypt, out of the house of bondage'" (Ex 20: 1-3). God identifies himself as the One who has just demonstrated his love by delivering Israel from slavery. The motive he gives for keeping the commandments is that they have the same source as God's great saving actions, his love.

From this it follows that the power by which we are freed from sin is the truth that God is love. The power to live the new life in Christ is the power of the conviction that God is love, revealed in the sacrifice of the Lamb of God.

"LORD, I AM NOT WORTHY TO RECEIVE YOU..."

These words, part of the final preparation for receiving Holy Communion, are an adaptation of the words of the centurion who appealed to Jesus to heal his servant (see Mt 8: 5-13). Their use here indicates that the function of faith in receiving Holy Communion is essentially the same as its function in the healing of the centurion's servant. The saving power is in Jesus; faith disposes us to receive it. With these words we respond to the celebrant who identifies the eucharistic Lord as the Lamb of God. Both the confession of unworthiness and the petition of hope in the power of Christ's word of love to heal us from sin are made possible by

---

40. See CCC 2059-2062.

knowing the full truth about the Lamb of God who takes away the sins of the world.

This brief prayer contains the truth about man and the truth about God. On man's part, it is the truth about sin. It is striking to consider how consistently God's presence provokes a sense of unworthiness. Unless one has faith in God's mercy, the tendency is to think that the all-holy God cannot tolerate the presence of sinners. In truth, it is sinners who find God's presence intolerable, for the light of God's presence exposes the darkness of men's sins.

After they had disobeyed God's commandment and eaten the forbidden fruit, Adam and Eve became afraid of God and hid themselves when they heard him. "I heard you in the garden; but I was afraid, because I was naked, so I hid myself" (Gn 3: 10). They had always been naked in God's presence and it had not been the cause of fear. So it is not nakedness as such that produced this servile fear.

The Catechism teaches: "They become afraid of the God of whom they have conceived a distorted image – that of a God jealous of his prerogatives" (CCC 399). To be aware of one's complete dependence on God – this is the meaning of their nakedness – can bring servile fear only if the image of God one has is of a despot.[41] In reality, there is nothing to fear from a God of love. Adam and Eve, and their descendents, are acting in ways that are consistent with their doubt about God's love. To live in servile fear of God, who is omnipresent, is to live in unending anxiety.

"BUT ONLY SAY THE WORD…"

It is clear that God sees things differently. Jesus lived in the company of sinners. He sought them out, for it was his mission to save them. The Gospels depict how frequently this was a source of consternation for those around Jesus who adhered to a theology that

---

41. This is the theme of Father Dominique Barthélemy's remarkable book, *God and His Image*, recently brought back into print by Ignatius Press.

God's holiness requires complete separation from sinners.[42] The distinction between sin and sinner is the key to grasping Jesus' behavior. God's holiness does indeed bring about the destruction of sin, but this is at the service of the rehabilitation of sinners, reconciliation, and communion with God.

In light of previous reflection on the Passover lamb, our confession of being unworthy means: I am not innocent; I renounce all claims to innocence. I see myself as having caused the spilling of the blood of the unblemished Lamb of God. I see that Peter's references to Jesus as the One whom "you killed" (Acts 2: 23; 5: 30) applies to me. By my sins I am "author and minister of all the sufferings that the divine Redeemer endured." By my sins I have laid "violent hands on him."[43] He is the Lamb whom my sins have pierced.[44]

There is, of course, a great difference between recognition of one's unworthiness and the re-establishment of a relationship broken by sin. The Prodigal Son's confession, "Father, I have sinned against heaven and against you; I no longer deserve to be called your son," was a condition for his being reinstated as son, but not its cause. The cause was his father's mercy. For the prodigal this mercy was a surprise. He had hoped for much less, for too little, in hoping to be treated simply as a servant. This would already be a mercy, for it would alleviate his immediate suffering. His father saw more deeply, though, and from the suffering of his own heart, overwhelmed and recoiled within by the rejection of his love, over not having a son to love, he knew that sooner or later his son would come to a place of deep regret for not having that unique bond with his father. From the merciful heart of the father came the undeserved gift of reconciliation and the fullness of communion between the two.

God's mercy is not a surprise discovery for those with Christian faith. In contrast with the prodigal son, when we say the prayer

---

42. See Mk 2: 16; Lk 7: 34, 39 and 15: 2; Jn 9: 31-34.
43. CCC 598.
44. See CCC 1432.

"Lord I am not worthy to receive you…" we can be confident that the Lamb of God will speak his word of merciful love. He has already spoken it. He is the Word of God. God is Love, and love revealed in the context of suffering and sin is mercy. Jesus is the Word of Mercy, the Logic of Divine Love, the Incarnation of mercy,[45] and he instituted the sacrament of the Eucharist in order to make divine mercy present in the Church. The truth about sin and the truth about God's love are fully revealed in the death of the Lamb of God so that we can know what God knows and be one with him in this knowledge. The revelation of God's love in the paschal mystery makes it possible for us to be God's associates in our own return to him, in our conversion.

> *And it is love that enables man, in contemplating the cross, to see in it an exact reflection of his immeasurable guilt, and "pierced with fear" (Psalm 119: 120) to deliver himself up to the severity of judgment, so as no longer to wage his own war against truth, but to take sides with the truth against himself.*[46]

SO THAT WE MAY LIVE IN THE CERTAINTY OF BEING LOVED

God's Word of love revealed in the Lamb who was slain by and on account of sin is no less effective in taking sins away than it is in commanding creation and demons. This makes it possible for us to pray the Our Father with audacious boldness that anticipates his positive response.

> *This power of the Spirit who introduces us to the Lord's Prayer is expressed in the liturgies of East and of West by the beautiful, characteristically Christian expression:*

---

45. See *Dives in misericordia*, 2.
46. Hans Urs von Balthasar, *Prayer* (New York: Sheed and Ward, 1961), p. 183.

> parrhesia, *straightforward simplicity, filial trust, joyous assurance, humble boldness, the certainty of being loved.* [47]

As the Lamb of God, Christ takes away the sins of the world by giving us the definitive demonstration of God's love. This is the proof of love that was needed for man to overcome every temptation to be suspicious about God's love. This love was demonstrated "to the end" (Jn 13: 1) in the paschal mystery that is re-actualized in the sacramental offering of his sacrifice. That demonstration of love is the source of the humble boldness that characterizes all Christian prayer, especially those that come in the Mass after the eucharistic prayer, when the Incarnation of mercy becomes present to us in the Eucharist.

"Lord, I am not worthy to receive you, but only say the word and I shall be healed" – this prayer contains the truth about man and the truth about God as these are revealed in the mission of the Lamb of God who takes away the sin of the world. The Church wisely gives us this prayer to prepare us in faith to receive the Lamb of God in Holy Communion.

"Faith, in its deepest essence, is the openness of the human heart to the gift" of God. [48] Faith is already the gift of God, but it is the gateway to all other gifts. By faith we know the gift God wants to make of himself to us, out of love, because he has revealed himself as the Lamb who takes away the sin of the world so that we might live in the affirmation and peace of the certainty that we are loved by God.

---

47. CCC 2778.
48. *Dominum et Vivificantem*, 51.

"A Two-edged Sword"

Why We Should Read the Scriptures Every Day

Monsignor James Turro

A Proper State of Mind for Reading the Bible

One must begin one's encounter with the Bible with full awareness of its divine inspiration. It is a "letter from God" to us and it bears witness to God and his purposes. Since it is God himself who is communicating with us, we must be fully receptive and ready to do as he asks. That must be our state of mind as we read.

We must be aware of the fact that the human beings God charged to articulate his message were subjects of particular cultures and language groups; they expressed themselves in words and ways particular to the culture in which they lived, and these are not always words and ways to which we are accustomed.

There is a probing question that we should bring to our reading of Scripture. Simply put, it is this: what is it that God expects of me, so that I may be saved? One must approach every reading of

Scripture prepared for the surprises God has in store for us at each reading.

Occasionally one sees a statue of Our Lady at the moment of the Annunciation: her hands are raised toward heaven. This posture suggests to us the attitude of receptivity we are to take when we read Scripture. Mary is a model for us in our reading of Scripture. We must be prepared to say, as she did: "Be it done unto me according to thy word" (Lk 1: 38). In fact Mary encouraged just that ready response when at the wedding feast at Cana she said simply: "Do whatever he tells you" (Jn 2: 5). This is the mindset which should accompany our every reading of the Scriptures.

The role of the Church in our reading of the Bible cannot be minimized, much less ignored. The plain truth is that there are parts of Scripture that defy our best efforts to understand them. One of the purposes of the Church is precisely this: to construe Scripture authoritatively for God's people. It is the belief of Christians that the Scriptures are Christ-centered. At the heart of its message is the fact that salvation comes from Christ. This is the unifying truth that gives Scripture its coherence.

As one reads Scripture, one must make an effort to find an application to one's personal life. One ought to engage two questions: "What is this text saying?" and "How does it apply to me?"

THE BIBLE IN THE LIFE OF THE CHRISTIAN

The New Yorker magazine once displayed a cartoon showing a man in a bookstore inquiring about Bibles. The clerk replies: "The Bible?… that would be under self-help." For the Catholic Christian, the Bible is infinitely more than a self-help manual. To put it bluntly, if precisely, it is the Word of God. If for no other reason, it must loom large in a person's life experience. No thought of it lying on the shelf gathering dust. It must have a thunderous impact on the way one lives. The Bible can also provide the spur one sometimes needs for prayer.

In one of the documents of the Second Vatican Council (*Dei Verbum*), a most unusual illustration is used. It speaks of the table of the Word of God and the body of Christ. The image is that of eating. It is remarkable how often, when that particular document is speaking of the Scriptures, reference is made to food and eating and drinking. The Word of God is spoken of as food for the soul and as a pure fountain of the life of the spirit.

In this document, the Church is conceived as striving constantly to probe the deeper meaning of God's Word in the Scriptures. One of the Church's main thrusts is to feed the people with the food that is Scripture. To deliver this nourishment is the point of the Church's preaching and teaching.

It would be a mistake to imagine that the Church connects Scripture exclusively to the liturgy. In the mind of the Church, as declared by the Council, the Bible has a life and a relevance beyond the liturgy and preaching. It also finds a home in the private lives of God's people.

Saint Ambrose speaks of the experience which a person can have in this way: "We speak to him when we pray; we listen to him when we read the divine oracles [Scripture]."

There ought to be a depth to one's reading of Scripture. It ought to go beyond a leisurely perusal of the text. Ideally, it should be a deeply disciplined focus on the text which results in prayer.

It is a fact that some people think of prayer and Scripture as two disparate realities and never the twain should meet. This goes counter to the Church's longstanding practice – evidenced most notably in monasticism – the practice of combining the reading of God's word with prayer.

The Christian today is immersed quite obviously in a most secular environment. Safeguarding one's Christian identity requires being in constant touch with God, as that link is detailed in Scripture.

One must foster in oneself a deep awareness of God speaking to us through his word in Scripture. This realization would only enhance one's efforts to bring into being a better world.

THE BIBLE COMES TO US OUT OF THE DISTANT PAST

It is important to realize – rather it is necessary to take into account as one peruses the text of Scripture – that the teaching of Scripture is filtered through the customs and idioms of a culture that is, at points, drastically different from ours. So, for example, when Jesus admonishes his audience to "call no man father" (Mt 23: 9), we are certainly not to understand him to mean that an individual dare not call his male parent "father." The text means, rather, that God must be understood as being even more a father to a person than that person's physical father. When one reads in Matthew (5: 29), "If your right eye causes you to sin, tear it out and throw it away; it is better for you to lose one of your members than for your whole body to be thrown into hell," one must construe this as saying that one must prefer one's spiritual welfare to one's physical well-being.

Hyperbole and metaphor also must be recognized in one's reading of Scripture. For example, Jeremiah is in one instance depicted as warning the inhabitants of Jerusalem that they could expect a catastrophic attack by the Babylonian army. The prophet stood up before the people holding a pottery jug, which he proceeded to smash by dropping it to the ground. This he hoped would have a salutary effect on his audience. Speaking for God, he said, "So will I break this people and this city, as one breaks a potter's vessel, so that it can never be mended" (Jer 19: 10-11).

One finds similar striking expressions in our Lord's preaching: "It is easier for a camel to go through the eye of a needle than for someone who is rich to enter the kingdom of God." To say, as some have, that a particular entrance to the city of Jerusalem was so named is to substitute a lifeless, earthbound view of Scripture for the lively meaning of his word that God intends us to embrace.

THE BIBLE AND THE CHURCH

It is important that in reading the Bible we take from it the meaning that the Church finds in a particular chapter and verse. The splintering of Christianity into a host of sects and denominations results from people pretending to find in texts of Sacred Scripture meaning that they want to find rather than the meaning that God intends. It is the role of the Church to construe the authentic meaning of Scripture for the common man. One thinks of Philip, who came upon an Ethiopian attempting to read the Scriptures without notable success. "Now there was an Ethiopian eunuch, a court official of Candace, that is, the Queen of Ethiopia, in charge of her entire treasury, who had come to Jerusalem to worship and was returning home seated in his chariot. He was reading the prophet Isaiah. Philip ran up and said 'Do you understand what you are reading?' He replied, 'How can I unless someone instructs me?'" (cf. Acts 8: 27-31). The Church is charged by God and instructed by him to construe the Scriptures unerringly for us.

At certain points in the reading of Scripture, it becomes necessary, more often than not, in order to unlock the full meaning of the text, to resort to collateral reading, that is to say, reliable Scripture manuals and commentaries.

THE REWARDS OF BIBLE READING

Saint Augustine referred to the Scriptures as "letters from home." This implies the latent blessings and satisfaction that God means the Bible to convey to our lives. It reassures us that there is meaning and purpose to our existence and that unmitigated happiness awaits the one who lives by God's will.

It may be, however, that one has at some earlier time in one's life made an abortive attempt to read the Bible on a regular basis, only to find that the Bible seemed not especially helpful in deciphering the conundrums of life; or, perhaps, it seemed impossible to decode the Bible's message. At times it can happen that, even if one succeeds in catching its meaning, it appears that the Bible was speaking of a God who seems quaint or limited in our world of high technology. The study of Scripture seeks to eliminate the misunderstandings that surface when one does not advert to the historical and cultural circumstances of the world in which the Bible was written. These circumstances can differ widely from those of today's world. Today's Christian must be prepared to make a concerted effort to study the Bible so that God can be perceived as speaking to us through the biblical stories and other biblical writings.

THE BIBLE AND THE WORSHIP LIFE OF THE CHRISTIAN

From the very beginning, the Bible has been at the core of Christian worship. There is an account of typical worship, traceable to Justin Martyr, that describes Christian worship in the earliest times – the middle of the second century A.D.: "And on the day called Sunday there is a meeting in one place of those who live in the cities or the country and the memoirs of the Apostles or the writings of the prophets are read as long as time permits. When the reader has finished, the one who presides, in a discourse invites and urges us to the imitation of these noble things" (*First Apology* 67).

Bible reading and preaching based on it remain at the core of Christian worship to this day. Also, reading Scripture helps the Christian by fostering a deeper understanding of God, the world, and God's will for his people. Extending one's contact with Scripture beyond one's hour of Sunday worship, into one's everyday existence, can only be enriching. It is true of Scripture that the appetite comes with the eating. If one persists in the effort to master the Scriptures, success will crown one's effort.

The Literary Splendor of the Scriptures

One ought not to suppose that the Bible is one great mass of ponderous prose that requires strong resolve to read through. To be sure, not every line in the Bible is high literature, but there are segments that compare very favorably with and at times surpass the usual secular literary classics. Consider the intensity of feeling in the Song of Songs: "Set me as a seal upon thy heart"; "Arise, make haste, my love, my dove, my beautiful one and come for lo, the winter is past, the rain is over and gone" (8: 6 and 2: 10-11). The psalms, also, are the repository of delightful images. "O Lord, our Master, how the majesty of thy Name fills all the earth" (Ps 8: 1).

One must wonder if the laments over Saul and Jonathan have ever been equaled, much less surpassed: "How are the mighty fallen! Tell it not in Gath, publish it not in the streets of Ashkelon, lest the daughters of the Philistines rejoice;... You mountains of Gilboa, never dew, never rain fall upon you. Never from your lands be offerings of first fruits made, the shield of Saul bright with oil no more..." (2 Sm 1: 19-21). "Saul and Jonathan, lovely and comely in their lives and in their death they were not divided. They were swifter than eagles, they were stronger than lions. You daughters of Israel, weep over Saul, who dressed you in scarlet, who decked out your apparel with ornaments of gold... I grieve for you, Jonathan, my brother, beloved by me beyond all love of woman. Never woman loved her only son as I loved you. O how the mighty have fallen and the weapons of war perished" (2 Sm 1: 23-27).

At the news of Absalom's death, David is choked with sorrow and can say hardly more than the boy's name: "And with that the king went up to the room over the gate in bitter sorrow and wept there. And thus he said: 'O my son Absalom, my son, my son

Absalom. Would to God I had died instead of you, O Absalom, my son, my son'" (2 Sm 19: 1).

Isaiah reports God's wrath against the king of Babylon as follows: "I will rise against them – it is Yahweh Sabaoth who speaks – and wipe out name and remnant from Babylon. No offspring, no posterity, it is Yahweh who speaks. I will turn it into marshland, into a place for hedgehogs; I will sweep it with the broom of destruction. It is Yahweh Sabaoth who speaks" (14: 22-23). Elsewhere in Isaiah we find: "How art thou fallen from heaven, O radiant one, son of the dawn. Hewn down to the ground, prostrate O terebinth of the nations" (Is 14: 12).

Impossible to pass over is Ruth's delicate expression of loyalty charged with affection for her mother-in-law: "For withersoever thou shalt go, I will go and where thou shalt dwell I also will dwell. Thy people shall be my people and thy God, my God" (Ru 1: 16).

Nor is the New Testament bereft of beautiful literature. Consider the Sermon on the Mount, with its shocking reversals. The poor are declared blessed, as are those who are hungry now. The rich have received all the consolation that will come to them. Those who are filled now will be hungry. Do not forget the story of the prodigal son, which in some five hundred words weaves a tale of wretchedness and human grandeur, loneliness and a cordial welcome home.

CONCLUSION

The serious reading of Scripture for the earnest Christian is not a leisure-time diversion. God has spoken; all must attend to his word. And one cannot be satisfied just to apprehend the message. It must be vigorously acted upon. No sitting on one's hands; one must give it a decisive and fervent response. And be forewarned – one cannot take the Bible in hand and begin to read it and remain unscathed. It makes a gigantic difference in the life of one who gives oneself to it. "For the word of God is living and active, sharper than any two-edged sword, piercing to the division of soul and spirit, of joints and marrow and discerning the thoughts and intentions of the heart" (Heb 4: 12).

MAKING SENSE OF SCRIPTURE

The Hidden Richness of Biblical Texts

PETER GIRARD, O.P.

On the holiest night of the Church year, when all appears to be enveloped in darkness, the new fire bursts forth in order to illumine the paschal candle. It is at this solemn moment that the Church announces Christ's dominion over time and history: "Christ yesterday and today, the beginning and the end, Alpha and Omega: all time belongs to him!" This prayer, a recapitulation of Hebrews 13: 8, 1 Peter 4: 11 and 5: 11, and Revelation 21: 6 and 22: 13, found in the 1951 rite as it was restored by Pope Pius XII, is accompanied by the inscription of the wax with Alpha and Omega, the symbols of time and eternity. Here the Church proclaims that Christ, the creator of time, has also entered into time through the resplendent mysteries of his incarnation and redemption. Christians, therefore, responding to the light of revelation, acknowledge a unique conception of time that places Jesus Christ at its absolute center, giving fullness of meaning to all that occurs from Genesis to the *Parousia*.

In order to appreciate fully our Catholic tradition of the

interpretation of biblical texts, we must begin with the acknowl-edgment that Jesus Christ remains the Alpha and Omega of human history. Without reverencing this truth, our study of the Scriptures, no matter how well intended, will inexorably devolve into a demy-thologizing of culturally bound and historically restricted texts. Our Catholic tradition of scriptural interpretation, on the other hand, respecting the harmony of *fides et ratio*, discovers the full and hidden richness of biblical texts by recalling that the Eternal Logos alone satisfies man's one, supernatural end, union with the Trinity. So the Church does not approach the study of biblical texts by assuming that they are bound by time or culture; neither does she understand them as simply the product of inspired human authors. Rather, we begin our discovery of the hidden richness of the Scriptures by reverencing the truth that Jesus Christ, the perfect revelation of the Father's glory (cf. Jn 14: 8-11), speaks to every age in order to draw all human beings to himself.

First, we must recall that *God himself* is the primary author of all Scripture. The biblical texts were neither whispered by mantic oracles nor simply the musings of enlightened men. Rather, God uniquely used the writers of the Scriptures as instruments of his revelation through their own time, history, culture, language, and experience. So while the matter of biblical texts varies widely according to the human writer, the form of divine revelation is common and never changes. Therefore, we can confidently state that God is the author of each word of Scripture from Genesis to Revelation, even as each text necessarily reflects the distinc-tiveness of the time, culture, language, and experience of the human writer. Since the Scriptures are truly the Word of God, we would deny ourselves the ability to discover the hidden richness of biblical texts by asserting that they remain merely the writings of human historians, poets, philosophers, and theologians.

Some have argued that while it is fitting to think of the Scrip-tures as divinely inspired in some way, it is preposterous to assert that every word of Christ in the Gospels, for example, was actually uttered by him in history. The reasoning here is that since the Gospel writers could not have known or would not have remembered the words of Jesus decades after they were spoken, they were "inspired" to write down a reverent approximation. Perhaps the Lord's Last Discourse on Holy Thursday night (John 14-17) is the most apt example. It seems impossible, some might argue, that Saint John could have recalled the exact words of Jesus at such length and detail from that evening. However, this line of thinking inevitably leads us back to asserting that human beings are the primary authors of these unique texts. We must hold that God remains the primary author of all Scriptures, as Saint Peter writes: "no prophecy ever came by the impulse of man, but men moved by the Holy Spirit spoke from God" (2 Pt 1: 21).

On that night of the First Holy Mass, the Lord promised to send the Advocate to teach them all truth and to "remind them of everything he told them" (cf. Jn 14: 25-26; 15: 26-27; 16: 8-15). It is through the Holy Spirit sent by Christ himself, therefore, that the human writers of Scripture were directly inspired to write the texts without error. So it is certainly reasonable to hold that the Holy Spirit inspired Saint John to recall accurately the words of Jesus on Holy Thursday night. Such an approach preserves the inerrancy of the Scriptures while avoiding any semblance of the magical. Catholics need not be ashamed of the claim that the words of the Last Discourse are the actual words of Christ and not simply a pious, albeit "inspired," approximation. The guidance of the Church by the Holy Spirit assures the inerrancy of the Word while affirming the unique character and necessary participation of the human writer.

Others may claim that apparent contradictions in the details of biblical texts either render divine authorship as absurd on the one hand or posit the human element as negligible on the other. Either point of view, however, misunderstands how God uses the time, history, culture, language, and experience of the human writer to reveal his eternal truth. For example, Saint John's account of some of the details of the Last Supper differs from the synoptic versions. Of course, given the nature of the Holy Spirit's guidance of the Church, we cannot claim that these accounts are simply human remembrances. Neither should we, in an attempt to preserve divine authorship and inerrancy, claim that the differences are not truly present. Rather, the key is recalling how the Alpha and Omega of history inspires each writer within time to reveal what remains eternally true. Given the limitations of our external senses, several eyewitness accounts of an historical event will certainly produce varying recollections. So it is not *contra fidem* to assert that different human writers of biblical texts may proffer varying and even seemingly inconsistent details. However, given the guidance of the Holy Spirit, Christ uses each human writer's experience within history to inerrantly reflect a unique facet of his eternal truth. So apparent contradictions in biblical texts are not really contradictions at all: they are distinctive ways of expressing aspects of eternal truth according to the experience of the human writer.

So we Catholics confidently hold that all of Scripture contains truth for all times, even though each of the texts was written at a certain point within history. It is without hesitation that the priest or deacon kisses the sacred text and asserts, "The Gospel of the Lord!" Since any word (even the Logos himself) remains essentially "spoken" and not simply statically existing, we Catholics hold that the presence of Christ in the Scriptures is *not in the printed page per se*, but blossoms with fecundity *whenever the texts are spoken*. As it remains part of the nature of the Logos to be eternally spoken and so the perfect reflection of the Father's glory, so his presence bursts forth when the Scriptures *are spoken* either to oneself or to another. The deacon holds the Gospel Book before the people in procession not because Christ is present "within" its adorned pages, but rather to signify that the Eternal Logos *will be proclaimed* very soon. Our Eastern brethren signify this truth well when the priest announces before the proclamation of the Word: "Wisdom, let us be attentive!" In the liturgy of the West, the Gospel Book is reverenced only *after* the Word has proceeded forth from the pulpit, not before. Pope Benedict XVI has continued the custom of his predecessor in blessing the people with the Gospel Book (a tradition taken from the East), but only *after* the Word has been spoken. Candles are traditionally present at the pulpit *only during the time when the Gospel is being proclaimed* and not before. In addition, it is interesting to note that once the Word has been proclaimed from the pulpit, the Gospel Book disappears entirely from the liturgy. There is no rubric directing a "Gospel recessional" or subsequent enshrining of the Gospel Book. Rather, now that the Word has been spoken, the presence of Christ has blossomed forth!

For some years it was rather popular for churches that had emptied niches of devotional statuary to fill them with Bibles, lectionaries, or Gospel Books, referring to them as "shrines of the Word of God." Very often a sanctuary lamp was lit near the texts – to convey the presence of Christ in the Word – in imitation of the practice our tradition dictates of placing a lamp near the tabernacle. This innovation was supposedly intended to reverence the presence of Christ in the Liturgy of the Word as he is reverenced in the Liturgy of the Eucharist. However, noting the significance of *lex ordandi, lex credendi* in the spiritual lives of Catholics, we can see that this liturgical innovation actually distracts the faithful from the reality of Christ's presence in the Word *as spoken*. We do not encounter the presence of Christ in the Scriptures by praying before the texts resting within a niche. Rather, we experience the blossoming of his graces when the Eternal Word *is proclaimed* to us as "living and active" (cf. Heb 4: 12).

The Eternal Logos, the perfect reflection of the Father's glory, came to "testify to the Truth" (cf. Jn 18: 37) so that human beings could embrace the supernatural end for which they have been created. While the Logos himself is eternally spoken, the Scriptures are revealed precisely so that human beings can be saved.

Man is created *imago Dei* and, therefore, with an intellect both desirous and capable of assenting to truth. Man's reason can embrace truths of nature and those revealed by God commensurate with its abilities. The supernatural virtue of faith, given in baptism, allows the intellect to assent to the highest truths with certainty, even those which elude the full grasp of reason alone. It is most fitting and in accord with the manner of our creation, therefore, to use our human intellects to ponder the truths of both nature and revelation (*fides quaerens intellectum*). We Catholics are neither pure rationalists nor fideists with respect to revealed truth. As Pope Benedict XVI has so often emphasized, we acknowledge the harmony of *fides et ratio*: God reveals the truth to man, who necessarily and most fruitfully uses his intellect to ponder "the mysteries of the *fidei depositum*."

The *Catechism of the Catholic Church* (CCC 115-199) gives us guidelines for applying our intellects to the eternal truths revealed in the Scriptures. The Catechism, seeking to preserve the full richness of the Catholic tradition of interpreting Scripture, bases its approach upon the *four senses of Scripture* enunciated by the Alexandrian School of the patristic age. It is only through an appreciation of each of the four senses that the hidden richness of biblical texts becomes evident. Using only one or two of the senses to understand the Scriptures (as some scholars and interpreters do) would be analogous to using a microscope to study the moon. Given the size of the object (the moon), a microscope (designed for objects less sizeable) is simply not capable of giving an adequate analysis of the lunar surface. Similarly, since the Scriptures are the Word of God and not simply a word of man, *all of the senses of Scripture* (an adequate "tool") are required for proper reflection upon it.

The first sense of Scripture is referred to as the *literal* (or literary) *sense*; it is sometimes contrasted with the other three, which jointly are referred to as the *spiritual senses*. However, we should not be misled to think that the literal sense exists in contrast to the others. The literal sense exists complimentarily with the others precisely because the Word is spoken within a certain time, language, and culture. Biblical texts possess definite literary forms within historical and cultural contexts: thus, historical works that are written *as histories* should first of all be interpreted as such; Scripture written as poetry needs to be interpreted as poetry and *not* as history. Parables possess a unique literary form and should be interpreted according to that literary form rather than another. The literal form of any Scripture, moreover, is not accidental: God reveals himself according to specific literary forms, and we begin our interpretation by acknowledging this fact.

In *Divinu Afflante Spiritu* (1943), Pope Pius XII encouraged Catholic scholars to use scientific methods in the study of biblical texts. Therefore, the Church is not fearful of using hermeneutics, cultural studies, textual criticism, history, archeology, philology, and other disciplines in the examination of texts. Since biblical texts were written within a specific time, culture, and language, such studies assist our understanding of their literary form and contribute to their fuller interpretation. However, since God remains the primary author of the Scriptures, the Church does not assume that an historical-critical method can give a full interpretation of any text. Note that the literal sense does not imply a suspension of belief in the divine authorship of Scripture (as some suppose). The literal sense is simply an acknowledgment, given man's creation as *imago Dei* and the harmony of *fides et ratio*, that Scripture needs to be interpreted first of all according to the literary form it possesses, written within a historical context.

Catholics do not accept what some Christian fundamentalist or evangelical traditions call the "literal interpretation" of Scripture. In these Protestant approaches, human reason lacks a natural inclination toward beatitude and so the application of the intellect to biblical texts remains perilous at best. In these traditions, the richness of the Scriptures is experienced when you "hear the Word" at face value and "accept Jesus as your personal Lord and

Savior." In accepting Jesus as our personal Savior, Catholics do not deny the ability of the human intellect (in response to grace) to ponder the truths contained within the Scriptures according to symbolic language.

The second sense of Scripture is referred to as the *allegorical* (or typological) *sense*. This mode of interpretation recognizes that since Jesus Christ remains the center of time and history, we may draw allegorical connections between him and the persons, places, and events of the Old Testament. So when we read the Scriptures, we find allegories or types of Jesus (and Mary) prefigured, giving us fuller insight into the truths revealed within them. This sense of Scripture is rarely recognized in homiletics today, yet it remained the preferred mode of interpretation for homilies during the entire patristic era (96-750 A.D.). Through the mysteries of his incarnation and redemption, Jesus established himself as the center of all time and history. Everything that takes place before the incarnation of the Logos foreshadows, or prefigures, him. So it is not as if Christ came in the fullness of time simply to fulfill what had randomly happened to the Jewish people. Rather, *salvation history happened as it did in order to prefigure Christ*. Saint Paul recognized this when he identified Jesus as the "New Adam" (cf. Rom 5: 14; 1 Cor 15: 45-49) and the rock that Moses struck at Meribah as a prefiguration of the crucified Christ (1 Cor 10: 4). Saints Peter, Paul, and Luke all point to the tree of life in the garden of Eden as a prefiguration of the cross by using the Greek word *xylon* (wood) rather than simply *stauros* (cross) when describing the crucifixion (cf. 1 Pt 2: 24; Gal 3: 13; Acts 5: 30; 10: 39). The Church's liturgy, especially the liturgy of baptism, has always recognized the beauty of the allegorical sense. In the prayer over the baptismal font, the priest cites how the waters of the Red Sea during the Exodus and that of the Jordan at the entrance of the Promised Land prefigured the waters of baptism. In the *Akathistos* (c. 636 A.D.), Mary is honored by many sublime titles pointing to her prefigurement as *Theotokos*, including the "New Eve," the "Ark of the Covenant," and the "Burning Bush."

The third sense of Scripture is referred to as the *moral* (or tropological) *sense*. In this mode of interpretation, we see that God reveals eternal, unchanging truths contained within biblical texts. The moral sense reveals that God himself establishes the natural law, giving human beings a blueprint of how to grow in virtue and embrace their one, supernatural end. So while the Scriptures were written according to a certain time and culture, its moral prescriptions are not limited to the time of its composition. So the Decalogue (Ex 20: 2-17; Dt 5: 6-21), for example, was not written only for the people of Israel, but it was revealed by God to apply to all times and cultures. The moral guidance given in the parable of the Good Samaritan (Lk 10: 30-37), the woman caught in adultery (Jn 8: 3-11), or the washing of the apostles' feet at the Last Supper (Jn 13: 3-20) remains applicable to people of every time and place. So when I read the Scriptures, I will not discover its richness if I regard its moral teachings as simply helpful insights toward my personal self-actualization. Rather, I discover the true beauty of the biblical texts when I understand that they are the way God is drawing me ever closer to himself through growth in virtue.

The fourth sense of Scripture is referred to as the *anagogical* (or mystical; spiritual) *sense*. In this sense, we see that God reveals the meaning of salvation history with respect to man's final destiny. Just as Saint Paul reminds us that without the resurrection our faith is meaningless (1 Cor 15: 14 and 17), so the Scriptures are not merely a guide to a happy life on earth, but point us to the reality that man's end is union with the inner life of the Trinity. To ignore the anagogical sense is to reduce the Scriptures to no more than an ethical guide for living a happy life or forming a just society. When, for instance, liberation theology reduces Christ to simply a human liberator who primarily reveals a plan for revolution against oppression, it is certainly denying this fourth sense of Scripture. Neglecting the importance of this sense of Scripture has led to more violence and denigration of the human person than perhaps any other, especially since liberation theology uncritically accepts the tenets of Marxism and Communist forms of government in its embrace of Jesus as human "liberator." Rather, contained within the Scriptures are truths that point all human beings toward a *supernatural end* in heaven. Christ is the liberator from sin first of all, enabling human beings to embrace their end in heaven.

Catholics approach the study of Scriptures with confidence for two main reasons. First, we accept that these texts remain the eternal, inerrant Word of God and not simply the reflections of human beings. Second, we have been given a faculty of reason that, in harmony with faith, allows us to penetrate the hidden richness of the Scriptures through various modes of interpretation. However, one question remains in this respect: given our fallible intellects, how can I have confidence in one interpretation of Scripture over another? Who is to say which rational reflection upon the Scriptures is valid and not *contra fides*? First, we must reject the notion that each and every interpretation of Scripture is equally valid. While various interpretations are certainly necessary to give fuller understanding to the eternal truths revealed, there must be some way of discerning whether or not an individual interpretation is erroneous. Such discernment remains the only guarantee that human beings are not led astray by a heterodox interpretation of Scripture.

Knowing that the Church would need such infallible discernment, the Lord commissioned one of his apostles to be the *Petros* of the Church, giving him the charism of "binding and loosing" (cf. Mt 16: 18-19). It is the Magisterium that guarantees orthodoxy in matters of scriptural interpretation through the charism bestowed upon Saint Peter and his successors. Here we can see that the institution of the papacy remains both necessary and reasonable, given the limits of the human intellect and the manner in which God reveals himself. The Magisterium would be unnecessary if individual human beings were capable of interpreting Scripture without error, or if revelation comprised oracular utterances accessible only through gnosis. However, since God reveals himself in a way that can be apprehended by *ratio* in harmony with *fides*, the Church necessarily needs a guide by which scriptural interpretations can be embraced or rejected. The teachings of the Magisterium, therefore, could be defined as the *infallible, rational reflection upon the Scriptures.* So Catholics really do not have "two sources of truth" (Scripture and Magisterium), as some might misleadingly claim. Rather, the source of all truth is Jesus Christ, the center of time and history, revealed within the Scriptures. The Magisterium is the necessary, infallible, rational reflection upon the Scriptures, guaranteeing that the Bride of Christ will not be led astray on her journey to see the Bridegroom.

Throughout history, the See of Peter has continued to exercise its unique charism in three respects. First, the Magisterium judges the *canonicity* of texts claiming to be Scripture. Although the Muratorian Fragment (170 A.D.) gives a listing of scriptural texts and the Council of Nicea (325) was held without addressing this issue, it later became clear that certain Christian communities were embracing divergent texts as canonical. Primary among these communities were the Gnostics of Egyptian monasticism, from which many books claiming canonicity (now referred to as the *Nag Hammadi* texts) emerged. It was the North African councils of Hippo (393) and Carthage (397) that established a definitive listing of canonical books, citing seventy-two books as truly inspired by the Holy Spirit and constitutive of the *depositum fidei* for the universal Church. The later councils of Ephesus (431) and Trent (1545-63) would consider this exercise of the Magisterium through Hippo and Carthage as normative when defending canonical issues of their own times. The Magisterium exercised this charism of infallible, rational reflection with respect to canonicity in the fourth century, but never since: the listings of Hippo and Carthage remain *unchanged* in the Catholic canon to this day.

The Magisterium also exercises its unique charism in its approval of translations of biblical texts. Much to the consternation of some who have proposed various translations in the English-speaking world, the See of Peter reserves the right, according to its office, to approve all translations of the Scriptures. Given what we have said concerning the fallible nature of individual interpretation, we can see that the Magisterium's role here is neither merely administrative nor extrinsic to its charism. As we have stated earlier, God chose to reveal his eternal truths according to a specific language and culture. If a proposed translation, therefore, substantially alters the meaning of the text as revealed in the original language, it must be rendered inauthentic and not constitutive of the *sacra doctrina*. Saint Jerome assisted the Church in this respect with his definitive translation of the Scriptures from the Hebrew and Greek into Latin (the *Vulgate*, 405). Employing the skills of competent scholars, the Magisterium discerns which translations authentically communicate the eternal truths revealed by God within biblical texts.

Finally, the Magisterium exercises its charism in its teachings about faith and morals. In its rational reflection upon the Scriptures, using every means of *ratio*, the Holy See infallibly proclaims the *depositum fidei* in order to keep the Bride of Christ on a safe path on her journey to meet the Lord. So Church teaching is never extrinsic to the Scriptures or an alternative source of truth, as some may claim. Rather, every teaching of the Magisterium, whether this be "ordinary" or "extraordinary," remains an infallible, rational reflection upon what is revealed through the Scriptures. In this respect, we can see why the Magisterium is absolutely necessary for the Church as she makes her pilgrim way to meet the Lord. As we learn more about the nature of creation and as technology poses new challenges to the dignity of the human person, the Magisterium proclaims eternal truths as they touch the lives of human beings in every age. Whereas human cloning is not explicitly mentioned in the Scriptures, it is the Magisterium, employing the skills of scientists, philosophers, theologians, and other scholars, which proclaims the truths of the faith in this regard. It is interesting to note that in our own time, when reproductive research diminishes the dignity of man to a degree never before seen, it remains the Magisterium alone which speaks out against human cloning, embryonic stem cell research, and other inherently destructive technologies.

While on the road to Emmaus on Easter Sunday evening, two disciples encountered the risen Lord as they walked (cf. Lk 24: 13-35). Here Jesus says something with respect to the interpretation of Scripture that we perhaps overlook. As these disciples did not appear to understand the fullness of how the Old Testament served as a prefigurement, Jesus, "beginning with Moses and all the prophets, interpreted to them in all the Scriptures the things concerning himself" (Lk 24: 27). Shortly after, when appearing to the Eleven, Jesus makes the same point: "These are my words which I spoke to you, while I was still with you, that everything written about me in the law of Moses and the prophets and the psalms must be fulfilled. Then he opened their minds to understand the Scriptures..." (Lk 24: 44-45). Thus, Jesus' very first instruction to his Church after the resurrection concerns the fruitful and faithful interpretation of the Scriptures!

Catholics are sometimes derided for "not knowing the Scriptures." There is truth to this claim only in the sense that many Catholics do not take the time to read and ponder the hidden richness contained within the biblical texts. However, it profits no one to read the Scriptures, even for many hours each day, if one does not understand the nature of how the Scriptures were written, how to interpret them recognizing the harmony of *fides et ratio*, and how the Magisterium guards the Church against error. A fundamentalist or evangelical preacher does not "know" the Scriptures simply because he can quote passages from memory.

Rather, one discovers the true refulgence of Scripture when one acknowledges that God is the primary author who revealed himself according to a certain time, culture, and language. One can discover the hidden richness of the biblical texts when studying them according to all four senses of Scripture, recognizing the necessary role of the Magisterium as guide. Catholics should claim their rightful place: walking with the risen Christ on the road to Emmaus, ready to have their hearts set aflame by the hidden richness of the Scriptures!

Praying Your Magnificat

Lectio Divina *with* MAGNIFICAT *Meditations*

Peter John Cameron, O.P.

Whenever we take up a text for spiritual reading, we do so filled with *expectation*. There is a reason why we reach for a book by a Father of the Church, a saint, or a recognized spiritual master, old or new. We expect not only to find there sage counsel, inspiring thoughts, solace, wisdom, or guidance – even more, we expect to *meet someone*. The hope of spiritual reading is to have an *experience* that returns us to that initial moment when we were first attracted to Jesus Christ and we became certain that he is the One we have been looking for all our life. We desire to renew that meeting with the Lord. We want the Newness we knew in that moment to take hold of our life again so that it becomes our life, once and for all. And we find that possibility offered to us in the words of Christ's close friends who have expressed their relationship with him in enduring spiritual treatises written for the good of all people.

Spiritual books are a mercy, for we are forgetful people. So easily we get distracted and sidetracked. Our lives become filled with the peripheral, the ephemeral, the inconsequential. We constantly require a way to get back to what matters, to regain our focus, our recollection. I keep on a bookshelf in plain sight at all times a short stack of spiritual masterpieces that help "jumpstart" me whenever I begin to feel spiritually sluggish, arid, or slack. I rely on the proven power of these books (amazingly, all of them little) to bring me back to REALITY. Where would we be without such spiritual life-preservers to hang onto when we find ourselves adrift? We enter into spiritual reading with the conscious anticipation of finding an antidote for our daydreaming, our preoccupation, our going astray. We turn to the masters of the spiritual life, making our own Christ's cry from the cross, "I thirst!"

It is the humble person who stretches out a hand for a spiritual book. Tracts on spirituality have nothing to offer the self-sufficient, the self-assertive, the individualistic self-made man or woman. To look for a book by a saint is to search for truth, meaning, fullness that otherwise eludes us because it is not inside us. When I open the cover of such a volume I open up my heart, acknowledging my inability to make sense of my life, my self, by myself. I need help. I need direction. Most of all, I need a companion on this journey of faith – someone who has gone before me and who can testify to the genuineness of it all. I cannot be fully myself without another. Spiritual reading is a way of depending. When I take up a spiritual treatise, yes, I am looking for an answer, but not to the question that I *ask* as much as to the question that *I am*.

SPIRITUAL READING, WITNESS, AND ENCOUNTER

Thus, I turn to the classics of spirituality looking to become one with an author who loves Jesus Christ and who is conformed to him in friendship. More important than the writer's advice is our longing to partake of the writer's *belonging* to the Lord. In other words, what attracts us to a particular spiritual text is the witness of the person who wrote it. Our Holy Father Pope Benedict XVI gives us a compelling way to conceive of the notion of "witness." In his apostolic exhortation *Sacramentum Caritatis*, the Holy Father states that "we become witnesses when, through our actions, words and way of being, Another makes himself present" (85). We love the writings of the mystics and ascetics precisely because through their words and way of being Jesus Christ himself becomes present to us. We don't come away merely with a message or intriguing theological insights – rather, spiritual reading effects in us a greater closeness with the Person of Christ. It deepens our communion with the Lord at the level of our affection, not just our intellect.

Of course, this is not surprising since, as Pope Benedict XVI explains in the opening paragraph of his first encyclical, *Deus Caritas Est*, "being Christian is not the result of an ethical choice or a lofty idea, but the encounter with an event, a person, which gives life a new horizon and a decisive direction." If being Christian itself is the result of an encounter with the Person of Christ, then all of the many different means that Christ employs to draw us to himself as Christians must engage the dynamics of encounter, including the means of spiritual reading.

We come to recognize just how true, how vital this is when we reflect on our own life. The Catholic philosopher Louis Lavelle makes an observation that we can confirm in our own experience:

> *The most significant event in the lives of most of us has almost always been an encounter with another human being who suddenly threw new light upon our lives, changed its direction and meaning, gave it balance and an inflection that it had hitherto been unable to achieve. It is not necessary to have lived with this person in long familiarity to attain such a result. A very brief contact can be sufficient. True*

> *influence is that of* pure presence; *it is the discovery of one's own being through contact with another being.* [1]

This is exactly what our heart longs for as we confide ourselves to a spiritual author. Through such sacred reading we ask in effect to have an encounter with another whose life has been completely transfixed and transfigured by Jesus Christ. We read with the humble hope of having new light thrown upon our lives. Silently we beg for changed direction, new meaning, restored balance, life-giving inflection. To be human is to be made for a Presence – that is the contact we crave as we delve into the Church's treasured texts.

As the editor-in-chief of MAGNIFICAT, I have often been struck by readers eager to tell me about the new "friends" they have met in the meditations. A young married couple I know first made the acquaintance of Caryll Houselander in the pages of MAGNIFICAT, and now they read her writings (which they have collected) when they pray together every day. A number of people first came to know of Monsignor Luigi Giussani, the founder of the ecclesial movement Communion and Liberation, by reading his writings in MAGNIFICAT, and several – including a young man who is an inmate in a North Carolina prison – claim that his writings have completely changed the way they approach their Catholic faith and their life. How many were thrilled to discover spiritual authors they had never heard of before through the meditations of MAGNIFICAT: writers like Venerable Louis of Grenada, Blessed Elizabeth of the Trinity, Father Jean-Pierre de Caussade, S.J., Père Lacordaire, O.P., Father Walter Ciszek, S.J., Raïssa Maritain, Jacques Fesch, and Father Maurice Zundel, not to mention the more "obscure" but profound authors.

Of course, the very reason why we believe in God at all – the

---

1. Louis Lavelle, *Evil and Suffering* (New York: The Macmillan Company, 1963), p. 137.

instigation for our belief – is the witness of a holy person – an encounter with a "pure presence" that happened to us, changing our life. The Catholic theologian Josef Pieper makes the fascinating point that

> *in all belief, the decisive factor is* who it is *whose statement is assented to; by comparison the subject matter assented to is in a certain sense secondary. If we pursue this consistently, it follows that belief itself is not yet "purely" achieved when someone accepts as truth the statement of one whom he trusts, but only when he accepts it for the simple reason that* the trusted person states it... *The will of the believer is directed toward* the person of the witness. [2]

It is trust in the personal witness of the one who writes that prompts us to take up a spiritual tome in the first place.

Pope Benedict XVI confirms this when, in speaking about the apostles, he notes that, before they were sent out to preach, they had to "be" with Jesus, establishing a personal relationship with him. On this basis, says the Holy Father, "evangelization was to be no more than the proclamation of what they felt and an invitation to enter into the mystery of communion with Christ" (General Audience, March 29, 2006). For, as the Pope reminds us, the Lord Jesus, in his preaching and teaching, does not communicate any contents that are independent of his own person, as a teacher or a storyteller would usually do.

WHY WE READ

The act of reading remains an irreplaceable way that human beings grow and learn and advance into maturity. There is

---

2. Josef Pieper, *Faith, Hope, Love* (San Francisco: Ignatius Press, 1997), pp. 31, 38, 42, 45 – emphasis added.

something about the process that gradually changes, develops, and perfects us. To be "well-read" is to be a person of a certain undeniable stature.

The poet Rainer Maria Rilke once wrote a letter in which he recommends a particular book to a friend of his. What he says about this book applies as well to the whole enterprise of reading, which in turn sheds light on the special project of spiritual reading. He writes:

> *The more often one reads [this book], the more everything seems to be contained in it, from life's most imperceptible fragrances to the full, enormous tastes of its heaviest fruits. In it there is nothing that does not seem to have been understood, held, lived, and known in memory's wavering echo; no experience has been too unimportant, and the smallest event unfolds like a fate, and fate itself is like a wonderful, wide fabric in which every thread is guided by an infinitely tender hand and laid alongside another thread and is held and supported by a hundred others. You will experience the great happiness of reading this book for the first time, and will move through its numberless surprises as if you were in a new dream. But I can tell you that even later on one moves through these books, again and again, with the same astonishment and that they lose none of their wonderful power and relinquish none of the overwhelming enchantment that they had the first time one read them. One just comes to enjoy them more and more, becomes more and more grateful, and somehow*

better and simpler in one's vision, deeper in one's
faith in life, happier and greater in the way one lives. [3]

The possibility of such gratitude, vision, faith, and happiness propels us to the Christian spirituality section of the bookstore.

The author Charles Lamb once observed, "I love to lose myself in other men's minds... Books think for me." While we do not want to renege on our responsibility to think for ourselves, we nonetheless do very often need to get out of our own thoughts – out of our own understanding and ideas which, as a result of the effect of original sin, become too narrow, rigid, and self-serving. As Christ's parables make clear, we remain for ever sheep, and thus to be ourselves we need a voice to follow. In the revered spiritual writings of the Church, we recognize the voice of the Good Shepherd calling us by name, beckoning us to himself. And we follow.

Father Adolphe Tanquerey († 1932), in his classic treatise on ascetical theology entitled *The Spiritual Life,* [4] makes the observation that spiritual writers are

> *benevolent* mentors *who reveal to us our defects with*
> *great discretion and kindness. They do this by placing*
> *before us the* ideal *we are to follow, enabling us by*
> *the light of this* spiritual mirror *to recognize our good*
> *qualities and our defects, the stages we have reached*
> *and those we have yet to traverse in the pursuit of*
> *perfection. Thus we are easily led to self-examination*
> *and to generous resolutions. (278)*

---

3. Rainer Maria Rilke, *Letters to a Young Poet* (New York: Vintage/Random House, 1986), pp. 19-21.
4. Adolphe Tanquerey, *The Spiritual Life: A Treatise on Ascetical and Mystical Theology,* trans. Herman Branderis (Tournai Society of St. John the Evangelist, Desclee & Co., 1930); hereafter, quotations from this work will be identified solely by page numbers given in the text.

THE PRAYER OF *LECTIO DIVINA*

The Church names this great hallowed tradition of sacred reading *lectio divina*. The *Catechism of the Catholic Church* teaches us that "*lectio divina* [is] where the Word of God is so read and meditated that it becomes prayer" (CCC 1177). However, this process of prayerfully pondering sacred texts extends as well to the writings of the saints and spiritual geniuses of the Church.

Archbishop Mariano Magrassi has pointed out that, in order to do *lectio divina* fittingly, we must allow all our vital energies to come into play. These will include our understanding and its ability to penetrate so that we can "read within"; the will and its capacity for commitment; the heart and its ability to respond affectively; the imagination and its unlimited creative power in order to reconstruct events.

When in *lectio divina* we plumb the depths of sacred writings with piety and meditative attention, then, says Saint Athanasius, the text in turn becomes a mirror in which may be seen the movements of one's own soul. We discover our truest self in the words we read.

But what writers to include in our non-scriptural *lectio divina*? The august professor of dogmatic and spiritual theology, Dominican Father Reginald Garrigou-Lagrange († 1964), in his monumental work *The Three Ages of the Interior Life*, provides a list of the saints and other spiritual giants whose works "we should not ignore" because "these works, though not composed under infallible inspiration, were written with the lights and the unction of the Holy Ghost." Garrigou-Lagrange's list of indispensable authors reads as follows:

> *The chief works of Saint Augustine, Saint Jerome, Cassian, Saint Leo, Saint Benedict, Saint Gregory the Great, Saint Basil, Saint John Chrysostom, Dionysius, Saint Maximus Confessor, Saint Anselm, and Saint Bernard. Very useful also is an acquaintance with*

what most concerns the interior life in the writings of Richard of Saint Victor, Hugh of Saint Cher, Saint Albert the Great, Saint Thomas Aquinas, Saint Bonaventure. Profit may always be drawn from the Dialogue *of Saint Catherine of Siena, the works of Tauler, and those of Blessed Henry Suso, Blessed Angela of Foligno, Blessed John Ruysbroeck, and Thomas à Kempis, the probable author of* The Imitation. [5]

Once I surveyed this list, I was deeply gratified (and relieved!) to realize that all of these authors have appeared in the pages of MAGNIFICAT!

A METHOD FOR PRAYING THE MEDITATIONS

So then, what do we do with this Meditation of the Day that we find following the prayers of the Mass each day in the pages of MAGNIFICAT? How can we incorporate it into our daily prayer life so as to make the most of it and capitalize on its riches? The seven simple steps I will propose provide a very straightforward schema or technique that can easily become second nature to you and to the rhythm of your daily prayer.

1. Before reading the meditation, turn to the Lord in prayer

Begin with a prayer asking God to open your mind and heart so that you can hear his voice and receive whatever insight or instruction he wills to impart to you. The heart of all prayer is begging God to show us the meaning of our life. That meaning often appears in a very explicit and direct way in the sacred texts which the Holy Spirit puts before our eyes. However, we require a

---

5. Reginald Garrigou-Lagrange, O.P., *The Three Ages of the Interior Life* (Rockford: Tan, 1989), pp. 249-50.

proper disposition in undertaking spiritual reading. Father
Tanquerey gives this instruction/correction to "the pious reader":

> *Let him be on his guard against* curiosity, *which seeks
> to learn novelties rather than to profit spiritually. He
> must beware of* vanity, *which prompts one to seek
> acquaintance with things spiritual in order to be able
> to speak about them and thus gain a reputation. He
> must beware of* censoriousness, *which prompts one to
> listen or read, not in order to gain profit, but to criti-
> cize the matter or the literary form of the discourses.
> His sole purpose must be his spiritual gain. (279)*

2. Be aware of the connection between the meditation and the Gospel

How are the MAGNIFICAT meditations chosen? While MAGNI-
FICAT meditations aim to represent a healthy blend of writers
ancient and modern, the fact is that there is always a connection
between the Gospel of the Mass of the day and the selected meditation. Sometimes the way that the meditation corresponds to the
Gospel is not overt or explicit, and may even seem oblique, but
that is not unintentional. The point is to lead the MAGNIFICAT
reader into the depths of the scriptural passage (to explore the
spiritual sense of the text). By way of such a meditation, MAGNI-
FICAT endeavors to give the reader new eyes with which to "pierce
the pearl" of the Gospel – a way that goes beyond our presupposi-
tions and preconceptions about a Gospel passage we have heard so
many times. Often the title given to the meditation is indispensible
to seeing the link between the Gospel and the meditation. The title
has been deliberately chosen to tease the imagination of the reader
into recognizing the hinge between the Gospel and the meditation. Beginning your prayerful reading of the meditation by first
reflecting on the significance of the title – especially if at first it
comes across as puzzling – will aid you in laying bare all the
levels of meaning that unite the Gospel with the meditation.

3. Read slowly and attentively

Let the words of the Meditation of the Day penetrate you. Linger over them. Don't move on to the next line until the one you are considering makes a definite impact on you, until you feel its meaning. Saint Bernard says that we should read devoutly with piety, seeking not only to know divine things but to taste them. If it happens that something is confusing or causes you to question, allow yourself to proceed, but only after making the promise to return to that line later with the help of the light provided in the rest of the meditation. Be mindful that sometimes just a solitary phrase can pierce your heart like an arrow. Let it. That may be all that the Lord wants to give you out of these two or three hundred words. Saint John Eudes directs: Stop to consider, ponder, and relish the truths that make the greater appeal to you, in order to fix them in your mind, therefrom to elicit acts and affections.

4. Verify what is proposed by comparing it to your experience

Now comes the hard "work" of your *lectio divina*. If what the meditation proposes is "true," the reason you can be certain of it is because it is true *in your life*. At this point, then, ask yourself: How is the claim of this meditation verified in my own situation? What concrete evidence is there, as I reflect on my life experiences, that what God promises in this reading has happened or is happening? If our "I" is alert and alive, we are constantly comparing whatever is placed before us with our "heart" – that is, with our fundamental need for love, truth, beauty, goodness, justice, peace, and happiness. And if we live at the deepest level of our "I," with our humanity fully enlivened, we will not settle for anything less than what totally satisfies our heart (which always knows what is enough and what isn't). Therefore, I sense that a proposal is "true" if in some definite (if not definitive) way it satisfies my hunger for these key elements of life. The meditations in MAGNIFICAT are chosen expressly to address this condition of neediness of the human heart. But sometimes we miss the wealth of a meditation because we fail to do the hard work of "verifying" it – of comparing it to what my heart *really* desires, *really* longs for, *really* awaits with expectation. To help with this real work, Theophan the Recluse (a nineteenth-century Eastern Orthodox monk) gives some counsel: When you read, he says, do not just leave impressed on your mind a general idea of the author's argument. Rather, always turn what the author says into a personal rule to be applied to yourself. When we do this, the general idea we have formed always undergoes some shades of change. Don't be afraid to bring to your reading all the circumstances and concerns of your life. If Jesus tells us that all the hairs on our head are counted (and he does), and if this is true (and it is), then it follows that whatever is on our mind, whatever situation or problem we find ourselves in, is important to God. And we should not be surprised if somehow the Meditation of the Day speaks directly and specifically to that concern. I can't tell you the number of letters Magnificat has received in which readers are convinced that a given meditation was chosen just for them in order to address their particular issue or worry. Why not? I believe that can happen. God loves us that much.

5. Let reading erupt into prayer

Let what the Holy Spirit speaks to you sink into your soul. Saint Bernard suggests, "Let prayer interrupt reading." Or, in the words of Saint John of the Cross, "Seek in reading and you will find in meditation." Meditative reading is meant to lead to contemplation. As Father Tanquerey insists, the real purpose of spiritual reading is to sustain in us the spirit of prayer.

6. Express your thanks

All of the graces that pour forth from our spiritual reading come from the gratuitous mercy of God; we "deserve" none of them. Gratitude makes us humble and docile before the tender grace of God. Christ is always eager to speak to us; he knows that we cannot go on living if we do not hear his voice. But he will not violate our freedom or force his way into our heart. The more we cultivate a spirit of thankfulness for the solace and compassion we receive from the meditations that we read, the more we renounce the false, self-sufficient self, and the more we remain disposed to a more fervent union with the Lord. Christ's graces flow through thankfulness. When we take nothing for granted, God can give us everything. And he will give us everything we need. Thankfulness keeps us sensitive and attuned to the ways of the Spirit. With a thankful heart, we can hear even the tiniest whispers of God.

7. Put the Lord's word to you into practice

Immediately put into action whatever it is that Christ in his mercy reveals to you. A motto of the Dominican Order is, "Contemplate and then share with others the fruit of your contemplation." This is an apt rule of thumb for every disciple of Christ. Jesus promises unfathomable joys for those who keep his word (see Jn 8: 51). Our prompt and generous obedience in acting on what the Spirit tells us is the way that the word of God continues "to spread and grow" (Acts 12: 24).

THE FRUIT OF *LECTIO DIVINA*

How can we know if we are doing *lectio divina* with the meditations "correctly"? A theologian of the ninth century named Ardo Smaragdus says that *lectio divina*, when done properly, sharpens perception, enriches understanding, rouses from sloth, banishes idleness, orders life, corrects bad habits, produces salutary weeping, draws tears from contrite hearts, curbs idle speech and vanity, and awakens longing for Christ and the heavenly homeland. Has any of these things ever happened to you? If so, you are divinely-reading well!

Or, from the point of view of Saint Thomas Aquinas, we can look for the four objectives of *lectio divina*: (1) to teach the truth;

(2) to refute error; (3) to take from evil; and (4) to incite to good. The ultimate purpose of *lectio divina* is to bring people to perfection. "No wonder, then," remarks Father Tanquerey, "that the reading of spiritual books and of the lives of the saints has brought about conversions such as those of Augustine and Ignatius Loyola, and led to the highest degrees of perfection souls that would have otherwise never risen above mediocrity" (278).

Saint John of the Cross offers us this advice in conclusion: "If you desire to discover peace and consolation for your soul and serve God truly… attend to one thing alone, which brings all these with it, namely, holy solitude, together with prayer and spiritual and divine reading."[6] May your *lectio divina* of MAGNIFICAT meditations move you to become more grateful for heaven's countless graces. In your reading, may you be guided by God's infinitely tender hand. May *lectio divina* make you somehow better and simpler in your vision of reality, deeper in your life of faith, and increasingly happier and greater in the way you live. And once these things happen to you, make sure to write it all down for us so that we can read it. We need your witness! May the story of all your life become a MAGNIFICAT meditation in the making.

---

6. *The Collected Works of St. John of the Cross* (Washington, DC: ICS Publications, 1979), p. 673.

PRAYING TWICE

The MAGNIFICAT Hymns and Their Music

GENEVIEVE GLEN, O.S.B.

"Who sings well, prays twice." This adage, often attributed to Saint Augustine of Hippo (354-430), captures the experience we have of knowing we have prayed differently when we have sung our prayer. We have added to the spoken word another dimension of the many-faceted human spirit. We have said what we meant from a different place in the soul. Hymns are only one expression of sung prayer, but they are a familiar and satisfying way of combining word and sound to communicate with God from our depths. MAGNIFICAT provides sixty-two or sixty-four hymns in every monthly issue. The number depends on whether the month has thirty or thirty-one days. The hymns have captured readers' interest, provoked readers' questions, and inspired readers' prayer. The time has come to explain something about the use of hymnody in MAGNIFICAT prayer. We will look at what the hymns contribute to the daily Prayers for Morning, Evening and Night. We will examine why and how they are chosen. And, finally, we will explore the selection of appropriate music for singing the hymns. In the course of this brief survey, we will try to answer some of the questions readers have put to us in the years since MAGNIFICAT began publication.

THE HYMNS IN CONTEXT

The MAGNIFICAT hymns are part of the Prayers for Morning, Evening, and Night. We can best appreciate the hymns themselves if we back up and look at the way the prayers themselves are constructed. They follow the general format established for the Church's *Liturgy of the Hours*.[1] Like the official Hours, the prayers or offices[2] of MAGNIFICAT include both biblical and non-biblical texts. The Prayers for the Morning and Evening both consist of an opening verse with a Trinitarian doxology; a hymn; a psalm with an introductory antiphon (Bible verse) and a Trinitarian doxology; a Bible reading with a short responsory (another Bible verse); a Gospel canticle with an antiphon (yet another Bible verse); intercessions; the Lord's Prayer; and a closing prayer or blessing. MAGNIFICAT has added a brief reflection before the psalm. Prayer at Night has an introductory verse; an optional examination of conscience; a psalm with antiphon and doxology; a Bible reading with a fixed responsory; a Gospel canticle with antiphon; a closing prayer and final blessing.

The prayers or offices of MAGNIFICAT are shorter than those of the Liturgy of the Hours. They are also composed according to a

---

1. The most available English-language edition of the official *Liturgia Horarum* is the 4-volume set entitled *Liturgy of the Hours* published by The Catholic Book Publishing Company (New York) in 1975.
2. The older, Latin-based name for the Liturgy of the Hours is the Divine Office. We therefore sometimes refer to the Prayers for Morning, Evening, and Night as "offices." The task of the editor and assistant editor for the Daily Offices is to choose and assemble the hymns and biblical texts and to compose the other non-biblical texts for each prayer or office.

different set of principles. On the weekdays of Ordinary Time – that long season of the Church year between the Christmas season and Lent, and between Pentecost and Advent – each office takes an image or theme from the chosen psalm and muses on it through the lenses of other biblical texts, hymnody, non-biblical prayers, and the brief psalm reflection. On all the other days of the liturgical year, the unifying imagery is found in one or both of the readings from the Mass of the day or the life of a saint being commemorated. On Saturday mornings, when the liturgical rubrics permit, the Prayer for the Morning is always in honor of the Blessed Virgin Mary. The hymn is either a Marian hymn or another hymn that highlights the aspect of the Virgin's life commemorated in the prayer. This means that the offices serve as a way of listening to God through reflection on Scripture as well as addressing God in the words prayed. They are a form of the ancient Christian practice of *lectio divina*, that is, absorbing Scripture slowly and deeply by reading, meditating, praying, and, sometimes, simply being present to God in the quiet of contemplation. The practice of praying the Liturgy of the Hours as a form of communal or private *lectio divina* goes back to the hermit-monks of the very early Christian centuries. Praying the texts as *lectio divina* is still a valuable dimension of the liturgical Hours or the MAGNIFICAT prayers even when they are sung or recited in family or group settings. A pause for silent prayer could be made after the psalm and the reading.

PRAYING POETRY

The MAGNIFICAT hymns are integral to this process of reflection and prayer, whether the offices are prayed in solitude or in community. Therefore the hymns have been chosen as poetic reflections on the texts and images of the Bible selected as the focus for each prayer. Unlike the other texts of the offices, except the psalms, the hymns are themselves prayer woven in and through poems written to be sung. Poetry is a doorway into Mystery, the Mystery that lies at the heart of everyday life. Poetry speaks a different language than the informational prose of computer manuals, cookbooks, and directions for wrestling into usable shape those maddening household and children's items that come innocently labeled "Some assembly required." Informational prose tells us how to do something. Poetry, and especially religious poetry, invites us to be somewhere and with someone: to be in the presence of a Reality within but beyond ourselves and to surrender ourselves to that Reality in the communion of worship. The Reality is, of course, the Triune God.

Poetry also speaks a different kind of language than the conceptual prose of scientific explanations, even scientific theological explanations. Concepts speak from and to our reason. They seek to make as clear as possible the factual reality of subatomic structures or the movement of stars or the relationships among the persons of the Trinity – but there, concept begins quickly to slide into poetry, because reason alone cannot grasp the reality of God. Poetry does not shun reason, but it moves beyond it by abandoning the language of concept for the language of image. Poets often invite us to think differently about what we see and touch and taste and know by comparing it with other facets of reality. To take an example so common it has become commonplace, a beautiful and beloved woman might be compared with a rose, not because she really looks like one but because she evokes some of the same awe and longing evoked by the beauty of the rose. Image offers us a wider range of perception and speech than does concept. The human spirit, reaching for words to address, express, and touch the "something more" of which we are aware, most often makes use of the language of poetry as the least inadequate for the impossible task. In the words of one of the MAGNIFICAT hymns,

Too high for us, O Lord, your ways,
Too vast your works: to them
We reach with trembling words of praise
To touch your garment's hem. [3]

To get a sense of why we use this language of poetry to communicate and commune with the Mystery of God, we might translate that verse into prose: "O Lord, your ways are so different from ours that we can't really reach you. The only way we can contact you is to speak words of praise." Somehow, the prose speaks the truth, but it lacks the quivering sense of awe borne by the poetic text. It says all that is necessary, but it does not express the "more" we feel and can hardly say.

EXPANDING OUR UNDERSTANDING THROUGH POETRY

The Bible makes frequent use of poetry to speak of God and with God. The most ancient and beloved prayers of the Jewish and Christian tradition are the psalms we pray daily with MAGNIFICAT. The psalms are themselves poems, originally written to be sung, as are the canticles also used in MAGNIFICAT. "Canticle" means "song." The Bible is studded with canticles, which are really psalms that occur in books other than the psalter. Sometimes MAGNIFICAT, like the Liturgy of the Hours, uses a canticle in place of a psalm. Daily, we pray the three great Gospel canticles: the Canticle of Zechariah (*Benedictus*) in the morning, the Canticle of Mary (*Magnificat*) in the evening, and the Canticle of Simeon (*Nunc Dimittis*) at night. Sometimes the biblical antiphons and readings are also poetry: the prophets, the wisdom books such as Sirach and the Song of Songs, and occasionally the historical

---

3. "Oh, Who Can Know the Mind of God," Genevieve Glen, O.S.B. *Take with You Words* (Portland, OR: OCP Publications, 2002). MAGNIFICAT: Sunday 24B in Ordinary Time, Prayer for the Evening.

books of the Bible, make ample use of poetry when prose fails to convey the overwhelming mystery, power, and beauty of God's presence and humanity's response. You can recognize biblical poetry apart from the psalms and canticles by the way it is printed. Since MAGNIFICAT does not have the space to print them in verse form, we use a slash to indicate the end of each poetic line.

The poets of the Bible belong to times long ago and places far away. Christians of later ages have always sought mediators to bridge the gap between their own world, with its particular perspectives and vocabulary, and the world of the Bible. Hymns have often met that need. Those most often chosen for MAGNI-FICAT translate biblical images grown distant or, on the contrary, too familiar, into fresh language accessible to readers from another culture. At the same time, the hymns extend these images by musing on what they might mean for us as Christians. Consider, for example, this 1920 translation of a Russian hymn:

God, you are clothed with light,
As with a garment fair,
And in your holy sight
The saints your beauty wear;
The heav'ns and all therein express
The glory of your holiness.

Give me a robe of light
That I may walk with you:
Bright as the stars are bright,
Pure as their light is pure;
Whose texture sin shall never stain,
But ever undefiled remain.

O Christ, I lift my eyes;
Your love for me I own;

In your great sacrifice
Remains my hope alone;
The robe is mine, my soul to dress,
Of everlasting righteousness. [4]

On some Saturday mornings in Ordinary Time, MAGNIFICAT couples this hymn with a text from Isaiah (61: 10; 62: 2-3), a canticle that the Church often puts on the lips of the Blessed Virgin Mary. The hymn allows us to see in Isaiah's "robe of salvation" the Christ in whom we are clothed at baptism (Gal 3: 27), this same Christ as the robe of holiness worn by Mary and all the saints, and the robe of holiness which we aspire to wear, through Mary's intercession, with the whole Church brought to its final glory (cf. Rv 19: 8).

Thus the MAGNIFICAT hymns offer us their own reflections on and response to the texts of the Bible from vantage points far closer to us than the ancient Hebrew and Greek worlds of the Bible itself. As Christians, however, we never pray solely from the narrow platform of the present moment. One of the goals expressed by Pierre-Marie Dumont, creator and publisher of MAGNIFICAT, is that readers may find access to the breadth and depth of the Church's vast tradition through the liturgy, the prayers, the daily meditations, the lives of the saints, the choice of and reflections on art, and the articles. Christian hymnody offers a long and venerable tradition of poetic wisdom upon which MAGNIFICAT continues to draw in pursuit of this goal.

We make an effort to sample widely. We employ translations of hymn texts from the venerable traditions of Greek and Latin

---

4. "God, Thou Art Clothed with Light," trans. John Brownlie. *Hymns of the Russian Church* (London: Oxford University Press, 1920). MAGNIFICAT: Ordinary Time, Saturday Prayer for the Morning; Easter Season, Week 3, Saturday Prayer for the Morning. In this case, the hymn has been slightly altered to update archaic language. See the discussion of text alteration below.

hymnody, which extend from the early Church through the Middle Ages and beyond. We also borrow through translations from the vivid poetry of Italian hymnody (e.g., "All Creatures of Our God and King," Saint Francis of Assisi, c. 1181-1226); the clear strains of French hymnody (e.g., "As Joseph Lay Uneasy," Sister Marie de la Croix, O.P.), the powerful German hymnody of the Reformation[5] and later, especially through the brilliant nineteenth-century translations made by Catherine Winkworth (e.g., "Lift up Your Heads, Ye Mighty Gates," Georg Weissel, 1590-1635), and a smattering of selections from other European countries. Of course, we call most often upon the rich tradition of English-language hymnody, which dates back to Isaac Watts, the "Father of English Hymnody" (1674-1749), and has continued to flourish into our own day. It includes English hymns (e.g., "Christ Whose Glory Fills the Sky," Charles Wesley, 1707-1788, and "Tell out My Soul," Timothy Dudley-Smith, b. 1926), American hymns (e.g., "Lord of All Being," Oliver Wendell Holmes, Sr., 1909-1994, and "When from Bondage," Delores Dufner, O.S.B., 1984), Scottish hymns (e.g., "Come, Let Us to the Lord, Our God," John Morison, 1781), Irish hymns, sometimes in translations made by Irish authors (e.g., "Be Thou My Vision," eighth century, trans. Mary Byrne, 1880-1931), and Welsh hymns, also sometimes in translations made by Welsh writers (e.g., "Guide Me, O Thou Great Redeemer," William Williams, 1745, trans. Peter Williams, 1771).

Despite the wide sweep of our hymnological net, we have intentionally omitted a number of contemporary favorites, such as "Be Not Afraid" (Bob Dufford, S.J.). The reason is simple. Because MAGNIFICAT hymns must read well as poetry when said

---

5. Texts are carefully selected to reflect Catholic theology even when the texts' authors are not Catholic. Hymns inspired by the Bible often transcend the fragmentation of belief seen in the doctrinal works of different Christian denominations.

rather than sung, we have limited ourselves to texts that are more than quotations of biblical verses and that are written in poetic meter (see below). One strong movement in contemporary hymnody, initiated by composers like the St. Louis Jesuits in reaction to some really shoddy English hymns written in the early postconciliar period, returns to a very old English-language tradition by setting to music biblical texts very little modified. Those texts sing beautifully but read rather clumsily, so we have chosen not to use them in MAGNIFICAT. Another contemporary movement that has generated many striking hymns has integrated text and music in irregular meters akin to some styles of free verse. The texts of such hymns must be sung to their own tunes in order to convey their meaning. When read rather than sung, these texts tend to fall flat. An example would be Michael Joncas' highly popular "On Eagle's Wings."

Sometimes a hymn you have sung in church may read differently in the pages of MAGNIFICAT. In the interest of providing readers with a truly representative selection of the great tradition of English-language hymnody, we make every effort to find the most authentic version of every text. Without indulging in hymnological archeology beyond our resources, we choose the oldest version we can find. This task is not always easy. The practice of altering texts to suit an audience is almost as old as hymnody itself. The roots of some texts are untraceable, so you will sometimes see in MAGNIFICAT's index pages that a text is "attributed" or "ascribed" to an ancient author because no one actually knows for sure when or where or by whom the text was really written. In such cases, no one knows which version of the text is the most authentic, either. At other times, an altered version of a hymn has become so fixed in practice that the original would sound very odd if we used it. A favorite example is Charles Wesley's classic Christmas carol, sung far and wide as: "Hark the herald angels sing, / 'Glory to the newborn king'." Wesley actually wrote "Hark, how all the welkin rings,/ 'Glory to the King of kings'" (1739).

The alteration was made in 1753 by George Whitefield, another leader of the Methodist movement, and has been sung ever since. "Welkin" is a word probably already archaic in Wesley's day. It means "the vault of heaven."

Like this eighteenth-century example, many modern alterations have been made in the interests of updating archaic language that would not readily be understood or easily pronounced by singers of a later time. The editors of MAGNIFICAT's daily offices occasionally update archaic vocabulary or grammatical forms to make a text more user-friendly, but we do so with the greatest restraint, lest we lose the flavor of the author's genius. At times, we use altered versions because a hymnal editor has not indicated that it is altered or because we cannot find the original. In such cases, we have occasionally been alerted by a knowledgeable reader who has led us to the original. Recently, the copyright administrator of the hymn "Lord Christ, When First Thou Cam'st to Earth," himself the grandson of the hymn's author, W. Russell Bowie (1882-1969), notified us that we were using an unauthorized altered version of the original text. We had taken it from a major hymnal, unaware that it was neither authorized nor particularly authentic. We were delighted to discover and use the far more powerful original, whose meaning shines clearly through the archaic verb forms.[6] In other cases, readers have expressed distress at finding what they thought was an altered version of a hymn in MAGNIFICAT, when we had in fact chosen the original in place of an altered version commonly sung. Nevertheless, because we are more concerned with readers' best interests than with historical accuracy for its own sake, we did abandon this principle in one case. Several readers were disturbed by the theology found in Catherine Winkworth's 1862 translation of "Now Thank We All Our God," written around 1636 in German by the

---

6. MAGNIFICAT: Sunday 20C in Ordinary Time, Prayer for the Evening (Vigil), and Holy Thursday.

Lutheran pastor Martin Rinkart. The questionable text reads, in the original: "And free us from all ills/ In this world and the next." Readers were concerned about a possible implication that one could be freed from "ills," i.e., hell, in the next world. Although that would not have been Rinkart or Winkworth's meaning, we chose to revert to the more familiar, "And free us from all sin/ Till heaven we possess." [7] We are always grateful for readers' help, so that we can more faithfully serve their prayer.

POETRY READ, SAID, OR SUNG

The MAGNIFICAT hymns must meet a dual need. They must serve prayer whether they are sung or not. In the best of all possible worlds, all MAGNIFICAT readers would be blessed with good singing voices, a memory for music, and a library of tunes at their fingertips, but this is not the best of all possible worlds. Many pray alone, perhaps in places where they cannot pray aloud, perhaps in physical circumstances that hinder song, perhaps with the will but not the way to make music. Others cannot read music or have little access to printed music resources such as hymnals. For all those reasons, the Church, in her wisdom, provides poems as alternatives to hymns in the official English-language edition of the *Liturgy of the Hours* which inspired the prayers of MAGNI-FICAT. That example suggests that when one cannot sing hymns, one can read them or other texts as poetry. Moreover, the Church makes clear that liturgical music, unlike other forms of music, exists not for its own sake but for the sake of opening the way for participants to deepen their conscious awareness of what their worship means. [8] When music accompanies texts, it must support

---

7. MAGNIFICAT: Thanksgiving Day, Prayer for the Morning, and some Mondays in Ordinary Time, Prayer for the Evening.
8. See Vatican II's *Sacrosanctum Concilium (Constitution on the Sacred Liturgy)* 14; *Music in Catholic Worship* (US Bishops' Committee on the Sacred Liturgy, United States Conference of Catholic Bishops, 1982), pp. 23-24.

the meaning and purpose of the texts. Therefore, the words themselves have primacy, and music is their servant.[9] Where words alone are possible, then words suffice. God does not refuse to hear the prayers of those unable to sing them. Therefore, MAGNIFICAT seeks to provide hymn texts which can be prayed as poetry read silently, poetry recited, or poetry sung.

However, many readers do want to sing the hymns. The challenge is to join words to music, although MAGNIFICAT itself does not have the space to print music. Some choices presented themselves to us at the beginning of our work.

The first was to supply the meter for each hymn, which we do. The meter of a hymn is what dictates the hymn tunes to which it can be sung. At its most basic, meter is quite simply a syllable count. A hymn whose meter is 8686 has four lines: the first line has 8 syllables, the second 6, the third 8, and the fourth 6. Theoretically, any text whose meter is 8686, also called common meter or CM, can be sung to any common meter tune. "Our God, Our Help in Ages Past"[10] has a meter of 8686. Precisely because, as the name indicates, that is the most common meter used in English-language hymnody, the text can be sung to any number of tunes written in 8686. This very useful knowledge means that you might be able to sing that hymn to tunes you already know very well from other familiar common meter hymns, such as "Lord, Who Throughout These Forty Days" or "While Shepherds Watched Their Flocks by Night." Alas, nothing is quite as simple as it looks. As you may have learned in school, "meter" refers not only to the number of syllables in a line of poetry but also to the way stressed and unstressed syllables are arranged in the line. All common meter texts and tunes are written in iambic meter: a unit of 2 syllables, the first unstressed, the second stressed, repeated

---

9. *Music in Catholic Worship*, p. 23.
10. MAGNIFICAT: Lent, Week 5, Monday, Prayer for the Morning. This hymn is more commonly known as "O God, Our Help in Ages Past."

four times in the 8-syllable line and three times in the 6-syllable line. Therefore, they are relatively interchangeable, although you might find it disturbing to the ear to sing a non-seasonal text like "Our God, Our Help in Ages Past" to the tune of a lenten or Christmas hymn, like the examples given above.

In the case of other meters, though, you might try to sing a text you do not know to a tune you do, only to find that the result feels like driving a wooden-wheeled cart over cobblestones. An example is the hymn text "Blessing and Honor and Glory and Power" (Horatius Bonar, 1866). [11] The printed indication says that the meter is 10.10.10.10. If you try to sing it to the tune used for "The Voice of God Goes out through All the World" (Luke Connaughton, 1970), you would find yourself in the cart. The reason is that the text of "The Voice of God" is iambic, like the text of "While Shepherds Watch," but the text of "Blessing and Honor" is trochaic. It is made up of ten lines of 2-syllable units consisting of a stressed syllable followed by an unstressed syllable – the reverse of iambic meter. Therefore, it needs a tune where each strong beat is followed by a weak beat. The tune used for "The Voice of God" has a weak beat followed by a strong one. It will not do for "Blessing and Honor."

Therefore, unless you want to spend a great deal of time mired down in the frustrations of trial and error, it is helpful to have a little more information. Here, MAGNIFICAT had two further options. The first was to provide the name of a tune to which a particular hymn could be sung. Like the texts themselves, all tunes have names usually given to them independently of the hymn with which they were first used. For example, the tune used to sing the Christmas carol "Joy to the World" (Isaac Watts) [12] is called "Antioch." Texts and tunes are often written independently of each

---

11. MAGNIFICAT: Christmas Season Weekday, Prayer for the Evening.
12. MAGNIFICAT: Christmas Day, Prayer for the Morning. This carol also appears in the collection of Christmas carols printed in the Christmas Week issue.

other. Isaac Watts published the text "Joy to the World" in 1719. An American, Lowell Mason, made an arrangement of a tune drawn from portions of Handel's *Messiah*, named it "Antioch," and published it in 1836. Joined to Watts' text, it became popular enough to displace other tunes to which the text had been sung. If you know the tune "Antioch," you can use it to sing any text you find in MAGNIFICAT written in common meter (8686), provided you repeat the last line of the text several times to match the tune. "Antioch" is not the most practical example because of those repeats, but it gives you an idea of how different texts can be wedded to a single tune if you know the meter, which MAGNIFICAT supplies. It also shows one of the other factors that can complicate matching texts and tunes: repeats and refrains. To use a simpler example, if you know the long meter (8888) tune "Duke Street" because you have sung it with the text "Jesus Shall Reign Where'er the Sun" (Isaac Watts), [13] you can sing it with any other text in MAGNIFICAT written in long meter.

The second option, which was chosen by MAGNIFICAT, was to provide the name of a well-known hymn whose tune can also be used to sing a lesser-known hymn text printed in MAGNIFICAT. For instance, you might read on a Monday morning that the long meter hymn "Glory to You Who Safe Have Kept" can be sung to the tune used for "The God Whom Earth and Sea and Sky." The problem with this approach has been that English-speaking Catholics really do not share a common repertoire of hymns that everyone knows well enough to recognize and sing without music. There are at least sixteen major hardback hymnals in use in Catholic parishes in the United States, to say nothing of a plethora of throwaway paperback hymnals and missalettes with hymns. Some standard hymns appear in most major Catholic hymnals, but these hymns are not necessarily used by every congregation that uses

---

13. MAGNIFICAT: Tuesday Mornings in Ordinary Time, Prayer for the Morning, and Solemnity of Christ the King, Prayer for the Morning.

the books themselves. Even within a single parish, those who worship regularly at the vigil Mass on Saturday evening may know an entirely different set of hymns than do those who regularly participate in the 11:00 A.M. Mass on Sunday morning. While serious efforts are currently being made to provide national oversight of the burgeoning industry of liturgical music, it seems unlikely that American Catholics will ever be obligated to use one or two national hymnals whose contents become familiar to everyone.

We could have limited our selection of hymn texts to a handful of those well known by most Catholics. Some of you may remember when Catholic musicians were forced to do that very thing at Mass, when we were just starting to sing in the vernacular and knew very few hymns. Some of us have "Holy God, We Praise Thy Name," "Praise to the Lord, the Almighty," and "To Jesus Christ our Sovereign King" indelibly engraved upon our inner ear because we sang them every single Sunday. They are all fine hymns, but even the finest do not bear repetition fifty-two times a year, come Ordinary Time, Advent, Lent, or Easter. We chose instead to provide a variety of hymns – our database presently includes close to a thousand – for the sake of a rich and variegated exploration of scriptural and theological images, even though we knew we were risking the frustration that does indeed beset those who would like to sing but are unable to locate appropriate music. To remedy the frustration, MAGNIFICAT is currently at work on a project to produce CDs containing a wide selection of hymns for each season so that readers can learn by listening. These CDs will not include every hymn printed in MAGNIFICAT, but they will provide a basic collection of tunes in the most frequently used meters, which readers will then be able to use to sing other texts in the same meter.

Mind, Heart, and Voice

The MAGNIFICAT hymns are above all prayer. Both words and music are there to engage the mind and heart in what ancient Christian wisdom called "the work of God," that is, the daily round of hymns, psalms, biblical readings, and prayers that make up the prayer the Church offers at significant times of the day. The mind is spurred to thought by what the voice sings or says. The heart, taken in the biblical sense as the seat of human wisdom in which reason, imagination, intuition, and emotion work together to make God's sense out of life, is taken deep into Christ's heart as we pray this round of word, song, and silence in union with him, as members of his Body. [14] MAGNIFICAT can provide only the script for the voice – the poetry of hymnody and psalm and certain biblical readings, the prose of reflections and prayers. MAGNIFICAT readers supply the mind and heart. The Holy Spirit transforms the interaction of the believing mind, heart, and voice into the prayer of Christ ascending like incense to the Father.

---

14. See the *General Instruction of the Liturgy of the Hours* (Congregation for Divine Worship, 1971), pp. 6-8.

"MY SOUL IS LONGING FOR THE LORD"

The Psalms as Timeless Prayers
of the Human Heart

M. TIMOTHEA ELLIOTT, R.S.M.

"O God, you are my God, for you I long; for you my soul is thirsting. My body pines for you like a dry, weary land without water." This first verse of Psalm 63 [1] expresses the soul's acute longing for God in the metaphor of parched land. It uses three different verbs (long, thirst, and pine) to relate the intensity of desire. Psalm 42 chooses another metaphor: "Like the deer that yearns for running streams, so my soul is yearning for you my God. My soul is thirsting for God, the God of my life; when can I enter and see the face of God?" (Ps 42: 1-2). The first word of this psalm in Hebrew is *'arag*, which by its very sound imitates the gasping or panting of the deer in search of life-giving water.

Biblical Hebrew, the ancient language in which the psalms were originally written, is a very economical language. The sum total of its vocabulary is about three thousand words, a number

---

1. Quotations from the psalms are taken from the 1966 Grail translation which is used in the liturgical books of the Liturgy of the Hours.

that would probably not encompass the entries in the *Oxford Unabridged Dictionary* up to the letter "B." Despite this fact, the vocabulary of longing in the psalms has a total of ten different words, each one with a unique nuance of meaning. Here we may note only a few: "to desire with tempestuous energy"; "to long deeply for"; "to crave"; "to desire to take pleasure in"; "to want"; "to cling to with inward devotion"; "to desire with hope, confidence, trust."

In the anthropology of the Old Testament, longing or desiring is connected with the "soul" in a significant way. The Hebrew word which is ordinarily translated "soul" is *nephesh*. However, *nephesh* does not carry the same connotation as our contemporary understanding of "soul." In Hebrew thought, an individual was a body-person, not a composite being with a soul distinct from the body. The *nephesh* denoted the total person as he is animated by a spirit of life. The *nephesh* does not live in the body but expresses itself through the body. Until roughly the first century before Christ, there was no generally accepted belief in life after death among the Jewish people. There are a few intimations that there will be some sort of continued existence for the just and righteous; however, the texts are late and vague, and they do not define the nature of that existence. [2] Hebrew thought did not admit the concept of an immortal soul existing separated from the human body.

For a moment, let us go back to the Book of Genesis and the account of the creation of man. God formed him from the clay of the earth and blew into him the breath of life. That breath of God entered man's mouth and lodged in his throat. The understanding was that when man died, God drew back his breath. The word *nephesh*, which in the Old Testament Scriptures is frequently translated as "soul," can also mean "throat," "thirst," and "desire."

---

2. Cf. Wis 3: 1-5, composed in Greek in the first century B.C.E., and 2 Mac 12: 44.

The connection here is that the soul (*nephesh*) *is* a thirst for God; the human person by his or her nature longs, yearns, and pants for God.

Now, let us turn to the subtitle, "The Psalms as Timeless Prayers of the Human Heart." The earliest psalms date from approximately 1300 B.C. They were written gradually over an extended period of time and tested against the faith of Israel before their number was fixed at one hundred fifty around 90 A.D. and they were received into the canon of Scripture as we have them today. The title of the book we call the Psalms in Hebrew is *T*ehillim*, a word that literally means "praises."

That title, "Praises," might seem a little odd to us who know that the Book of Psalms contains many different types of prayer that do not necessarily come under our normal definition of "praise." There are, of course, psalms that praise, but there are also psalms of thanksgiving, psalms of complaint or lament, penitential psalms, psalms of trust and petition, psalms for pilgrims, meditative wisdom or Torah psalms, psalms that celebrate the coronation, wedding, or victory of a king, blessings, processional psalms, and, yes, even "cursing psalms." All these forms of prayer come under the heading "Praises."

Article 2639 from the *Catechism of the Catholic Church* is helpful for understanding how all of these forms of prayer can be collected under the title *T*ehillim*, "Praises." Article 2639 defines praise this way:

> *Praise is the form of prayer which recognizes most immediately that God is God. It lauds God for his own sake and gives him glory, quite beyond what he does, but simply because HE IS. It shares in the blessed happiness of the pure of heart who love God in faith before seeing him in glory. By praise, the [Holy] Spirit is joined to our spirits to bear witness that we are children of God, testifying to the only Son in*

> *whom we are adopted and by whom we glorify the*
> *Father. Praise embraces the other forms of prayer*
> *and carries them toward him who is its source and*
> *goal: the "one God, the Father, from whom are all*
> *things and for whom we exist."*

We might ask ourselves now why the Church continues to use these "old prayers" composed by ancient Semites, dusty nomads, people whose culture and language are so alien from our own. After all, we have some very nice, newer prayers – "Christian" prayers that we learned from our parents. Why do we cling to these "antiques"? Old does not necessarily mean better, does it?

The answer becomes clear as we read and pray the Psalms. They are "grown up" prayers, prayers that increase in meaning through years of praying. We constantly discover new meanings. They are prayers that read the motions and motives of our souls, the heights and depths of human experience. Saint Athanasius of Alexandria in his letter to Marcellinus [3] referred to the psalms as a "mirror of the soul." He wrote: "[The Psalter] possesses an extraordinary grace peculiar to itself – it reflects the movements of each soul, its vicissitudes and amendments, all represented and portrayed within the book itself." Saint Ambrose wrote, "All with eyes to see can discover in it [the Psalter] a complete gymnasium for the soul, a stadium for all the virtues, equipped for every kind of exercise; it is for each to choose the kind he judges best to help him gain the prize." [4] In the psalms we can find sentiments appropriate for every stage of prayer from the beginner to the most advanced stage of contemplative prayer.

The psalms dare to pose the hard questions that we all have: "How long, O LORD, will you utterly forget me?" (Ps 13); "My

---

3. In sections 15 to 27 of his letter to Marcellinus, Saint Athanasius gives a wonderful listing of the psalms which are appropriate to pray for every possible occasion.

4. From the *Explanations of the Psalms*, Ps 1: 4, 7-8 (CSEL 64, 4-7).

God, my God, why have you forsaken me?" (Ps 22); "Why do the wicked prosper while the just go mourning?" (Ps 73). These prayers have been meaningful for more than three thousand years, to people of widely differing times and cultures. Throughout this long period of time, they have taught us how to pray. They serve to stretch our hearts in the ways of prayer. Let us focus upon three aspects: they offer us images of the God to whom we pray; they enlighten us about the ends or motives of prayer; they give us the language to interpret our spiritual experiences.

IMAGES OF GOD

Divine revelation enables us to have a correct image or concept of God. Many of our mental or conceptual images of God come from our early childhood and the way our parents and teachers spoke of God to us. Some other images come from religious art – like the white-haired, bearded old man (God) extending his pointed finger toward Adam in Michelangelo's creation scene painted in the Sistine Chapel.

It is important for us to recall that the Book of Psalms is not only a book of prayers; it is also divine revelation. The psalms not only speak to God, but also speak about him; they reveal him to us. Recently, I read through all one hundred fifty psalms in an afternoon and noted only the names and the images they offered for God. The variety and wealth were utterly amazing. There were some that might be called "severe": lawgiver, judge, warrior, vindicator, avenger, chastiser, hunter, God of vengeance, the Holy One of Israel. There are royal images: King, King of Glory, Creator King of all the earth, Maker of Princes, Protector of his people, one who anoints and blesses, the Most High, Lord of Hosts, Restorer of Fortunes. There are images of strength and protection: Father, Fortress, Shield, Stronghold, Refuge, Guide, Shepherd, my Rock, my salvation, guardian of my life, savior, the one who holds me with his right hand, the mighty one of Jacob.

There are images like Teacher, Healer, Light, Counselor, Covenant Lover, one who laughs at the wicked who plot against him, "my exceeding joy," a farmer who plants his people in the land, a mother, a bird lifting its little ones upon its wings, redeemer, builder, miracle worker, "my strength and my song," forgiver, and fulfiller of my desires.

These are only a few, and they invite us to know God and to approach him in all the richness of who he is. These images of God reveal his divine attributes in ways that we can readily understand. Repeatedly we read, "God is good and his covenant love endures forever" (Ps 136: 1); "He is merciful and compassionate, slow to anger and abounding in love… He knows of what we are made" (Ps 103: 8, 14); "He fulfills the desire of all who fear him, he also hears their cry, and saves them" (Ps 145: 19).

THE ENDS OF PRAYER

Anyone who was catechized with the *Baltimore Catechism* knows that there are four ends of prayer: praise and adoration, petition, reparation, and thanksgiving. For many of us, petition dominates. Petition is real prayer, and it honors God who is our loving Father. When we ask for what we need, we affirm that he is kind, compassionate, provident, and generous in supplying our needs. But if our prayer is limited to petition, the relationship does not grow very much. God is more than the "operator" who answers our 911 calls. The psalms press out the borders and invite us into other forms of prayer.

The first end of prayer is praise and adoration

Let us begin with praise and adoration. The *Catechism of the Catholic Church* defines praise as "the form of prayer which recognizes most immediately that God is God." It recognizes that he is Creator and I am a creature, and I am simply glad that he is. It is a mature, unselfish form of prayer. Quite simply, praise is adoration with joy – not with fear, or awe, but simply joy. We need to be exercised in praise, and the psalms have many examples. Approximately one-fourth to one-third of the psalms are psalms of praise.

The word *Halleluyah* is most frequently associated with psalms of praise. The word itself is a call to praise. Literally it means, "all of you, come and praise Yahweh!" As the crown of God's creation, the human being summons all of creation to give voice with him to God's goodness, his beauty, his mighty acts of salvation. These psalms traverse creation from the angelic spheres, through the starry nights and sun-filled days, from highest mountains to the depths of seas. They examine all forms of life on the earth and note how a provident God provides food and shelter for each of his creatures (Ps 104); they even delight in the majesty of storm (Ps 29). Some of these psalms meditate upon the "strong arm and outstretched hand" of the Almighty as he leads his people forth from Egypt, provides for them in the desert, and enters into covenant with them. His acts of salvation from their enemies and the gift of the land of his promise to Abraham stir their hearts with wonder at his great fidelity.

The second end of prayer is petition

More than one-third of all the psalms in the Bible are prayers of petition. The majority of these psalms are classified as "laments" or "prayers of complaint." God must have known that we would need so many and wanted to assure us that it was all right to pray in this way.

Complaint psalms are for very urgent situations. They begin with an ardent cry to God: "O God, come to my assistance! LORD, make haste to help me!" (Ps 70: 1); "Out of the depths I cry to thee, O LORD, LORD, hear my voice!" (Ps 130: 1); "My God, my God, why have you forsaken me?" (Ps 22: 1). They issue from a firm conviction that the person or the nation is in a covenant relationship with God. This covenant bond is firm, solid, unbreakable. The God of the covenant is loving, provident, and faithful, and when he sees my need he will respond.

The need or the crisis represented in these psalms is urgent – it is a life-and-death situation. There is no time to waste on fancy words. The complaint psalms are characterized by bold, demanding language. God is addressed only in imperatives, and never with the polite form that uses "please." In a desperate situation (like drowning) there is no time for many words. "Help!" is enough.

An enemy of some kind threatens. It may be a person (a false witness at a trial, someone who is injuring me personally, cheating me) or a natural disaster like flood or famine. It may be disease, sickness, or physical death itself. The enemy may be spiritual, physical, or social. In order to emphasize the deadly threat of the enemy, the Psalmist often uses exaggerated metaphors to characterize him. The enemy, for example, may be portrayed as a wild beast ready to devour me, a hunter or a fowler armed with bow and arrows, a "man of blood" who seeks my life, a pack of wild dogs, or an overwhelming flood.

> *Save me, O God!*
> *For the waters have risen to my neck.*
> *I have sunk into the mud of the deep*
> *and there is no foothold.*
> *I have entered the waters of the deep*
> *and the waves overwhelm me.*
>
> (Ps 69: 1-2)

Initially we think that here is a drowning person. But the next verse tells us that this is a metaphor for a personal enemy.

> *More numerous than the hairs on my head*
> *are those who hate me without cause.*
> *Those who attack me with lies*
> *are too much for my strength.*
>
> (Ps 69: 4)

After the description of an enemy, the prayer moves on to petition. What does the Psalmist want God to do about this situation?

In your great love, answer me, O God,
with your help that never fails:
rescue me from sinking in the mud;
save me from my foes.

Save me from the waters of the deep
lest the waves overwhelm me.
Do not let the deep engulf me
nor death close its mouth on me.
...
Do not hide your face from your servant;
answer quickly for I am in distress.
Come close to my soul and redeem me;
ransom me pressed by my foes.

(Ps 69: 14-18)

Closely associated with the petitions, we often find "suggestions" as to what God might do to the enemy. Ordinarily, these are just "suggestions." Psalm 69 goes on to say, "Let their eyes be darkened, so that they cannot see... may their camp be a desolation, let no one dwell in their tents... let them be blotted out of the book of the living; let them not be enrolled with the righteous" (Ps 69: 24, 26, 29). The Psalmist does not fear to express anger, hurt, or any other passion with God. He knows that God can handle it. The conviction here is that there is no topic or feeling that can not be brought to God in prayer. He will receive it, and our covenant relationship established in baptism is so strong, it will not be broken.

At times we are surprised to find a little "holy blackmail" in these psalms of complaint. Moses himself was an expert at this type of prayer. After the incident of the Hebrew people worshiping the golden calf, God wished to annihilate the whole nation and start over with Moses. Moses stood in the breach and said, "Now wait a minute. What about your promises to Abraham, Isaac, and Jacob? Are you going to go back on your word? Besides, what will the Egyptians say? Did you bring these people out into the desert to kill them?" In other words, "God, your reputation is at stake." Many of the complaint psalms say things like, "If I die, who will praise you? No one praises you from Sheol" (Ps 6: 6).

Finally, the complaint psalm will swiftly change from petition to praise and thanksgiving. The conviction is that once God knows our sorrow, our danger, he will act swiftly. The prayer and the pray-er undergo a kind of conversion. The cry, the honesty of the prayer, turns everything over to God with hope, and then in utter confidence moves on with thanksgiving and praise. Psalm 69 moves on from its "suggestions" and petitions to these sentiments:

> I will praise God's name with a song;
> I will glorify him with thanksgiving.
> …
> The poor when they see it will be glad
> and God-seeking hearts will revive;
> for the Lord listens to the needy
> and does not spurn his servants in their chains.
> Let the heavens and the earth give him praise,
> the sea and all its living creatures.
>
> (Ps 69: 33-35)

The third end of prayer is contrition and reparation

The third end of prayer is contrition and reparation, best expressed in the penitential psalms. These psalms belong to the category of complaints or laments. In this case, however, the enemy is sin, and the enemy is within us. There are seven psalms that belong to this category – the so-called seven penitential psalms (Psalms 6, 32, 38, 51, 102, 130, and 143). All follow the same structure, though the order of the elements in these psalms may vary:

1. A cry to God: "LORD, rebuke me not in thy anger, nor chasten me in thy wrath." Both Psalm 6 and 38 begin this way. "Have mercy on me, O God, according to thy steadfast love" (Ps 51). "Hear my prayer, O LORD; let my cry come to Thee!" (Ps 102).

2. The mention of the enemy – sin: "I acknowledged my sin to thee and did not hide my iniquity" (Ps 32). "Against you, you only have I sinned… In sin did my mother conceive me" (Ps 51: 6a, 7b).

3. Petition: "Wash me thoroughly from my iniquity and cleanse me of my sin" (Ps 51). "I confess my iniquity and I am sorry for my sin" (Ps 38: 18).

4. Movement toward praise and thanksgiving and, in the case of these psalms, an apostolate of witnessing to the mercy of God: "Then I will teach transgressors your ways and sinners will return to you" (Ps 51). "Blessed is he whose transgression is forgiven, whose sin is covered" (Ps 32). "I will instruct you and teach you the way you should go; I will counsel you with my eye upon you" (Ps 32).

The fourth end of prayer is thanksgiving

Israel's law required sacrifices of thanksgiving for favors received. Whenever a person had been delivered by God from a serious illness, a natural disaster like a crop failure or flood, from a false accusation in a lawsuit, that person was obliged to go up to Jerusalem at the time of one of the great annual feast days (Passover, Pentecost, or Tabernacles) and offer a sacrifice of thanksgiving. This was not a private matter. The individual was instructed to gather the entire household, wife, children, servants, friends, and relatives, everyone who was aware of the sickness or life-threatening situation. They would take a lamb or a goat to be sacrificed in the Temple and some bread and wine. The whole entourage would be present for the sacrifice of thanksgiving. After the animal was sacrificed, part would be given to the priests, the blood and inner organs would be offered on the altar, and the rest would be roasted there in one of the large ovens that were within the Temple precincts. Then everyone present would sit down and have a meal together. In the midst of this setting, the person healed or delivered in some way would stand up and offer a psalm of thanksgiving. The purpose of this public act of gratitude was to witness to the goodness of God, to witness to the fact that he hears our prayers, and that there is reason to have great hope in him. "What God has done for me, he will do also for you." Psalm 116 is a wonderful example of a psalm of thanksgiving.

> *I love the Lord for he has heard*
> *the cry of my appeal*
> *for he turned his ear to me*
> *in the day when I called him.*
>
> *They surrounded me, the snares of death*
> *with the anguish of the tomb;*
> *they caught me, sorrow and distress.*
> *I called on the Lord's name.*
> *O Lord my God, deliver me!*
>
> *How gracious is the Lord, and just;*
> *our God has compassion.*
> *The Lord protects the simple hearts;*
> *I was helpless so he saved me.*
>
> *Turn back, my soul, to your rest*
> *for the Lord has been good:*
> *he has kept my soul from death,*

*my eyes from tears
and my feet from stumbling.*

*I will walk in the presence of the Lord
in the land of the living.
I trusted, even when I said:
"I am sorely afflicted,"
and when I said in my alarm:
"No man can be trusted."*

*How can I repay the Lord
for his goodness to me?
The cup of salvation I will raise;
I will call on the Lord's name.*

*My vows to the Lord I will fulfill
before all his people.
O precious in the eyes of the Lord
is the death of his faithful.*

*Your servant, Lord, your servant am I;
you have loosened my bonds.
A thanksgiving sacrifice I make:
I will call on the Lord's name.*

*My vows to the Lord I will fulfill
before all his people,
in the courts of the house of the Lord,
in your midst, O Jerusalem.
Praise the Lord!*

(Ps 116)

THE PSALMS GIVE US THE LANGUAGE
TO INTERPRET OUR SPIRITUAL EXPERIENCES

Saint Augustine referred to the psalms as "the prayer book of the Holy Spirit," and rightly so. He wrote, "God praised himself so that we would know how to praise him." In the *Confessions* (Book 9, part 4) Saint Augustine wrote, "O, in what accents I spoke to you, my God, when I read the Psalms of David! Those faithful songs and sounds of devotion permit no swelling pride. I was yet a catechumen and novice in your love... What cries I raised to you in those Psalms! I was on fire toward you, and eager to proclaim them, if possible to the whole world, *nor can anyone hide himself from your heat.*" [5] In his *Confessions* Saint Augustine frequently used the language of "being set on fire" by the words of the psalms, and he describes how they prompted the expression of his most intimate sensations (*Confessions* 9.8).

The *Confessions* begin with a quotation from Psalm 4 and thereafter there is not a page, there is hardly a paragraph, that does not contain some quotation from a psalm. He found in them the language that enabled him to speak of his journey to faith, and the transformation that God accomplished in him even as he prayed them. In his other theological writings he quotes the psalms more than ten thousand times.

I am certain that each of us has a few psalms to which we return frequently for our prayer. They contain images, thoughts, and sentiments that we find consoling because they express something very personal about our relationship with God. We have all had the experience of praying a psalm on a particular day and finding that a verse "leaps off the page," so to speak, and we find ourselves saying, "Yes, that is exactly what I experience today";

---

5. *The Confessions* I/1, introduction, translation and notes by Maria Boulding, O.S.B. (New City Press, Hyde Park, NY 1997); in the series from the Augustinian Heritage Institute, *The Works of Saint Augustine: A Translation for the 21ˢᵗ Century*, series editor John E. Rotelle, O.S.A.

"Oh, yes, that is what I know to be so true of God!" As we read the psalms, they also read our inmost thoughts and sentiments. Saint Athanasius said it so well, "The psalms are the mirror of the soul."

Saint Ambrose wrote a marvelous definition of a psalm, and it is with his words that I wish to conclude.

> *A Psalm is the prayer of praise of the people of God,*
> *the exaltation of the LORD,*
> *the joyful song of the congregation,*
> *the cry of all humanity,*
> *the applause of the universe,*
> *the voice of the Church,*
> *the sweet-sounding confession of faith,*
> *entire surrender to (divine) power,*
> *blessed freedom,*
> *a cry of happiness,*
> *an echo of joy.*
> *A psalm softens wrath, relieves care, and lightens sorrow.*
> *It is a weapon at night,*
> *teaching in the day,*
> *shield in fear, a festival celebration in holiness,*
> *an image of quietness,*
> *the pledge of peace and harmony.*
> *The psalm arises at day's beginning and is still sounding*
> *at day's end.*
>
> (St. Ambrose, *Explanatio Psalmi* 1, CSEL, 64.7)

FAITH OF OUR FATHERS

The Pilgrim Way of Life

ANN T. ORLANDO

Beginning in March 2007, His Holiness Pope Benedict XVI has often greeted pilgrims at his weekly general audience in the Vatican with a discussion of one of the Church Fathers. [1] The Holy Father's attention to them through this series of talks at general audiences highlights the continuing significance of the Church Fathers for our faith. They have influenced almost all aspects of our faith, including doctrine, liturgy, practice, ecclesiology, sacramentology, Christology, and Marian devotion. As friends of MAGNIFICAT, we feel their influence every time we reach for our MAGNIFICAT. The very structure of the Mass, the liturgical seasons, and prayer in the morning and evening follow the patterns they developed; the MAGNIFICAT's Meditations frequently use the

---

1. These general audiences can be found on the Vatican website at http://www.vatican.va/holy_father/benedict_xvi/audiences/index_en.htm. If the Holy Father has already spoken about one of the Fathers mentioned here, a specific reference to the date will be given.

Church Fathers as a rich mine of our spiritual legacy. By rein-forcing the continuity with our spiritual heritage, MAGNIFICAT follows the advice of Saint Vincent of Lerins († 450, feast day May 24) to the children of the Church, that they should cultivate the "rosebuds" of prayer and spirituality bequeathed to us by the Fathers of the Church.[2]

Because it would be impossible to present everything that is meaningful about the Church Fathers[3] in a single paper, here we will focus on an especially congenial theme for the Church Fathers and friends of MAGNIFICAT: how to lead a prayerful life. These great theologian-saints often described the prayerful life to their contemporaries as the pilgrim life in homilies, sermons, poems, and treatises. In these ways, they left behind "rosebuds" for us. Before we turn to our discussion of the prayerful life, however, we should briefly consider who are the Church Fathers.

WHO ARE THE CHURCH FATHERS?

No one we now consider a Church Father thought of himself in that way. It is only in hindsight that later generations turned to some of the earlier great Catholic saints and teachers to distin-guish them as Church Fathers. The Church still maintains Saint Vincent's criteria for the designation "Church Father": antiquity, orthodox doctrine, ecclesial approval, and holiness of life.[4]

By antiquity we now understand the period from the death of the apostles to before the Middle Ages. Historically and culturally the Church Fathers were shaped by the Roman Empire and late

---

2. Vincent of Lerins, *A Commonitory*, 57, trans. C. A. Heurtley, Nicene and Post-Nicene Fathers, Second Series 2, vol. 11 (Peabody: Hendrickson, 1995), p. 148.

3. Boniface Ramsey, *Beginning to Read the Fathers* (New York: Paulist Press, 1985). This is an excellent introduction to the Church Fathers.

4. Vincent of Lerins, *A Commonitory*, 152. It should be noted that Saint Vincent himself is now considered one of the Church Fathers.

antiquity. Most scholars [5] start this period in the Church's history with the third pope, Saint Clement of Rome [6] († 98, feast day November 23). When the period ends is more uncertain, but most scholars end it somewhere between Pope Saint Gregory the Great († 604, feast day March 12) and Saint John Damascene († 754, feast day December 4). This span of six hundred years starts with the period of intense martyrdom by the Roman authorities that ended in 312, during the reign of Emperor Constantine the Great. After this date, the Church entered a period of great flourishing in Roman society. Because the Church Fathers lived before the schism between the Catholic and the Orthodox Churches, all of these great saints discussed here are venerated both by the Orthodox and by Catholics. [7]

The second criterion, orthodox doctrine, means that what the Church Fathers taught was in keeping with sound Catholic teaching. An examination of the Magisterium reveals the reliance on the Church Fathers who often gave the definitive statement of sound doctrine. For example, Pope Saint Leo the Great [8] († 461, feast day November 9) bequeathed to us the clear understanding of Jesus Christ as having two natures in one person. The Fathers taught in many ways, including sermons, letters, biblical commentaries, and scholarly treatises. Sermons are listed first among their works because the overwhelming majority of Church Fathers were bishops. [9] Their primary concern was to lead their people to holiness. As a result they wrote well-argued pieces against various heretical movements. The Fathers almost always wrote such pieces

---

5. The academic study of the Church Fathers is known as patristics or patrology.

6. Benedict XVI, *Clement of Rome*, General Audience, March 7, 2007.

7. John Damascene articulated the doctrine that we venerate saints but do not worship them; only God is to be worshiped.

8. Benedict XVI, *Pope St. Leo the Great*, 5 March 2008.

9. Among the notable non-bishops mentioned here were Saint Hippolytus and Saint Benedict of Nursia. However, they can be taken as the exceptions that prove the rule.

in response to perceived problems. As in the case noted above, Pope Saint Leo developed the two natures in one person Christology to counter heresies that questioned Christ's humanity.

The third criterion, ecclesial approval, is reflected in several ways. First is the continuing reliance the Church has in every subsequent generation on the teaching of the Fathers. The importance of what they wrote has been so compelling that all succeeding generations have carefully preserved their teaching, so that we have an extensive collection of their works. These works were preserved not as museum pieces from an earlier era, but as working papers for later theologians. For instance, the great medieval theologian Saint Thomas Aquinas († 1274, feast day January 28) referenced one or another of the Church Fathers on almost every page he wrote. In our own time, we can see ecclesial approval in the use of the Fathers' teachings in the *Catechism of the Catholic Church.* One of many examples is Pope Saint Leo the Great and our understanding of Jesus Christ as true God and true man, as discussed in the Catechism (CCC 464-469). Another aspect of ecclesial approval is the later Church's recognition of their personal holiness by declaring them saints. [10]

We come finally to the fourth criterion: holiness of life, or the personal intimacy with God cultivated by the Fathers in themselves and others. As friends of MAGNIFICAT, we are touched perhaps most directly by this criterion. The order of the Mass we celebrate today owes much to the early liturgical developments of Fathers such as Saint Hippolytus († 236, feast day August 13). In his *Apostolic Tradition*, he gives us prayers for the Mass, most of which we would recognize as familiar today. For instance, at the

---

10. While most of the Church Fathers were subsequently venerated as saints, not all were – Origen and Tertullian being notable examples of those who are not.

beginning of the offertory, Hippolytus records the following exchange between the bishop or priest and the people: [11]

> Bishop: The Lord be with you.
> People: And with your spirit.
> Bishop: Lift up your hearts.
> People: We have lifted them up to the Lord.
> Bishop: Let us give thanks to the Lord.
> People: It is right and just.

A notable characteristic that Saint Hippolytus shared with all of the Fathers is that he did not see himself as inventing something novel. Rather, he saw himself as standing in the tradition of Scripture and the apostles to carry forward the message of the Good News: thus the title *Apostolic Tradition*. Also, like most of the earliest Church Fathers, Saint Hippolytus gave witness to his faith by suffering martyrdom.

The time of martyrdom in the early Church lasted from the very beginning of the Church (Saint Stephen in the Acts of the Apostles) until Constantine the Great became emperor of the Roman Empire and established toleration for Christians in 312. Saint Hippolytus died during a time of intense persecution in Rome; a companion in martyrdom with him was Pope Saint Pontian. [12] Later generations have honored them together on the same feast day, as we continue to do today. The burial places of martyrs became gathering places for Christians to celebrate the liturgy. The most famous of these places are the catacombs just outside of Rome, which can still be visited today. Among these is a catacomb named for Pope Saint Callistus († 222, feast day

---

11. Hippolytus, *The Apostolic Tradition*, iv. 3, ed. Gregory Dix and Henry Chadwick (London: Alban, 1992), 7.
12. The relationships among Hippolytus, Pontian, and Callistus are complex and not well understood. A good discussion is found in: Ronald Heine, "Hippolytus, Ps.-Hippolytus and the Early Canons," *Early Christian Literature*, ed. Frances Young, et al. (Cambridge: Cambridge University Press, 2004), pp. 142-51.

October 14), which may be the burial site for himself, Pope Saint Pontian, and perhaps Saint Hippolytus. Murals depicting the sacraments of baptism and Eucharist surround the tombs, emphasizing the importance of the sacraments in the early Church.

An example of our reliance on early practices is found in our contemporary Rite of Christian Initiation of Adults. During the 1960s when the bishops wanted to revitalize the Church's approach to adult baptism, they looked to this early period in the Church for a model. The current structure of pre-catechumenate, catechumenate, lenten purification and mystagogia accompanied by the rites of acceptance, election, and initiation are precisely the approach developed by the Church during its early centuries as a persecuted Church. Today's catechumens in our open churches are following in the footsteps of those ancient catechumens who learned about Christianity and were baptized in the catacombs.

After the time of martyrdom in the Roman Empire, once the Church could be openly in Roman society, monastic movements for men and women grew rapidly. As the martyrs had been before them, monks, nuns, and other devout Christian ascetics were considered the "heroes" of the faith. The most influential and popular book of this period was the biography of the monk Antony († 356, feast day January 7) written by Saint Athanasius [13] († 373, feast day May 2), bishop of Alexandria, Egypt. *The Life of Antony* remains one of the most important and popular biographies of a saint today. Another vitally important contribution associated with Saint Athanasius is the Nicene Creed, which we say every Sunday and holy day at Mass. As a young priest, Saint Athanasius attended the Church Council in Nicea, at which the Creed was written. [14] As a bishop, he worked hard to promulgate

---

13. Benedict XVI, *St. Athanasius*, General Audience, 20 June 2007.

14. The Creed written at the Council of Nicea was modified at the Council of Constantinople in 381; this modified Creed is the one we profess at Mass. Saint Gregory Nazianzus presided over the Council of Constantinople.

the acceptance of the Nicene Creed as the basic doctrinal statement of the faith.

To help monks and nuns live a prayerful life in community,
early abbots wrote rules for their communities. One of the most
famous and enduring rules was written by Saint Benedict of
Nursia [15] († 547, feast day July 11). He developed his rule to guide
the life of the monks in the monastery he established at Monte
Cassino, south of Rome. Nearby, his twin sister, Saint Scholastica
(† 547, feast day February 10), established a similar convent for
women which also followed Benedict's rule. We know a great
deal about Benedict and Scholastica because, just as Athanasius
wrote a life of the monk Antony, another Church Father, Pope
Saint Gregory the Great, wrote a life of Benedict. Benedict's rule
has been the foundational building block for Catholic monastic
communities ever since the sixth century. Today, Benedictine
communities of men and women continue to follow in the footsteps of Christ by following the rule. An important part of the rule
is the order in which the psalms are to be prayed during the day
through the seasons of the liturgical year. This is seen today in the
Liturgy of the Hours, a version of which for laity is provided in
MAGNIFICAT for prayer in the morning and evening. Thus, we pray
morning and evening in communion with each other and in
continuity with centuries of prayerful Christians. Benedict's rule is
also justly famous for its injunction to offer hospitality to poor
people and pilgrims, "because in them more particularly Christ is
received." [16]

---

15. Benedict XVI, *St. Benedict of Norcia*, General Audience, 9 April 2008.
16. Benedict of Nursia, *The Rule of St. Benedict in English* 53.15, ed. Timothy
Fry (Collegeville: Liturgical Press, 1982), p. 74.

PILGRIMAGES

In the earliest Church, during the time of the martyrs, pilgrimages were brief journeys to the burial sites of martyrs. Thus, for instance, through clandestine visits to the sites, the early Christians in Rome preserved the memory of where Peter and Paul had been martyred and buried. Once that time of martyrdom was over, Christians could travel more easily to distant holy sites. Of course, the primary pilgrimage destination was Jerusalem. One of the earliest pilgrims to the Holy Land was Saint Helena († 330, feast day August 18), the mother of the Emperor Constantine. In her pilgrimage to Jerusalem she discovered the True Cross (celebrated on September 14). She also procured the funds from her emperor-son in 325 to build basilicas on Calvary and in Bethlehem, the Church of the Holy Sepulcher and the Church of the Nativity, respectively. These churches still stand and have welcomed throngs of devout Christian pilgrims (not to mention gawking tourists) ever since.

It was not only the powerful and wealthy who traveled to Jerusalem. We have the diary of a woman named Egeria, who made a pilgrimage from southern France to Jerusalem sometime in the fourth century. We know very little about Egeria, except that she kept a detailed account of her pilgrimage. Her diary is a remarkable record of the ancient Holy Week liturgy; she has given us a vivid account of the Triduum celebrations in the fourth century. When read today, what strikes us is not the differences but the similarities between her account and our contemporary practice. Her description of the adoration of the cross on Good Friday bears a very close resemblance to our practice each Good Friday in every Catholic parish:

> *The bishop duly takes his seat in the chair, and a table covered with a linen cloth is placed before him; the deacons stand round the table, and a silver-gilt casket is brought in which is the holy wood of the Cross. The*

casket is opened and (the wood) is taken out, and the wood of the Cross is placed upon the table. Now, when it has been put upon the table, the bishop, as he sits, holds the extremities of the sacred wood firmly in his hands, while the deacons who stand around guard it. It is guarded thus because the custom is that the people, both faithful and catechumens, come one by one and, bowing down at the table, kiss the sacred wood and pass through. [17]

Although these pilgrimages to Jerusalem and other holy sites became very popular in the fourth century, the Church Fathers of the fourth and fifth centuries developed another understanding of pilgrimage: the pilgrimage of our life to the heavenly Jerusalem. As important as all of the Church Fathers are, the Church in subsequent centuries has come to recognize eight as being preeminently important. Four wrote in Greek, and, in addition to Saint Athanasius, they are Saint Basil the Great [18] († 379, feast day January 2), his brother, Saint Gregory of Nyssa [19] († 394, feast day March 9), and their friend Saint Gregory Nazianzus [20] († 390, feast day January 2). The other four wrote in Latin: in addition to Pope Saint Gregory the Great, they are Saint Ambrose [21] († 397, feast day December 7), Saint Jerome [22] († 420, feast day September 30)

---

17. Egeria, *Journal*, XXXVII.2, trans. Louis Duschesme, found at http://users.ox.ac.uk/~mikef/durham/egeria.html.
18. Benedict XVI, *St. Basil*, General Audiences, 4 July 2007 and 1 August 2007.
19. Benedict XVI, *St. Gregory of Nyssa*, General Audiences, 29 August 2007 and 5 September 2007.
20. Benedict XVI, *St. Gregory Nazianzus*, General Audiences, 8 August 2007 and 22 August 2007.
21. Benedict XVI, *St. Ambrose*, General Audiences, 24 October 2007.
22. Benedict XVI, *St. Jerome*, General Audiences, 7 November 2007 and 14 November 2007.

and Saint Augustine of Hippo [23] († 430, feast day August 28). Taken together, these eight Fathers of the Church contributed in countless ways to our understanding of theology and our spirituality. Among the things they forcefully taught was that our life is a pilgrimage. By this they did not mean that pilgrimage could be used as an analogy of or a metaphor for life. Rather, they understood Christian life as truly a pilgrimage. In this way, they saw a journey to the earthly Jerusalem as the metaphor for the real pilgrimage of life to the heavenly Jerusalem. [24]

Thus, these great Fathers were very careful to define what they did not mean by pilgrimage. For instance, Saint Gregory of Nyssa tells us that "pilgrimage" should not be primarily understood as a journey to see holy places. Saint Gregory was concerned that travelers might think that simply by visiting Jerusalem, one could become holier. Gregory notes rather pointedly, "When the Lord invites the blest to their inheritance in the kingdom of heaven, He does not include a pilgrimage to Jerusalem amongst their good deeds." [25] For Gregory, just making the journey to Jerusalem does not make a person holier, since "change of place does not bring one closer to God, but where you are, God will come toward you." [26] Gregory does not completely discourage pilgrimages to the Holy Land, as long as they are undertaken in the proper spirit of a prayerful life. After all, Gregory himself went on a pilgrimage to Jerusalem. However, it is not the places where Christ's life

---

23. Benedict XVI, *St. Augustine of Hippo*, General Audiences, 9 January 2008, 16 January 2008, 30 January 2008, 20 February 2008, and 27 February 2008.
24. Dee Dyas, *Pilgrimage in Medieval English Literature 700-1500* (Cambridge: D. S. Brewer, 2001). This book is a scholarly work on this understanding of pilgrimage in the early Christian centuries.
25. Gregory of Nyssa, *On Pilgrimages*, trans. William Moore, Nicene and Post-Nicean Fathers, Second Series, vol. 5 (Peabody: Hendrickson, 1995), p. 382.
26. Ibid.

unfolded, but the truth of Christ's life that is fundamental to our faith. "Before we saw Bethlehem we knew Him being made man by means of the Virgin; before we saw His Grave we believed in His Resurrection from the dead; apart from seeing the Mount of Olives, we confessed that His Ascension into heaven was real." [27]

Gregory of Nyssa was not alone in cautioning that places in themselves do not make our faith stronger. There is the famous story of Saint Ambrose discouraging Saint Monica († 387, feast day August 27) from going to the tombs of the martyrs because many of these places had become more like tourist attractions than places of veneration and worship. Instead, Ambrose wanted Monica to focus on him for whom the martyrs had died. This story about Monica and Ambrose is told by Monica's son, Saint Augustine, in Book VI of his *Confessions*. A little later he tells the story of Monica's death. At the conclusion he asks his "fellow citizens" with him on pilgrimage to the eternal Jerusalem to pray for his mother and father. [28]

SAINT AUGUSTINE AND THE PILGRIMAGE OF LIFE

Pope Benedict XVI called Saint Augustine "the greatest Father of the Latin Church." [29] A measure of his prominence is found in the *Catechism of the Catholic Church* [30] which references Saint Augustine more often than any other theologian from any era. His importance to our spiritual life is exemplified in MAGNIFICAT, where Saint Augustine makes regular appearances in the

---

27. Ibid., p. 383.

28. Augustine, *Confessions*, IX. 37.

29. Benedict XVI, *St. Augustine of Hippo* (1), General Audience, 9 January 2008. Available at http://www.vatican.va/holy_father/benedict_xvi/audiences/2008/documents/hf_ben-xvi_aud_20080109_en.html.

30. *Catechism of the Catholic Church*, Index of Citations, 742-743.

Meditations. More than any other Church Father, Augustine taught that life is a pilgrimage. [31]

Augustine famously wrote about his own life as a pilgrim in his *Confessions*. This is a deeply revealing account of his life of sin and falling away from God, and how God drew him into the Catholic faith. He relates how Saint Monica and Saint Ambrose were instrumental in God's plan for his salvation. Monica prayed for her wayward son for nineteen years while Augustine was separated from the Church. During this time, Augustine's life was filled with ambition and lust. The turning point came when he met Ambrose and listened to Ambrose's preaching on Scripture. Augustine says of Ambrose, "This man of God welcomed me with fatherly kindness and showed the charitable concern for my pilgrimage that befitted a bishop." [32] After study as a catechumen, Augustine was baptized by Ambrose at the Easter Vigil in 387.

Later, when Augustine himself was a bishop, he often spoke and wrote about the Christian as a pilgrim, about the pilgrim in the earthly society, and the pilgrim Church. In all cases, Augustine was referring to our journey to the heavenly kingdom, not a trip to the earthly Jerusalem. In fact, for all he had to say about many subjects, Augustine had very little to say about the earthly Jerusalem. His goal was, and he wanted our goal to be, the heavenly Jerusalem. In concert with the other great Church Fathers, Augustine wrote that the earthly Jerusalem "stood as a sign of the heavenly city it foreshadowed." [33]

Augustine divided people into two groups: those who are on

---

31. J. Van Oort, *Jerusalem and Babylon: A study into Augustine's "City of God" and the Sources of His Doctrine of the Two Cities* (Leiden: Brill, 1991). Van Oort has cataloged all the occurrences of "pilgrim" and "pilgrimage" in Augustine, pp. 132-42.

32. Augustine, *The Confession*, V.xiii.23, trans. Maria Boulding (New York: New City, 1997), p. 131.

33. Augustine, *Exposition of the Psalms*, Part III, Vol. 17, Psalm 64: 1, trans. Maria Boulding (New York: New City Press, 2003), p. 265.

pilgrimage to the heavenly Jerusalem and those who are not. Those not on pilgrimage think happiness can be found in this world, while those who are on pilgrimage know that true happiness is realized in the eternal Jerusalem. Those who do not live a life of faith have only this imperfect world to call home. They "cannot truthfully call themselves pilgrims on earth, for they are in the place where they are born according to the flesh; they have no city anywhere else and hence are not foreigners on earth but earthlings."[34] They are not on pilgrimage to the heavenly homeland, and so death is a passage *from* life. For the pilgrim, on the other hand, death is a passage *to* life. For Augustine, our life as a pilgrim is not measured by birth and death. Rather, our pilgrim life begins when we are baptized and ends with eternal life. By virtue of our baptism we become strangers and wanderers on earth, searching for our true homeland. Baptized Christians who, through God's grace, try to lead a righteous life are those "who on this pilgrimage sighed with holy longing for their heavenly country."[35]

Augustine did recognize that although true pilgrims may not be of the world, they are certainly in the world. Thus the pilgrim is affected by the world's cares and concerns. And so Augustine gives practical advice to the pilgrim concerning the things of this world. For instance, in his *Tractates on the Gospel of St. John*, Augustine addresses the pilgrim's attitude to money: "For you money will be an instrument of pilgrimage, not a stimulus of greed, which you should use for necessity, not for the enjoyment of pleasure."[36] In this same work, he goes on to say that we should use money the way a traveler uses a wayside inn, not with

---

34. Augustine, *Expositions of the Psalms*, Part III, Vol. 19, Psalm 118 (8): 1, trans. Maria Boulding (New York: New City Press, 2003), p. 372.
35. Ibid.
36. Augustine, *Tractates on the Gospel of St. John*, XL.10. *Erit tibi nummus instrumentum peregrinationis, non irritamentum cupiditatis; quo utaris ad necessitatem, non quo fruaris ad delectationem.*

the purpose of remaining, but rather, use it temporarily and then move forward. What must always travel with us on our pilgrimage are: "the divine Scriptures, the assembling of the people, the cele-bration of the sacraments, holy baptism, and singing God's praises." [37] These are the things to which we should cling as we travel on our pilgrimage of life.

Among the items that belong in our baggage are some things that you might well expect: the Bible and the sacraments. But Augustine also includes the assembling of the people as important to our pilgrimage. Our pilgrim companions are found in an ever-widening circle of family, friends, and Church. We are pilgrims even in our own home, and "the family which lives by faith is journeying toward the celestial city." [38] Augustine knows that the faithful family and the earthly family live side by side; further, he acknowledges that both families use the good things of the world necessary for life, and that both seek happiness and peace. But while the earthly family uses these things as an end in themselves, the pilgrim family uses them simply as a means to help them on their journey.

Families, of course, live together in a broader society. The society of pilgrim families is the pilgrim Church. Augustine frequently referred to the Church as the "heavenly city while in its state of pilgrimage." This pilgrim Church "gathers together a society of pilgrims of all languages, not scrupling about diver-sities in [human] manners, laws and institutions." [39] What holds this society of the pilgrim Church together is commonality of faith, hope, and love. That commonality is manifested by how Christians on pilgrimage pray together. "For witness the prayer of the whole city of God in its pilgrim state, for it cries to God by the

---

37. Ibid.
38. Augustine, *City of God*, XIX.14, trans. Marcus Dods (New York: Modern Library, 2000), 693.
39. Ibid., XIX.17, 696.

mouth of all its members, *Forgive us our debts as we forgive our debtors*." [40]

THE PILGRIM AT PRAYER

The hallmark of the pilgrim is continual prayer in union with the whole Church. But how to pray continually, given all the cares of this earthly life? Augustine analyzes this question and carefully answers it in a letter he wrote to a wealthy Roman widow, Proba. He wrote this letter more than sixteen hundred years ago, and in so doing left a "rosebud" for us. The letter opens with: "Recalling that you asked and that I promised that I would write something for you on praying to God... I must now at last pay my debt and yield to your pious desire in the love of Christ." Augustine himself notes that Proba is "among the nobility of this world, a wealthy woman, and the mother of such a large family." [41] Wealth in and of itself, says Augustine, need not be an impediment to prayer and the holy life, and he gives Zacchaeus (Lk 19: 1-10) as an example.

He asks Proba to consider what is true life and happiness. He suggests to Proba that "you should regard yourself as desolate in this world, however great the happiness with which you are living in it." [42] He reminds her that wealth and worldly honors only encourage a desire for more of them, that she will never be satisfied with them. Thus, these things cannot make Proba happy, no matter how much wealth and good fortune she may have. The happy life is in "that person who has everything he wants and does not want anything improper." [43] It may be proper to want some wealth, says Augustine, as long as it is not desired in itself, but needed to meet family obligations. However, even as she engages

---

40. Ibid., XIX.27, 708.
41. Augustine, *Letter 130*, 1.1, trans. Roland Teske (New York: New City Press, 2003), p. 184.
42. Ibid., 2.3, 185.
43. Ibid., 5.11, 189.

in worldly activities to meet the needs of her family, Proba should understand the words "pray without ceasing" (1 Thes 5: 17) to mean "desire without ceasing the happy life." [44]

Augustine notes that amid the cares and concerns of this world, the desire for the eternal happy life can "in a sense cool down." Thus, taking time "at certain hours by the words of prayer we call the mind back to the task of praying… in that way we remind ourselves to aim at that which we desire." [45] These moments of prayer should be brief, so that we do not lose our focus. Augustine encourages "frequent prayers, but very brief ones." [46] The form of prayer does not need to be wordy. He tells Proba that the divine Scripture has already given us the words we need. In particular, all our intentions are found in the Our Father. [47] These intentions are the ones that lead us to the genuinely happy life. Augustine concludes his letter by asking Proba "to pray earnestly for us, too." [48]

CONCLUSION

How does Augustine's advice, written so long ago, apply to us as friends of MAGNIFICAT? First, we might think of MAGNIFICAT as the guidebook for our pilgrim life. Most of us need a guidebook when we journey to a new place, and our life as it unfolds each day is always a new place. MAGNIFICAT gives us daily directions and mileage markers to keep us on the right path in our pilgrimage. MAGNIFICAT helps us heed Augustine's advice to say short, frequent prayers during the day. MAGNIFICAT also encourages us to recognize that we do not travel alone. We have the companionship in prayer of our fellow pilgrims in the Church,

---

44. Ibid., 9.18, 192.
45. Ibid., 9.18, 192.
46. Ibid., 10.20, 193.
47. Cf. ibid., 13.24, 195.
48. Ibid., 14.31, 199.

and the intercession of all those pilgrims who have gone before us. Following the ancient daily and seasonal liturgical paths developed by the Church Fathers, MAGNIFICAT guides our steps to the heavenly Jerusalem and true happiness.

THANKS BE TO GOD

Developing a Grateful Magnificat *Heart*

MARILYN QUIRK

Mary said,
"My soul proclaims the greatness of the Lord;
my spirit rejoices in God my Savior.
For He has looked with favor on his lowly servant;
From this day all generations will call me blessed.
The Almighty has done great things for me,
and holy is his name."

(Lk 1: 46-49)

Mary's magnificent hymn of praise, the *Magnificat*, gives us a view into her heart and soul. We see her obedience, her faith, and her total love for the living God. As she sings her canticle, she looks back through the ages at God's faithfulness to his people; she looks at all the wondrous things he has done and then sees how she is part of his plan; she realizes in a new way his overwhelming love for her as he chooses her to receive his greatest gift – to bring God's promised Messiah into the world. And the only thing she can offer him in return is a heart overflowing with thankfulness and praise.

Mary, our Mother, wants to teach us to love and praise God as she does: with our whole heart, soul, mind, and strength. Let us learn from her as we look back and reflect upon the time just prior to her singing her beautiful song of praise.

> *In the sixth month, the angel Gabriel was sent from God to a town of Galilee named Nazareth to a virgin betrothed to a man named Joseph of the house of David. The virgin's name was Mary.*
>
> (Lk 1: 26-27)

The beautiful narrative of the Annunciation as told in the first chapter of Luke's Gospel tells of the angel Gabriel sent from God to invite his highly favored daughter, Mary, to become the mother of the Redeemer. This ordinary woman, extraordinarily graced by God from the moment of her conception, was told she would conceive and bear a son and name him Jesus. "How can this be...?" she asked. The angel told her in reply, "The Holy Spirit will come upon you and the power of the Most High will over-shadow you. Therefore, the child to be born will be called holy, the Son of God." Mary placed her life at the disposal of his plan and said, "I am the servant of the Lord, let it be done according to your word." [As a side note – I love the title with which Mary identified herself – servant. In Greek this word is δούλη (*doulé*), which means a female slave, a servant of servants, the lowest level of servitude.] Her surrender to the Lord was total.

This overshadowing of the Holy Spirit must have been the most incredible experience of union with God ever. I imagine she would have wanted to savor this moment for a good period of time. Yet Luke tells us "in those days" Mary set out in haste to visit her kinswoman, Elizabeth, whom the angel said was with child in her old age "for nothing is impossible with God." In faith, Mary began this arduous journey of nearly one hundred miles, which must have taken several days, to the hill country to a town of Judah. She went on the wings of the Holy Spirit to love and serve her aged cousin. Pope Benedict said this was the first eucharistic procession. One may also say that she was the first bearer of the good news of our salvation. When Mary entered Zechariah's house and greeted Elizabeth, the child within Elizabeth's womb leapt; "Elizabeth was filled with the Holy Spirit and cried out in a loud voice, 'Blest are you among women and blest is the fruit of your womb. But who am I that the mother of my Lord should come to me?'"

Because there were no easy forms of communication over distances at that period of time, the sight of Elizabeth, great with child, must have filled Mary's heart with joy. This was indeed confirmation of what the angel had told her about her cousin. How good it is for all of us to have a confirmation of what God has spoken quietly to our heart. It was not possible for Elizabeth to know through human eyes that Mary was pregnant. It was only by the revelation of the Holy Spirit that she knew Mary was bearing the Son of God. The exuberant joy of these two women must have filled that little home. I can only describe this moment as an explosion of grace. Mary, filled to overflowing with love and gratitude and joy, sang her *Magnificat* with great exultation. When she said, "my spirit *rejoices* in God, my Savior," the Greek word "rejoice" translates to jubilee joy – to jump or leap in great jubilation. She marvels at the faithfulness and mercy of God in redeeming the human race and with all humility acknowledges that the Almighty has done great things for her. She gives him the glory, taking none for herself.

The town where this event took place is called Ein Karim, which means "Garden Fountain" or "Vineyard Fountain." In visiting that little home in the Holy Land, one can see a well inside with the water flowing down into a fountain in the little village just below the shrine. It is called Mary's Spring. When Mary visited Elizabeth, a little spring burst forth, as often happens in places of her visitations. Water is a symbol of the Holy Spirit. Wherever she goes, the Holy Spirit is there as well. The following passage describes Ein Karim to me.

> *"You are an enclosed garden, my sister, my bride,*
> *an enclosed garden, a fountain sealed.*
> *You are a park that puts forth pomegranates,*
> *with all choice fruits;*
> *Nard and saffron, calamus and cinnamon,*
> *with all kinds of incense;*
> *Myrrh and aloes,*
> *with all the finest spices.*
> *You are a garden fountain, a well of water*
> *flowing fresh from Lebanon.*
> *Arise, north wind! Come, south wind!*
> *blow upon my garden*
> *that its perfumes may spread abroad."*
>
> (Song 4: 12-16)

MAGNIFICAT, [1] A MINISTRY TO CATHOLIC WOMEN, is a work of which I have been privileged to be a part since its beginning on the Feast of the Holy Rosary, October 7, 1981. MAGNIFICAT takes its inspiration from the Visitation, and before we had ever heard of Ein Karim, the Lord inspired us with this passage from Scripture. We are women whose lives have been transformed through God's mercy by "the love God poured into our hearts through the Holy Spirit that has been given to us" (Rom 5: 5). We have experienced a taste of the joy these two women, Mary and Elizabeth, shared as they came together. Through the grace and mercy of God, the Holy Spirit, given to us in baptism and confirmation, has been

---

1. MAGNIFICAT, A MINISTRY TO CATHOLIC WOMEN is a different organization from MAGNIFICAT® even though they share the same name. The trademark MAGNIFICAT is used under license from and is the exclusive property of Magnificat Central Service Team, Inc., A Ministry to Catholic Women.

stirred and fanned into a flame (2 Tm 1: 6), making us new crea-
tions in Christ. This personal encounter with the risen Christ has
impelled us to go and tell the good news to our sisters in Christ,
to evangelize and foster spiritual growth in women all over the
world.

Our Holy Father, Pope Benedict, in speaking to the Curia at the
end of 2007 identified a crucial need in the Church: to evangelize. He also stated that the Gospel cannot be implemented without
a personal encounter with Christ. He said further, "Whoever has
recognized a great truth, whoever has found a great joy should
transmit it. He cannot keep it to himself."

John Paul II told us (Rimini, Italy, April 2001) that Mary is the
privileged and sure means for encountering the Lord: "It is she
who prepares us to welcome His Word and makes us persevering
in prayer, in the expectation of the Spirit who inflames our hearts
and leads us to put out into the deep with courage, toward the
goals that the Lord is indicating."

As a mother, I care deeply about the spiritual well-being of my
children. I have learned that Mary, my heavenly Mother, cares
much more about my spiritual growth. Time and again I have
asked Mary to help me pray, to prepare my heart to receive the
Eucharist, to assist me in my ordinary duties, etc., and she has
more than answered my prayer. In the Apostles' Creed, we say
Jesus "was conceived by the Holy Spirit and born of the Virgin
Mary." This is also true in our lives. Mary was there at Cana inter-
ceding with Jesus: "They have no more wine." One interpretation
is the "wine" of the Holy Spirit. She was present at Pentecost,
praying with the apostles and disciples for the coming of the
Spirit. (When the Holy Spirit was poured out upon them, the joy
of those receiving the Spirit was so profound that some bystanders
scoffed, "They have had too much new wine.")

Father Cantalamessa, preacher to the papal household and a
regular contributor to the MAGNIFICAT publication, said in one of

his Advent homilies in 2007 that "all prayers and hymns to the Holy Spirit begin with 'Come!' This means that the Spirit is something that we have received and that we must receive again and again." The "Spirit who interiorly transforms us, gives us a taste of the praise of God, opens our mind to the understanding of the Scriptures, teaches us to proclaim Jesus 'Lord' and gives us the courage to assume new and difficult tasks in the service of God and neighbor." Mary, spouse of the Holy Spirit, teaches us openness and docility to the Holy Spirit in our everyday lives.

Mary's life was filled with unexpected twists and turns, joys and sorrows. She embraced each day and situation with total submission to the will of God. "I am the servant of the Lord, let it be done according to your word." Father Romanus Cessario says it best in his exquisite meditations in the 2008 Holy Week edition of MAGNIFICAT, "The *Via Matris*: The Way of Our Sorrowful Mother." Father Cessario writes that "although Mary was conceived immaculately she did not refuse to embrace the sorrows that she endured for the Lord's sake... Her 'Fiat' her prayer of submission to the divine plan, commits Mary to cooperating with her Son as he wins the world's salvation. The sorrows of Mary are meant to provide a source of encouragement for Christian believers. What the Mother of God experienced in faith becomes both a model and a support for us." She truly is the Woman of the Way and the Help of Christians. So often I have turned to her and meditated on her trials in life and been strengthened. How many of us, as parents, have had concerns for our children and grandchildren, and have entrusted them to her to watch over them. Mary is the first and foremost disciple, with virtues for all to emulate!

Saint Augustine tells us that we cannot be exempt from trials but that we progress through means of them. In the ministry of MAGNIFICAT we have received strength and inspiration from hearing the testimonies of so many women who have endured great obstacles and difficulties, have overcome them, and have grown spiritually through the power of the Holy Spirit and Mary's help. As Mary endured the depths of sorrow, she received the heights of joy and praise. Reflecting on her many trials gives us strength to endure and to grow in our own gratitude to God.

This year marks the twentieth anniversary of John Paul II's Apostolic Letter *On the Dignity and Vocation of Women*. The introduction opens with an excerpt from a prophetic message to women given at the close of the Second Vatican Council, December 8, 1965.

> *"The hour is coming, in fact has already come, when the vocation of women is being acknowledged in its fullness, the hour in which women acquire in the world an influence, effect, and a power never hitherto achieved. That is why, at this moment when the human race is undergoing so deep a transformation, women imbued with the Spirit of the Gospel can do much to aid mankind in not falling…"*

The word "imbued" means to soak, to saturate as if one were dyeing a garment. God's plan for us is to be saturated with his Holy Spirit – as Mary is.

Women have been given by God great power to influence for good or for evil. We see this in the Scriptures and in our society and culture today. The late Archbishop Sheen said that "woman is the measure of the level of our civilization." As go women, morally, so goes the culture. She is a standard bearer. As we see the moral decline in our culture today, we also see that godly women can make a difference in influencing our culture for good. I have witnessed that when a woman surrenders her heart to the Lord and his purposes for her life, dramatic changes often happen within her family and sphere of activities.

In John Paul II's Apostolic Letter on women he wrote, "in order to intervene in the history of his people, God addresses himself to women…" And also, "In the Spirit of Christ… women can discover the entire meaning of their femininity and thus be disposed to making a 'sincere gift of self' to others thereby finding themselves."

I believe God is speaking this message to the hearts of women all over this world. Let us pray that we respond in this critical hour. I believe it is only through the grace of God in the power of his Spirit that we as women can pull down the strongholds that allure us to seek ourselves in following the ways of the world. Jesus said, "Whoever finds his life will lose it and whoever loses his life for my sake will find it" (Mt 10: 39). I like to think of this passage in this way: in seeking ourselves we lose our selves, but in losing ourselves in Christ we discover who we are. It is only in Christ that we can find our true identity and fulfillment. "Self-help" programs apart from Christ, striving to have the perfect body or to rise on the corporate ladder, will never gain for us true peace. Our position or beauty, etc., is not our worth; it is only Christ and his plans for us that will bring true happiness.

Again, John Paul II said, "Only by the power of the Holy Spirit who 'overshadowed' her was Mary able to accept what is impossible with men, but not with God" (cf. Mk 10: 27). God, the Almighty, is calling all of us, men and women, to unite with him in a life of holiness – to walk with him as Enoch and all the holy men and women in the Scriptures walked – to imitate the lives of the saints of the past and the saints who are living among us today. This is the universal call to holiness the Church proclaims. As Mary teaches us, however, holiness cannot be accomplished by our efforts alone. We must cooperate with God's grace. He initiates and we respond. How do we cooperate and respond to his grace?

I believe it is by living a life of prayer. "There is no holiness without prayer. In fact, as we see in the lives of the saints, Christians are worth as much as they pray" (John Paul II, Rimini, Italy, April 2001). Prayer must become an essential part of our day. Making it so begins with a decision on our part that time alone with God must be a priority. In all of our busy lives we need to carve out a portion of our day to God – to seek his kingdom first and his righteousness, and all things will be given to us besides (Mt 6: 33). This will mean finding a time and place to meet with God alone: "When you pray, go to your room, close the door and pray to your Father in secret. And your Father who sees in secret will repay you" (Mt 6: 6). These are the words of Jesus, who by his words and example teaches us to pray. Seeking God in personal prayer will always be rewarded – if we are faithful to a little, he will give us more. Prayer will be the joy and strength of our lives.

In 2001, John Paul II exhorted us to "'put out into the deep' of prayer in order to 'put out into the deep' of mission. Mission that does not spring from contemplation is doomed to frustration and failure… Contemplation which does not give birth to mission will eventually wither" (John Paul II, Vatican, June 22, 2001). In other words, we must "Be" before we "Do." Prayer must always precede apostolic activity.

What happens to us as we pray? Why is it so important? I have tried to identify, from my personal experience, six gifts God gives us as we pray. You may want to add to this list.

1. Fellowship with God

It is inconceivable to us how much God desires to commune with us. Saint Augustine said that God thirsts that we may thirst for him. It is in prayer that we come to know him and his personal love for us and to love him in return. Once we have experienced the joy of fellowship with him, nothing will be the same. We will only thirst for more. We have an open invitation to have each day a divine appointment with the Almighty. He desires for us "fullness of joy in his presence" (Ps 16: 11).

2. He Changes Us

In the presence of the living God, we are changed and transformed. "All of us, gazing on the Lord with unveiled faces are being transformed into the same image from one degree of glory to another" (2 Cor 3: 18). The word "transform" in Greek is μεταμορφεῖν (*metamorphein*), which is metamorphosis – the process through which a caterpillar is changed into a butterfly. God changes us in his presence. Bad habits are gradually softened and erased. More love for others comes into our hearts. Even our appearance can be altered as the Lord's light shines through us (see 2 Cor 4: 6). I have realized that, through prayer, God changes the desires of my heart. Looking back, I have seen how the direction of my life has changed. The things that I held important no longer attract me. It is amazing that we have only to say "yes" to him and dispose ourselves and he does the rest – he transforms us. This is the good news of salvation.

3. He Teaches Us

He renews our mind. "Do not be conformed to this world but be transformed by the renewal of your mind, that you may prove what is good and acceptable and perfect" (Rom 12: 2). Once again the word "transform" is metamorphosis. God's word is alive and active with power to enlighten and conform our minds to God's will as we read and meditate upon the Scriptures. "The revelation of your words sheds light, giving understanding to the simple" (Ps 119: 130). As we read God's word and reflect upon it, it is amazing how often a word or a passage will come "alive" to us with understanding and be a source of meditation for the day. The MAGNIFICAT missal is a great tool for us to read and meditate upon the Scriptures for each day. It is a perfect companion to carry with us in our purse or pocket. I look forward to the spiritual reflection that follows each day's reading, as well as the many hymns and beautiful images that accompany each issue. Father Peter Cameron's articles and meditations are both inspiring and spiritually nourishing.

4. He Guides Us

In prayer we come to recognize the Shepherd's voice that wants to lead and "guide us along right paths for his name's sake" (cf. Ps 23: 3). So often in prayer God will inspire us and direct us to do or not do certain things. We may be prompted to call or visit someone in need. Or we may have a decision to make that we want to take to prayer. I remember after Hurricane Katrina when we were in "exile" – not knowing if our home was destroyed or where we were to live. I was praying in an adoration chapel and the clear words came to me, "My home is by your altars" (cf. Ps 84: 4). I was filled with peace and joy, knowing it did not matter as long as I was with him.

5. He Strengthens Us against Temptations

Jesus, as he prayed in the garden prior to his passion, told his companions to "watch and pray that you may not undergo the test." He was preparing them for what was to come, but they did not understand. All of us are tempted, but prayer strengthens us to overcome temptations. In my own life, areas I have struggled with, through prayer, have somewhat been lessened and handling them has been a bit easier. One example is the proper use of my tongue: to respond with kindness when spoken to unkindly, not speaking too much (or too little), speaking the right words at the right time and in the right way. God is about the work of purification, and so we will never be free of temptation, but he will always give the grace to grow and overcome.

6. He Uses Us

The work of intercession on behalf of others is powerful. Battles can be won, wars can be stopped, lives can be changed through conversion, vocations to the priesthood and religious life can increase, family life strengthened, and life can be made sacred – all through prayer. God will inspire us to pray in a certain way for a particular situation, but we must be disposed by prayer to follow his directives.

Developing a grateful, *Magnificat* heart like Mary's will require us to decide to make God first in our lives. This will mean daily prayer, but also frequent participation in the sacraments. Most of us are blessed with the opportunity to attend daily Mass. This is such a gift to be able to receive the Lord – body and blood, soul and divinity – into our very being. Jesus said, "Whoever eats my flesh and drinks my blood remains in me and I in him. Just as the living Father sent me and I have life because of the Father, so also the one who feeds on me will have life because of me" (Jn 6: 56-57). What powerful words to meditate upon. Every one of us who wants to grow in Christ should make every effort to receive the Eucharist as often as possible. "The Eucharist is a priceless treasure… *The worship of the Eucharist outside of the Mass* is of inestimable value for the life of the Church" (*Ecclesia de Eucharistia*, John Paul II's encyclical on the Eucharist, section 25). Eucharistic adoration chapels, which are springing up all over with the encouragement that has come from Pope John Paul II and Pope Benedict, are great gifts. I live in the Archdiocese of New Orleans, where Archbishop Alfred Hughes, a native of Boston, has set up an office to promote eucharistic adoration. I am blessed to live in a place where there are three adoration chapels within a ten-minute drive from my home. It is a taste of heaven to have this opportunity. Eucharistic adoration has become a great joy in my life and has expanded my participation in the Holy Mass. These chapels are fountains of grace for the Church. They seem to build community as well.

We are blessed in the Church to have the great sacrament of reconciliation. The discipline of monthly confession (more frequent if needed) is a great means of spiritual growth and grace. Nothing gives us greater gratitude and love in our hearts for God than receiving his forgiveness and mercy. I love the words of Jesus regarding the sinful woman who anointed his feet: "I tell you, her sins which are many are forgiven, for she loved much; but he who is forgiven little, loves little" (Lk 7: 47).

All of us need some kind of faith community in order to grow and be strengthened spiritually. In a culture increasingly secular, it is important to have holy bonds of friendship and prayer so that we can grow in holiness and bring the Gospel into the marketplace. The presence of a joy-filled, loving Christian provides a powerful witness. My involvement in various growth and prayer groups within the Church has helped to deepen my faith and inspire me by the lives of those trying to live a godly life. Participation in conferences and events like the "Pilgrimage of Hope" bless the faithful with renewed spiritual strength to press on to live and proclaim the kingdom of God in our midst.

We are living in difficult times – some say these are times of darkness but of great light. "The light shines in the darkness and darkness has not overcome it" (Jn 1: 5). We are those who are to be the lights in the midst of the darkness.

At the opening of the one hundred and fifty year jubilee celebration in Lourdes, France, as papal envoy Ivan Cardinal Dias stated: "The Virgin Mary invites us once again today to be part of her combat legion against the forces of evil. The struggle between God and his enemy still takes place more so today than at the time of Bernadette, one hundred and fifty years ago." He quoted Cardinal Karol Wojtyla's words on November 9, 1976 (six months before he became pope): "We are today before the final struggle between the Church and the Antichurch, between the

Gospel and the Anti-Gospel." Cardinal Dias continued, "One thing that remains certain: the final victory belongs to God and that will happen thanks to Mary the Woman of Genesis and of the Apocalypse who will fight at the head of the army of her sons and daughters against the enemy forces of Satan and will crush the head of the serpent" (*Inside the Vatican*, February 2008).

Let us ask Mary to pray for us and to walk with us along the way of her Son. Let us ask her to help us be a people of hope, a people of joy and gratitude in the knowledge of our God "who is able to accomplish far more than all we ask or imagine, by the power at work within us, to him be glory in the Church and in Christ Jesus to all generations forever and ever. Amen" (Eph 3: 20-21).

I close with words from Saint Ambrose: "Let Mary's soul be in each of you to proclaim the greatness of the Lord. Let her spirit be in each to rejoice in the Lord."

NAVIGATING BY THE STARS

The Saints as Spiritual Guides for Daily Living

RALPH MARTIN

The saints have always been an important part of our life as Catholics. For many reasons we honor them, admire them, and ask their intercession. At the same time there has been a tendency to look at their lives and accomplishments as so special and heroic that they are unattainable for us "average" Catholics. There are some saints, though, who not only provide a heroic example but actually teach us how to embrace the unique call to holiness that each of us has received; they impart to us a wisdom that helps us to undertake and continue to make progress on the journey to full union with God. Some of these saints are called Doctors of the Church.

A Doctor of the Church is first of all a saint, but a saint who was specially called by God to carry out a teaching ministry of such value that the whole Church becomes attentive to it. Some of the thirty-three Doctors of the Church have made their contribution primarily in the area of scriptural exegesis or commentary, some by countering heresy and engaging in apologetics, some by constructing syntheses in dogmatic or moral theology. Some, however, make their contribution in the area of "spirituality" – that body of wisdom and insight that helps us respond to God and grow in union with him.

One of the most remarkable – and in my experience, least commented on – legacies of Pope John Paul II was his bold call for the whole Church to reconnect with our mystical tradition, especially as it is expressed in the writings of the Doctors of the Church. As many people know, he did his own doctoral dissertation on John of the Cross, who is generally recognized as one of the greatest mystics and writers on the spiritual journey. It was John Paul II also who, in 1997, took the bold step of recognizing Saint Thérèse of Lisieux as a Doctor of the Church.

This call to reconnect with the mystical tradition of the Church was sounded clearly in his important Apostolic Letter that was issued at the close of the Great Jubilee Year on January 6, 2001. In this Letter, *Novo Millennio Ineunte (The Beginning of the New Millennium)*, John Paul wrote:

> *The great mystical tradition of the Church... shows how prayer can progress, as a genuine dialogue of love, to the point of rendering the person wholly possessed by the divine Beloved, vibrating at the Spirit's touch, resting filially within the Father's heart. This is the lived experience of Christ's promise: "He who loves me will be loved by my Father, and I will love him and manifest myself to him" (Jn 14: 21). It is a journey totally sustained by grace, which nonetheless demands an intense spiritual commitment and is no stranger to painful purifications (the "dark night"). But it leads, in various possible ways, to the ineffable joy experienced by the mystics as "nuptial union." How can we forget here, among the many*

shining examples, the teachings of St. John of the Cross and St. Teresa of Avila? (32)

John Paul II issues this call in relationship to two important realities: the "universal call to holiness," which he identifies as being one of the truly major themes of the Second Vatican Council, and the hunger for meaning that is characteristic of even our most de-Christianized societies.

Novo Millennio Ineunte (NMI) is a remarkable document. It is at the same time one of the most accessible of John Paul's documents for the average reader and one of his most important. It is his attempt to "decipher what the Spirit is saying" to the Church, since the beginning of the Second Vatican Council. It is very much a "vision statement" or "mission statement" for what John Paul believes the Spirit has been doing with us these past forty years, and a guide for what lies ahead. In short, John Paul senses that the Spirit has been preparing us for the challenges the Church will face in the third millennium by leading us into three, as he calls them, "rediscoveries." One of these rediscoveries is that of the universal call to holiness.

Deeply embedded in Catholic culture for many centuries has been the sometimes unspoken, but deeply rooted, belief that everyone is called to holiness, but that *real* holiness is primarily for priests and nuns. John Paul cites the Council text that states that everyone in the Church, including laypeople, is called to the fullness of holiness.

But the gift (of holiness in baptism) becomes a task, which must shape the whole of Christian life: "This is the will of God, your sanctification" (1 Thes 4: 3). It is a duty which concerns not only certain Christians: "All the Christian faithful, of whatever state or rank, are called to the fullness of the Christian life and to the perfection of charity" (Constitution on the Church, *40*) (NMI 30).

The pope insists that such a call to holiness isn't an optional extra for some, but is intrinsic to Christian life.

> *To ask catechumens: "Do you wish to receive Baptism?" means at the same time to ask them: "Do you wish to become holy?" It means to set before them the radical nature of the Sermon on the Mount: "Be perfect as your heavenly Father is perfect" (Mt 5: 48).*
>
> *As the Council itself explained, this ideal of perfection must not be misunderstood as if it involved some kind of extraordinary existence, possible only for a few "uncommon heroes" of holiness. The ways of holiness are many, according to the vocation of each individual. I thank the Lord that in these years he has enabled me to beatify and canonize a large number of Christians, and among them many lay people who attained holiness in the most ordinary circumstances of life. The time has come to re-propose wholeheartedly to everyone this* high standard of ordinary Christian living*: the whole life of the Christian community and of Christian families must lead in this direction (NMI 31).*

It is in this context – of a rediscovery of the urgency of embracing the universal call to holiness on the part of everyone in the Church – that the pope calls us to reconnect with the spiritual resources in our tradition that will enable us to do so. He tells us quite specifically what he expects we will discover as we reconnect with our spiritual tradition. He tells us that we will be led into a depth of Trinitarian union that the mystics call "spiritual marriage." He tells us that our tradition will reveal to us that, although our own effort is necessary, it is not sufficient and the whole response to God and our continued perseverance on the journey is totally dependent on his grace. He also tells us that there will be painful dimensions to this journey as it involves deep purification, but that it is at root a joyful journey that is beyond value in its fruits.

He is specific about the resources in our tradition that he has in mind. At *Novo Millennio Ineunte* 32, he specifically mentions John of the Cross and Teresa of Ávila, and elsewhere in the document (NMI 27), Thérèse of Lisieux and Catherine of Siena. He is thinking primarily, it seems, of those Doctors of the Church whose main contribution is to offer wisdom about how to make progress on our journey to full union with God.

For the past fifteen years, I have felt called to study these Doctors of the Church (in addition to the Doctors already mentioned, we should also note Saint Bernard of Clairvaux and Saint Francis de Sales) because I know that no knowledge is more valuable on this earth than that which has been revealed to us about how to make progress on the journey! As I have studied and prayed through these writings, I have been struck not only by the beauty of the vision and the wealth of practical insight, but also by the great harmony of teaching among these different saints. Even though they write over many centuries, in different cultures, in various languages, there is a remarkable harmony among them, and when you bring them all together to form an overall picture of the journey, you find an amazingly helpful and convincing map of the spiritual journey. I have tried to construct such a map in a way that is accessible to everyone without compromising the depth of the teaching. [1]

In the limited space available to us, let us "sample" a little of this wisdom, which truly will help us navigate our spiritual journey.

---

1. My book that brings together the wisdom of these Doctors of the Church is titled *The Fulfillment of All Desire: A Guidebook for the Journey to God Based on the Wisdom of the Saints*. It is published by Emmaus Road Publications, Steubenville, Ohio, and is widely available.

WISDOM ABOUT SIN

How helpful it is to have as our guide the wisdom of the saints concerning sin!

As we begin the spiritual journey, the struggle against sin may be particularly intense. Ignorance about right and wrong needs to give way to true understanding. Conversion has to deepen. Deeply ingrained habits have to be exposed to the light and the power of grace. New habits have to be established.

Bernard of Clairvaux gives a striking summary:

> *We have seen how every soul – even if burdened with sin (2 Tm 3: 6), enmeshed in vice, ensnared by the allurements of pleasure, a captive in exile, imprisoned in the body, caught in mud (Ps 68: 3), fixed in mire, bound to its members, a slave to care, distracted by business, afflicted with sorrow, wandering and straying, filled with anxious forebodings and uneasy suspicions, a stranger in a hostile land (Ex 2: 22), and, according to the Prophet, sharing the defilement of the dead and counted with those who go down into hell (Bar 3: 11) – every soul, I say, standing thus under condemnation and without hope, has the power to turn and find it can not only breathe the fresh air of the hope of pardon and mercy, but also dare to aspire to the nuptials of the Word, not fearing to enter into alliance with God or to bear the sweet yoke of love (Mt 11: 30) with the King of angels.* [2]

---

2. Bernard of Clairvaux, *On the Song of Songs*, sermon 83, no. 1. I recommend the four-volume edition of this work published by Cistercian Publications in Kalamazoo, MI. The translations of Bernard used in this essay are from this edition.

Bernard, excruciatingly aware of the condition of the soul apart from God, nevertheless knows that every soul, without exception, however deeply mired in the mud of sin and disordered lives, is called not only to begin the journey to union with God, but to complete it successfully by attaining spiritual marriage, that state of deep habitual union with God that brings with it great joy (even in the midst of suffering) and wonderful apostolic fruitfulness.

Besides initial hope, the saints teach us some really basic but very helpful principles. First of all, they teach us, *sin never helps*! Sin always presents itself as a solution to a problem we are having, but it never is a solution; it always makes the problem worse. We are short of money and are tempted to steal to relieve financial pressure. We are plagued by sensual temptations and are tempted to give in to restore "peace." We are involved in an embarrassing situation and are tempted to lie to avoid embarrassment. We are hurt by someone and are tempted to hate to assuage our anger. Sin always wounds the soul, further darkens our intellect, and further distances us from the light and joy of God. Sin often also makes matters worse in our social interactions! Lies are found out, and the embarrassment is doubled. Money is stolen, embezzlement is discovered, and jail follows. Hatred for others locks us in a prison of misery and hurts us even more than it hurts the ones we hate. Unforgiveness is singled out by the saints as a significant block to progress on the spiritual journey.

I have a colleague at the seminary where I teach, a very distinguished colleague, who occasionally remarks that part of her mission as a teacher is to "state the obvious." Even though it seems obvious to emphasize the principle that sin never helps, it often is not obvious to many of us, and it is immensely helpful to get clear about it.

As the psalm puts it:

> *Who shall ascend the hill of the LORD?*
> *And who shall stand in his holy place?*

He who has clean hands and a pure heart,
   who does not lift up his soul to what is false,
   and does not swear deceitfully.

(Ps 24: 3-4) [3]

TURNING AWAY FROM SERIOUS SIN

Obviously, turning away from serious sin is one of the first things that needs to happen in true conversion. As Saint Francis de Sales writes: "What is your state of soul with respect to mortal sin? Are you firmly resolved never to commit it for any reason whatsoever?... In this resolution consists the foundation of the spiritual life." [4]

Francis recommends that a person in such a situation – coming back to the Lord from a life that included serious sin – consider the possibility of making a "general confession." This entails making an appointment with a trusted confessor and going over one's whole life as a way of making a fresh start. Francis acknowledges that this is not absolutely necessary, but he strongly advises it.

He also points out how important the regular practice of the sacrament of reconciliation can be in making a real change in our lives. He points out, though, that for the sacrament to be really efficacious it is important that we prepare for going to confession and be sincere and serious about wanting to turn away from sin. "Often they make little or even no preparation and do not have sufficient contrition. Too often it happens that they go to confession with a tacit intention of returning to sin, since they are

---

3. All of my quotations from Scripture are from the RSV translation unless otherwise indicated.
4. Francis de Sales, *Introduction to the Devout Life*, Preface. There are several "abridged" or "edited" versions of this book available. I recommend the unabridged version published by Doubleday's Image Books, with the translation of John K. Ryan.

unwilling to avoid its occasions or use the means necessary for amendment of life." [5]

If one has become enmeshed in deep patterns of sin, it may take a while and entail a struggle to become free – we have the inspiring and insightful account of Augustine's own struggle in his *Confessions* to guide us here – but availing ourselves of the means of grace and embracing the necessary wisdom will eventually bring us freedom.

LETTING GO OF THE AFFECTION FOR SIN

One of Francis' most helpful insights is his teaching on the affection for sin. He points out that oftentimes we might turn away from serious sins in our life and try hard not to commit them, but still nurture affection for such sin, which greatly slows down our spiritual progress and disposes us to future falls.

He points out that, although the Israelites left Egypt in fact, many did not leave it in affection; and the same is true for many of us. We leave sin in effect, but reluctantly, and we look back at it fondly, as did Lot's wife when she looked back on the doomed city of Sodom.

Francis gives an amusing but telling example of how a doctor, for the purpose of health, might forbid a patient to eat melons lest he die. Such patients, therefore, abstain from eating them, but

> *they begrudge giving them up, talk about them, would eat them if they could, want to smell them at least, and envy those who can eat them. In such a way weak, lazy penitents abstain regretfully for a while from sin. They would like very much to commit sins if they could do so without being damned. They speak about sin with a certain petulance and with liking for it and*

---

5. Ibid., Pt. I, chap. 1.

think those who commit sins are at peace with themselves. [6]

Francis says this is like the person who would like to take revenge on someone "if only he could," or a woman who doesn't intend to commit adultery but still wishes to flirt. Such souls are in danger. Besides the real danger of falling into serious sin again, having such a "divided heart" makes the spiritual life wearisome and the "devout" life of prompt, diligent, and frequent response to God's will and inspirations virtually impossible.

What does Francis propose as the remedy for such remaining attachment to the affection for sin? A recovery of the biblical worldview!

Francis himself leads the reader of the *Introduction to the Devout Life* through ten meditations on these basic truths: focusing on all we have been given by God and the debt of gratitude we owe him, the ugliness and horror of sin, the reality of judgment and hell, the great mercy and goodness of Jesus' work of redemption, the shortness of life, and the great beauty and glory of heaven. Francis believes that there truly is power in the Word of God, and that meditating on the truth can progressively free us from remaining affection for sin.

The Scripture is clear:

> *How can young people keep their way pure?*
>   *By guarding it according to your word.*
> *With my whole heart I seek you;*
>   *do not let me stray from your commandments.*
> *I treasure your word in my heart,*
>   *so that I might not sin against you...*
> *I will meditate on your precepts,*
>   *and fix my eyes on your ways.*

---

6. Ibid., Pt. I, chap. 7.

I will delight in your statutes;
I will not forget your word.

(Ps 119: 9-16, NRSV)

The saints have a wonderful way of bringing the insight of Scripture into contact with the circumstances of our lives. Teresa of Ávila puts it this way:

> *A great aid to going against your [own] will is to bear in mind continually how all is vanity and how quickly everything comes to an end. This helps to remove our attachment to trivia and center it on what will never end. Even though this practice seems to be a weak means, it will strengthen the soul greatly and the soul will be most careful in very little things. When we begin to become attached to something, we should strive to turn our thoughts from it and bring them back to God – and His majesty helps.*[7]

We need to make the prayer of Scripture our own: "So teach us to number our days/ that we may gain wisdom of heart" (Ps 90: 12, NRSV).

Francis knows that as long as we are alive in this body, the wounds of original sin and our past actual sins will cause affection for sin to spring up again and again. But it is our response to this bent of our nature toward sin that is determinative of the progress we make on the spiritual journey. We need to grow in our hatred for sin so we can resist it when it makes its appeals. Catherine of Siena talks of the two-edged sword with which we fight the spiritual battle: one side is hatred for sin; the other is love for virtue.

---

7. Teresa of Ávila, *The Way of Perfection*, chap. 10, no. 2. I recommend the edition of Teresa of Ávila's writings published by the Institute for Carmelite Studies in Washington, D.C., translated by Fr. Kieran Kavanaugh.

The vigorous effort that the saints urge us to make in the struggle against sin is firmly grounded in the Scriptures.

> *Submit yourselves therefore to God. Resist the devil and he will flee from you. Draw near to God and he will draw near to you. Cleanse your hands, you sinners, and purify your hearts, you men of double mind... Humble yourselves before the Lord and he will exalt you. (Jas 4: 7-10)*

We need to determine, with the help of God's grace, never freely to choose to offend him. Francis makes clear that such purification of the affection for sin must extend to venial sins also. (Venial sins are lesser sins, as opposed to mortal sins, that damage our relationship with God but don't destroy it.)

VENIAL SIN

Teresa, Bernard, and Francis all acknowledge that there will probably always be some inadvertent venial sins that we commit, without full reflection or choice. As Bernard puts it: "Which of us can live uprightly and perfectly even for one hour, an hour free from fruitless talk and careless work?" [8]

They all also teach, though, very clearly and strongly, that, insofar as it lies in our power, we need to resolve never freely to choose to offend God, even in a small matter, if we are to make progress in the spiritual life.

Both Francis and Teresa point out that, to fall into some involuntary lie, out of embarrassment, for example, is one thing; but to maintain an affection for telling little lies, or to choose freely to do so, is a significant obstacle to making progress, and truly offensive to the Lord.

Affection for venial sin, just as affection for mortal sin, should

---

8. Bernard of Clairvaux, *On the Song of Songs*, sermon 12, no. 11.

214

gradually disappear from our lives as we make progress on the spiritual journey. As Francis de Sales puts it:

> *We can never be completely free of venial sins, at least so as to continue for long in such purity, yet we can avoid all affection for venial sins... We must not voluntarily nourish a desire to continue and persevere in venial sin of any kind. It would be an extremely base thing to wish deliberately to retain in our heart anything so displeasing to God as a will to offend him. No matter how small it is, a venial sin offends God.* [9]

To nourish affection for venial sin, Francis points out, weakens the powers of our spirit, stands in the way of God's consolations, and opens the door to temptations. At the same time, Francis doesn't want to engender a morbid scrupulosity about the myriad temptations and sometimes inadvertent venial sins that are part of life in this world. He assures us that inadvertent venial sins and faults are "not a matter of any great moment" if, as soon as they occur, we reject them and refuse to entertain any affection for them.

Francis makes clear that the process of purification will continue throughout our life, and so "we must not be disturbed at our imperfections, since for us perfection consists in fighting against them." [10]

Hatred for sin is important. Confidence in the mercy of God is even more important. "May the LORD, who is good, grant pardon to everyone who has resolved to seek God, the LORD, the God of his fathers, though he be not clean as holiness requires" (2 Chr 30: 18b-19).

Thérèse of Lisieux makes clear that growth in the spiritual life is usually a gradual process; Jesus is patient with us, "for He

---

9. Francis de Sales, *Introduction to the Devout Life*, Pt. I, chap. 22.
10. Ibid., Pt. I, chap. 5.

doesn't like pointing everything out at once to souls. He generally gives His light little by little." [11]

Thérèse also speaks of a "joyful resignation" to the lifetime struggle with faults.

> *At the beginning of my spiritual life when I was thirteen or fourteen, I used to ask myself what I would have to strive for later on because I believed it was quite impossible for me to understand perfection better. I learned very quickly since then that the more one advances, the more one sees the goal is still far off. And now I am simply resigned to see myself always imperfect and in this I find my joy.* [12]

Thérèse's resignation was not one of despair, discouragement, passivity, or lack of effort, but a humble acceptance of her creaturely imperfection despite her efforts, infused with joy by her hope in God's transforming love eventually bringing her to perfection.

In the last days of her life, when she was virtually suffocating from tuberculosis, Thérèse was corrected for an impatient remark to a sister whom she found "tiresome." Her response? "Oh! how happy I am to see myself imperfect and to be in need of God's mercy so much even at the moment of my death." [13]

Realistically, Francis says, there will probably be falls along the way, but God can use even these to deepen our humility. "Imperfections and venial sins cannot deprive us of spiritual life; it is lost only by mortal sin. Fortunately for us, in this war we are always victorious provided that we are willing to fight." [14]

---

11. Thérèse of Lisieux, *Story of a Soul*, chap. VII. I recommend the edition published by the Institute for Carmelite Studies in Washington, D.C., translated by Fr. John Clarke.
12. Ibid., chap. VII.
13. Ibid., Epilogue.
14. Francis de Sales, *Introduction to the Devout Life*, Pt. I, chap. 5.

Francis, like many of the saints, wants to encourage us on the spiritual journey. This is a journey on which we are all called to embark; and God will give us the grace to make progress on this journey, if only we are willing to persevere, to fight the good fight.

> *As for the seed that fell on rich soil, they are the ones who, when they have heard the word, embrace it with a generous and good heart, and bear fruit through perseverance. (Lk 8: 15, NAB)*

Bernard wants us to know that even in the midst of the struggle – whether it be with mortal sin or venial sin, worldliness or temptation, perseverance in prayer or growth in virtue, loving or forgiving – we profoundly need to "lean on the Beloved." Bernard knows that to "fight against yourself without respite in a continual and hard struggle, and renounce your inveterate habits and inborn inclinations" is very hard, impossible really, without the help of the Lord.

> *But this is a hard thing. If you attempt it in your own strength, it will be as though you were trying to stop the raging of a torrent, or to make the Jordan run backwards (Ps 114: 3). What can you do then? You must seek the Word... You have need of strength, and not simply strength, but strength drawn from above (Lk 24: 49).* [15]

The words from Hebrews come to mind:

> *Therefore, since we are surrounded by so great a cloud of witnesses, let us also lay aside every weight, and sin which clings so closely, and let us run with perseverance the race that is set before us, looking to*

---

15. Bernard of Clairvaux, *On the Song of Songs*, sermon 85, nos. 1, 4.

Jesus the pioneer and perfecter of our faith, who for the joy that was set before him endured the cross, despising the shame, and is seated at the right hand of the throne of God. (Heb 12: 1-2)

The journey up to the summit of the mountain of God (or Mount Carmel, as John of the Cross calls it) is difficult. The saints know that it is impossible to attain the summit – spiritual marriage in this life, beatific vision in the next – without leaning heavily on the Beloved. As Bernard, in accord with his fellow Doctors, explains:

"Who shall ascend the mountain of the Lord?" (Ps 24: 3). If anyone aspires to climb to the summit of that mountain (Ex 24: 17), that is to the perfection of virtue, he will know how hard the climb is, and how the attempt is doomed to failure without the help of the Word. Happy the soul which causes the angels to look at her with joy and wonder and hears them saying, "Who is this coming up from the wilderness, rich in grace and beauty, leaning upon her beloved?" (Song 8: 5). Otherwise, unless it leans on him, its struggle is in vain. But it will gain force by struggling with itself and, becoming stronger, will impel all things towards reason... bringing every carnal affect into captivity (2 Cor 10: 5), and every sense under the control of reason in accordance with virtue. Surely all things are possible to someone who leans upon him who can do all things? What confidence there is in the cry, "I can do all things in him who strengthens me!" (Phil 4: 13)... "Thus if the mind does not rely upon itself, but is strengthened by the Word, it can gain

such command over itself that no unrighteousness will have power over it." [16]

The Good News is that the Beloved loves to be leaned on!

---

16. Ibid., sermon 85, no. 5.

"LEST THEY LOSE HEART"

Mary and Catholic Parenting Today

J. DAVID FRANKS AND ANGELA FRANKS

And whatever you do, in word or deed, do everything in the name of the Lord Jesus, giving thanks to God the Father through Him. Wives, be subject to your husbands, as is fitting in the Lord. Husbands, love your wives, and do not be harsh with them. Children, obey your parents in everything, for this pleases the Lord. Fathers, do not provoke your children, lest they lose heart.

(Col 3: 17-21)[1]

Magazines are filled with parenting advice, of widely varying quality. But when instruction to parents is divinely inspired, we can be confident of its worth. Yet what does it mean for children

---

1. All Scripture quotations are from *The Ignatius Bible: Revised Standard Version – Second Catholic Edition* (San Francisco: Ignatius Press, 2006). Here emphasis has been added, and the translation slightly modified.

to "lose heart"? How should fathers (and mothers) raise their children so that this does not happen?

Pop culture presents an answer in the form of the hip mother. This mother, whose wardrobe and texting mastery are barely distinguishable from her daughter's, allows her child's spiritedness to run free, enabling it with the newest iPods, cellphones, laptops, clothing styles (ever more boudoir-like), and so on.

This perspective is not wholly wrong. "Lose heart" is a translation of the Greek αθυμειν, "to become spiritless." The Vulgate of Saint Jerome translates this as *pusillo animo*: to have a contracted, small heart – from which comes our word pusillanimous. Saint Paul is telling fathers in the letter to the Colossians not to crush a child's spiritedness. But the Madison Avenue/Hollywood/consumerist understanding of "spiritedness" is a caricature. Authentic "self-expression" flows from a developed interior life; it cannot come from sliding seamlessly into the ready-made and interchangeable social roles on offer by pop culture. A child's unique personality gasps for air in the superficial sea of mass consumer culture.

It is one of the remarkable experiences of parenthood to realize that a child's personality is recognizable even from the womb. Parents are entrusted with these newly created personalities, which take flight on the wings of interior capacities formed according to the measure of true love. By contrast, pop culture encourages an artificial state of prolonged, indeed endless, immaturity – a constant pursuit of self-gratification – which is the antithesis of truly unique, personal spiritedness. The opposite of faint- or smallheartedness is not the license to do whatever feels good, which collapses freedom into the emptiness of being "pro-choice." Our unique personalities blossom only when we commit ourselves to loving in the truth – even when that is hard. The opposite of smallheartedness is great-heartedness (magnanimity).

Each Child – Called to Holiness, Called to Greatness

To crush the spirit of a child is a terrible violence. God has indeed loved each of us into existence: at the moment of conception, he creates an unrepeatable human person with an immortal soul, called to share the eternal festival of love that is the life of Father, Son, and Holy Spirit. [2] It is an awesome thing for a parent to contemplate the growing life in the womb and know that, whatever futility will creep into my projects, no power in the universe can erase this fruit of the mutual love my beloved and I share. Whatever my life comes to, we have generated a person who will never pass into nothingness. An immortal strides into existence under each mother's heart.

But what a responsibility! We fathers and mothers are given these little beloved immortals so that we may participate in bringing them to the stature of God's plan for their lives. In calling us all to share his undying happiness, God gives us each an absolutely unique vocation (calling), an irreplaceable role or mission in salvation history. To fulfill this vocation is to attain happiness; to fail one's vocation is to miss happiness. A vocational realism is required of every parent: our plans for our children count for nothing; we are agents of God the Father and of his wise and loving plan for our little ones. Our children truly have a concrete calling. This is first a call to a state of life in the Church: a call to the priesthood or to religious life or to the lay state (and this usually is a call to marriage). Within these states, each individual's unique personality can unfold in a singular way. We are now worlds away from the false show of individuality on display

---

2. To gain the barest glimpse of the beauty of this eternal Trinitarian love, this love stronger than death, consider the great loves of your life – for parents or spouse or children or friends. Then think what that intimacy would be like if our sinfulness and the sinfulness of those we love didn't get in the way.

in pop culture. We are in the deep, rich, life-giving soil of God's love.

Each unique vocation is a call to greatness, for to serve the mission of injecting God's love into the world is the greatest endeavor of all – even if our particular way of doing so is in the everydayness of family and community life. This is the central teaching of the Second Vatican Council: the call to holiness is universal. For laypersons, no less than for priests and religious, the Christian vocation is to spiritual excellence. [3]

It is clearer now: to cause a child to become pusillanimous, crushed in spirit, is a total inversion of what a parent should be doing. Every father and mother has the glorious opportunity to cultivate in children the taste for greatness, to encourage an eagerness for astonishing deeds of love (even if these will be accomplished along a "little way" far removed from television cameras). If parents do not lead their children to aim for human and Christian excellence, who will?

Every human being is endowed with the capacity to know and love: these are the spiritual powers that make us persons, make us *who*s amidst a world of *what*s. It is by virtue of these powers that our souls are immortal: our knowing and loving reach beyond all time and space. One act of true love has more of reality in it than the whole of the expanding material universe in its extent of forty billion light years. By our intelligence, our power of knowing, we are able to move around in the world with a sovereignty of action that no other animal in any way approaches. Subhuman animals live by instinct, and their scope does not extend beyond that part

---

3. The universal call to holiness is Christianity's unprecedented synthesis of aristocracy and democracy: every single human being (democratic element) is called to nobility of life (aristocratic element). See Chapter V (nos. 39-42) of Vatican II's Dogmatic Constitution on the Church *Lumen gentium* in Decrees of the Ecumenical Councils, Vol. II (Trent-Vatican II), ed. Norman Tanner, S.J. (Washington, D.C.: Sheed & Ward/Georgetown University Press, 1990), pp. 880-84, or at www.vatican.va.

of their environment they can sense. Humans live in the wide world of history and ideas. We image the very freedom of God. Every human being has been endowed with this dignity by God the Father. There is not an individual of the human species, from an embryo to a person in a persistent vegetative state, who does not possess these immense capacities. And these capacities to know and love are given precisely so that we may know and love other persons: man is made for love, as Pope John Paul II's theology of the body makes clear. We are made for the soaring nobility of true, self-sacrificial love.

This is another way of saying what Aristotle recognized: man is the social/political animal. We cannot physically or spiritually survive without being in community with other human beings. To say that we are social by nature, or that we are made for love, is to say that we cannot be happy without serving the true good of others. The whole sweep of human history, from the rise of cities in Mesopotamia all the way through globalization, is the story of this drive toward living out our necessary interconnectedness (though with sin constantly corrupting social forms). Therefore, being an excellent human necessarily includes being an excellent citizen. It belongs to parents to raise their children as patriots, loving what is good and true about their nation and resisting the elitist (anti-religious) decadence to which Western democracies seem prone. The consumerist individualism so dramatically seen in the lifestyle of the sexual revolution contracts the hearts of children by lowering their sights to mere self-gratification. Catholic parents can serve the graciousness of God by raising children who live within the wide horizons of the common good.

HAVING THE HEART TO FIGHT FOR THE COMMON GOOD

Understanding what magnanimity, or great-heartedness, is all about begins with understanding what freedom is for. Freedom is not meant to be bent toward the mere gratification of our egoistic impulses, which is what our consumer culture insists on: "If it feels good, do it." But in their deepest impulses, our children seek instead the higher path of divine love, in which alone freedom finds its home. Jesus lays out this path in the Sermon on the Mount, the great constitution of Christian life. This call to holiness, the call to love perfectly, can be fulfilled only from within the sacramental life of the Church. The Sermon belongs to the concrete context of the sacrifice of the cross and the sacramental system that flows from the side of the One who loves us to the end (Jn 19: 34) – the water being the water of baptism, the blood none other than the blood of the Eucharist. It is only by God's grace that we are able to love more than humanly: the Christian in the state of grace loves by the power of God's own love. This is what gives life to every Christian action in the world.

Now more than ever, with the unprecedented technological power leveled at the most powerless human life, our suffering world needs Christians to live out vigorously the divine love that animates their spiritual lives. This is why Vatican II, precisely as an engagement with the modern world, places the call to holiness at the center. Holiness has always been required, but in a globalized culture of death, it is required more urgently than ever: the powerless are being pulverized as never before, and the innocence of the young is being corrupted, in the "hook-up culture," as never before. [4]

So much depends on Christian heroism injecting God's love into the world and interrupting the corruption of interpersonal relations worked by the ideology of loveless sex and the culture of

---

4. It should be noted that two prongs of the new evangelization of the modern world are specially entrusted to the laity: the theology of the body and Catholic social doctrine. These are presented as Parts 1 and 2 of Pope Benedict's first encyclical, *God Is Love (Deus Caritas Est)*. Catholic parents must, in a conscious way, equip their children to carry out the new evangelization. They must learn the faith so that they may communicate it to their children. The *Catechism of the Catholic Church* is an indispensable starting point.

death. Catholic parents must raise children who are ready to do battle courageously for the sake of the unborn who are threatened by abortion and biotech experimentation, as well as the elderly and disabled threatened by euthanasia. Imagine the great-heartedness it would take to speak up for these victims of history in a high-school classroom. Or to tell the truth on a college campus about marriage as the union of one man and one woman for life and open to life. By contrast, consider the susceptibility to the hook-up way of life of children lacking great-heartedness. A sexual inferno is devouring even our middle-schoolers, especially our girls. No small part of having "friends with benefits" (FWB) is an epidemic of non-coital sexual activity, abject and depersonalizing as that is. And, of course, pornography is rendering boys and men incapable of attaining the glory and greatness of self-sacrificial love. To live the truth of love in a culture of death more and more requires a supernatural great-heartedness. Cultivating this in our children is possible only by the grace of the sacraments, by the grace of Christ our hope, as Pope Benedict has emphasized – especially in his second encyclical, *Spe salvi*, and in his apostolic journey to the United States. How could we go on without our Lord's assurance, "In the world you have tribulation; but be of good cheer, I have overcome the world" (Jn 16: 33)? We serve that great hope by leading our children into the arms of the good Lord Jesus – in the sacraments, in the daily prayer life so well fostered by MAGNI-FICAT. Being faithful instruments of God's loving will for our children, we parents show life to be a pilgrimage of hope.

When Saint Thomas Aquinas discusses pusillanimity in the *Summa theologiae*, he cites Colossians 3: 21. He points out that pusillanimity causes us to fall short of that which our powers make us capable of accomplishing. Recall the nobility of our spiritual powers of knowing and loving. Think what these powers are capable of when elevated and energized by grace. Consider the vocation given to each person as that person's unique way to live out these powers for the sake of true love. And then think of the

urgent need that everyone do their utmost to live out their vocation to love in this culture of death. This gives the fullest perspective on why it is a grave thing indeed to crush a child's spirit, to
lead children to withdraw from doing the good of which they are
capable. The flourishing of their personalities is inseparable from
their unique contributions to the defense of the common good – in
a time of massive assault on the most powerless and most
innocent.

TRUE FATHERHOOD:
CULTIVATING GREAT-HEARTEDNESS

"Fathers, do not provoke your children, lest they lose heart."
Though this injunction clearly applies to both fathers and mothers,
Saint Paul addresses fathers explicitly. This indicates the magnitude of the disorder that arises when the spiritual head of a family
abuses his authority. Saint Paul is clearly indicating that true
fatherhood is the opposite of paternalism, which is to lord it over
one's children, to keep them in a state of spiritual minority. This is
a perversion of fatherhood. A true father uses his authority so as
to serve the blossoming of the native powers of his children. [5]
There is nothing that a good father wants more dearly than to see
his children outdo him in the achievement of great things.
A French poet, Charles Péguy, puts it beautifully:

> It's never the child who goes to the field, who tills and who
> sows, and who reaps and who harvests the grapes and who
> trims the vine and who fells the trees and who cuts the
> wood.
> For winter.
> To warm the house in winter.

---

5. This is also true of priests, who are spiritual fathers, charged with fostering
the spiritual growth of their flocks.

But would the father have the heart to work if
    he didn't have his children.
If it weren't for the sake of his children.
And in winter when he works hard.
In the forest.
When he works the hardest.
With his billhook and with his saw and with
    his felling axe and with his hand axe.
In the icy forest.

His children will do better than he, of course.
And the world will go better.
Later.
He's not jealous of it.
On the contrary.
Nor for having come to the world, as he did,
    in an ungrateful time.
And to have no doubt prepared for his sons
    a time that is perhaps less ungrateful.
What madman would be jealous of his sons
    and of the sons of his sons.

Doesn't he work solely for his children.[6]

Serving the Birth from Above

Of course, both fathers *and* mothers are called to cultivate great-heartedness in their children, because both parents serve as instruments of God the Father's plan for their children. Indeed, we all stand to the Father as his children, though the baptized person is a child of the Father in a breathtakingly novel way. In

---

6. Charles Péguy, *The Portal of the Mystery of Hope*, trans. David Louis Schindler, Jr. (Grand Rapids, MI: Eerdmans, 1996), pp. 12, 17, 18.

admonishing those who would keep children from him, Jesus says, "Truly, I say to you, unless you turn and become like children, you will never enter the kingdom of heaven" (Mt 18: 3). Nicodemus' confusion in the Gospel of John could be ours: "How can a man be born when he is old? Can he enter a second time into his mother's womb and be born?" (Jn 3: 4). We have a hard time taking the word "children" to mean anything but little, immature people. But Jesus was not asking Nicodemus to re-enter his mother's womb, nor is he asking us to act immaturely. There is a spiritual meaning of childhood that is being revealed here, and it is a meaning that is coincident with being magnanimous, with having a mighty spirit or a great heart: "But to all who received Him, who believed in His name, *He gave power to become children of God*; who were born, not of blood nor of the will of the flesh nor of the will of man, but of God" (Jn 1: 12-13; emphasis added). We become children of God through baptism, which incorporates us into the life of God the Father, Son, and Holy Spirit. Jesus tells as much to Nicodemus: "Unless one is born of water and the Spirit, he cannot enter the kingdom of God" (Jn 3: 5). This is an astounding truth! As the Swiss theologian Hans Urs von Balthasar puts it, "God the Father empowers his Son to have us be begotten or born together with Him from God." [7] No wonder, then, that "whoever receives one such child in my name receives me; and whoever receives me, receives not me but him who sent me" (Mk 9: 37). In baptism, we are incorporated into (that is, made part of the Body of) Jesus Christ: we become "sons" in the Son, adopted children of God the Father. The fullness of great-spirit-edness is attained in the Spirit of adoptive sonship, and Christian parents have the immense privilege of cultivating that life of divine childhood. In procreation, a father and mother cooperate with God the Father in the creation of new life. But procreation is

---

7. Hans Urs von Balthasar, *Unless You Become Like This Child*, trans. Erasmo Leiva-Merikakis (San Francisco: Ignatius Press, 1991), p. 38.

inseparable from education: a Christian father and mother have the *even higher* calling to cooperate in serving the birth from above, the supernatural life of divine love that our children receive in baptism.

Jesus, the Eternal Child of the Father

The adult Jesus makes clear that spiritual childhood coincides with spiritual maturity. His whole consciousness is structured by his relationship with his Father. As Pope Benedict XVI says, Jesus has to be understood "in light of his communion with the Father, which is the true center of his personality; without it, we cannot understand him at all, and it is from this center that he makes himself present to us still today."[8] Jesus dwells continually in the bosom of his Father (Jn 1: 18). From that center he is sent out into the world, to carry out the Father's plan of loving kindness. "For God sent the Son into the world, not to condemn the world, but that the world might be saved through him" (Jn 3: 17). He remains always conscious of coming from another, namely, from the loving Father. "His entire existence is a 'sending' a 'mission' i.e., a relationship."[9]

Jesus' origin in the Father is a mystery of infinitely vital love, so he is always receptive of the Father's will: "My food is to do the will of him who sent me, and to accomplish his work" (Jn 4: 34). With childlike trust, he is obedient to all that the Father asks of him. The Father is not an abstract idea for Jesus. In fact, God is the most concrete reality of all. This concreteness does not in any way arise from bodiliness, but rather from God's being the

---

8. Pope Benedict XVI, *Jesus of Nazareth: From the Baptism in the Jordan to the Transfiguration*, trans. Adrian J. Walker (New York: Doubleday, 2007), p. xiv.
9. Joseph Cardinal Ratzinger, *Behold the Pierced One* (San Francisco: Ignatius Press, 1986), p. 22.

transcendently "personal" reality.[10] Saint Thomas Aquinas makes clear that persons are the most perfect things in all of nature.[11] When you look from rocks, to plants, to animals, you see an ascending likeness to the "substantiality" of being a person; movement comes more and more from the interior of the thing. A rock falls, but is not alive in its moving. Sap rises in a maple, but only with animals is there movement based on the interior reception of sensible stimuli. With the human animal, though, something marvelous happens: freedom breaks out. We are sovereign over our acts, able to act for truth and love.[12] Certainly, God is not any less personally substantial than we are. Indeed, he is the original fullness of all personhood, and in fact, God is *tri*-personal: Father, Son, and Holy Spirit. God is Love.

But for many people, even many Christians, God is not concretely personal but is rather an empty concept. For children, though, "God" is not a mere label. When parents are living icons of divine love, then their children know, existentially, the Love that is their ultimate source. When a mother smiles at her child, the glorious love of the Trinitarian life, which is at the heart of reality, shines through her love. All boys and girls sense that, just as Mom loves them – and this love structures their existence – so too does God love them concretely and personally.[13]

Jesus, the eternal Son, reveals his childlike awareness of the Father's concrete and ever-present love. "In short, the entire life of Jesus, right up to his death on the Cross, can be seen under the

---

10. As our teacher Father Matthew Lamb would put it, "God is an infinite act of loving understanding."

11. Aquinas, *Summa theologiae* I, q. 29, a. 3.

12. Angels are nothing but subsisting acts of knowing and loving – completely without bodies, but more substantial than any rock, plant, or subhuman animal.

13. Perhaps the deepest horror of abortion, and all other forms of child abuse, is that the child, who is utterly receptive to the reality of being, is assaulted, even killed, by the lie that at the heart of reality is not love, but rather a malignant evil that strikes at love.

sign of prayer and confidence in the Father." [14] That prayer is presented most directly in this wonderful passage related by both Saints Matthew and Luke:

> At that time Jesus declared, "I thank you, Father, Lord of heaven and earth, that you have hidden these things from the wise and understanding and revealed them to little ones; yes, Father, for such was your gracious will. All things have been delivered to me by my Father; and no one knows the Son except the Father, and no one knows the Father except the Son and any one to whom the Son chooses to reveal Him."

(Mt 11: 25-27, translation slightly modified; cf. Lk 10: 21-22)

This prayer sheds light on the adoptive sonship brought about by baptism. The Father has revealed mysteries to those who are childlike, who participate in his eternal Son's receptive obedience. The Father has delivered these spiritual children – the followers of Jesus – to the Son, for him to keep in his care. This care includes revealing the Father to us. God's providential plan is that we *all* become his children! Being faithful to this precious calling of the Father means preferring his will over our own and existing in an attitude of complete obedience concerning his plan for us. Docility to the Father's will in the Holy Spirit is the essence of spiritual childhood. Indeed, it is the essence of holiness, by which grows the Father's kingdom of love on earth, the Church: "Thy kingdom come; thy will be done..."

Parents raising their children so that they not "lose heart" develop in their children the ability to live in obedience to the wise and loving will of the Father. In their role as educators, Christian fathers and mothers serve the baptismal birth from above. Parents are honored with the task of shaping their children,

---

14. Elena Bosetti, *Luke: The Song of God's Mercy*, trans. Julia Mary Darrenkamp, F.S.P. (Boston: Pauline Books and Media, 2006), p. 90.

in their powers of intellect, will, and sense appetites, so that they are capable of self-sacrificial love, capable of living out the vocation that God has in mind for each of them, which is in fact the vital wellspring of their unique personalities. What a noble endeavor is family life! For this surpassing end, God the Father has bestowed upon parents a share in his authority [15] – not to rule tyrannically, but to rule as God rules: in a way that encourages great-heartedness. Indeed, Christian family life by grace embodies the Trinitarian life of love: "The Christian family is a communion of persons, a sign and image of the communion of the Father and the Son in the Holy Spirit." [16] Every marriage between baptized Christians is suffused and elevated by grace. Marriage lived faithfully and fruitfully transforms the world, for true love is the deepest reality. So the Christian family is the staging area of world-changing love. [17] Again, this is not by the measure of television celebrity, but by the measure of reality: nothing can change the world like Christian family life well lived, for the smallest act of true love has more of being than the wide world.

A Christian family generously welcomes into the world as many children as the Father wishes to give. And procreation is inseparable from education. The graciousness of Christian family

---

15. See the *Catechism of the Catholic Church* (CCC 2197).
16. CCC 2205.
17. When seen in the light of the common good, the importance of the family for the life of the world becomes very clear. Extending the teaching of John Paul II, Pope Benedict has been emphasizing the absolute centrality of the family for social justice. For example, in his 2008 World Day of Peace Message (which can be accessed at www.vatican.va), he notes that peace begins in the home (a theme dear to Blessed Mother Teresa): "Indeed, in a healthy family life we experience some of the fundamental elements of peace: justice and love between brothers and sisters; the role of authority expressed by parents; loving concern for the members who are weaker because of youth, sickness, or old age; mutual help in the necessities of life; readiness to accept others and, if necessary, to forgive them. For this reason, the family is *the first and indispensable teacher of peace.*"

life is the atmosphere in which the inner directionality of the human heart attains its initial fruition: to love and be loved in the truth. Christian parents cherish the supernatural freedom of their children given in baptism. Freed from sin, infused with God's own love, and trained in virtue, children are empowered to perform transfiguring acts in the home, in the community, in the nation, in the culture, in the world – to draw all humans into the loving embrace of Holy Mother Church and thus into the arms of the Triune God.

FREEDOM AS OBEDIENCE TO TRUE LOVE

It is the prompt, easy, and joyful living out of self-sacrificial love that constitutes Christian maturity: to lay one's plans and preferences before the Father, so that his will be done (his loving will for the salvation of the world). This is the maturity that is identical with spiritual childlikeness. Christian adulthood is essentially nothing other than receiving one's unique mission/vocation from God the Father and carrying it out. As we see in the life of Jesus, there is a unity "between the abiding dependency of the Son on the Father ('My teaching is not mine' Jn 7: 16) and the autonomously responsible mission which the Father entrusts to the Son – the unity, if you will, between being a child and being an adult." [18] Education in the home aims at this mature, dependent creativity in the service of love, which occurs according to the promptings of the Holy Spirit – inspiring moral beauty as glorious as a fresco by Blessed Fra Angelico or a violin sonata by Mozart. Indeed, this inspired life draws vital strength from immersion in high culture – an integral component of the MAGNIFICAT way of life.

A man is free only if he can give himself away, and this requires self-sacrifice. Here is the place for Christian discipline.

---

18. Balthasar, *Unless You Become*, p. 72.

Children are born naturally at the mercy of their passions, and their wills outrun their intellects. They do not have the ability to deny themselves immediate gratification for the sake of a higher good, so parents must direct them to *true* goods – not cater to the whims of a moment. Training a child in the virtues that alone can sustain true love requires consistency. Inconsistency might cause a child to assume that the ultimate authority – God – is also inconsistent and, thus, untrustworthy. But God's will is not arbitrary; it is wise and loving. Indeed, God's love is the source of his laws, which are meant to guide us to our happiness.

Think of a child who cannot behave at Mass. Such a child does what he wants; in some way, he is "free" – but only in the empty sense of individualist consumerism. His bad behavior does not open his horizons; rather, it closes them to all those things that can be gained through quiet receptivity. This child's deepest yearnings for truth, beauty, and love await – for their unfolding – the serenity of a peaceful heart. Parents serve this unfolding even through the little dramas of child development. One tough juncture in maintaining discipline is when children are just beginning to walk. Rookie toddlers, understandably, want to walk all the time. But a child who is allowed to walk around in church (or even in restaurants) on some occasions will want to do so all the time – and may throw tantrums when thwarted. Acquiescing after a tantrum, of course, is the worst outcome of all. An approach that has worked well for us involves a simple rule: our children are held by one of us until they can do all the things that everyone else in church is doing. (We do allow our younger kids to stand instead of kneel.) If they make noise, they are taken to the back of the church (but still held). Here fathers should make a special point of being involved: toddlers can start to feel pretty heavy after a while, and they can squirm mightily. Dads, put your muscles to work! Fathers have the first responsibility in maintaining discipline after all. This is why Saint Paul addresses fathers first in Colossians 3: 21. Children learn docility in the arms of their fathers.

We also discovered a nice by-product of insisting on good behavior in Mass: a child who can behave in Mass can behave just about anywhere! By focusing our disciplinary energies on church behavior, we get more bang for our parenting buck, so to speak. Our children's self-control was earned with often-wearisome repetition, and remonstration and punishment were occasionally required. But their (and our!) reward is a newfound freedom that opens up new horizons.

Developing such obedience requires sternness, but a sternness that flows from love, as it does with God the Father. If children grow up in an atmosphere of (wisely ordered and intelligible) love, they grow up to trust reality and to trust God. Toddlers confidently take mother's hand and follow her into a new situation – into a snow-covered field or into a pool, say – if they have internalized a trusting receptivity toward her. The family should be a school of love, training children to grow into Christian maturity on the basis of a deep and receptive trust of God's will for them: to follow wherever he leads.

Life is not a bed of roses for the loving Christian family, however. The drama of human, and certainly of Christian, existence occurs nowhere but in the cross, the ultimate wellspring of self-sacrificial love in our world. This is the paradox caused by our sinful resistance to God's love for us: our happiness, our personal flourishing in true love, can be found only in the cross – in giving of ourselves without reserve, without counting the cost in suffering. We can do this only through being caught up in Christ's self-sacrifice, in baptism and Eucharist. The big and little tragedies that occur in every family – through sin and through external disasters – must be weathered by everyone, young and old. Through what they suffer, children can learn to take their sorrows to Jesus, to place their little hearts in the Sacred Heart. Then God will expand their hearts to take on the contours of his own mighty heart. We all find ourselves only through losing ourselves in God. Parents have a special responsibility to model spiritual endurance and resilience in the face of tribulation; that endurance and resilience are made possible by the sacraments and prayer.

Taking Heart in Mary, Our Mother

In carrying out its vital function in Church and society, every family has an indispensable resource in the experience and counsel of the Christian community. The communion of saints watches over our every step, praying for us. Angels guard us. The Mother of God tenderly enfold us – parents and children – in her Immaculate Heart, so that we not lose heart.

It might be easy to dismiss Our Lady's relevance to our lives, or the relevance of the Holy Family for our families: Mary *couldn't* sin after all; her child is God. But we should not forget that God gives us just what we need to carry out our vocation, and the same was true for Mary. Her inability to sin only befits her as the Mother of the Most High God. Yet her Immaculate Conception was not only an honorific bespeaking God's generosity. It was also urgently needed for her to be able to face the trials that she would experience in being the Mother of the Redeemer.

Mary received Jesus as her Son without fully knowing what would be asked of both of them. She had to let him go on his mission, which left her behind in some way. When the woman in the crowd pronounced a blessing on his mother – "Blessed is the womb that bore you, and the breasts that you sucked!" – Jesus deflected attention onto the childlike qualities needed by all believers: "Blessed rather are those who hear the word of God and keep it!" (Lk 11: 27-28). Mary's motherhood of her flesh-and-blood Son is stretched to become a universal motherhood, but this can happen only through the loneliness of letting Jesus go away from her side and out into the world, out into the sin and death

238

tearing the world to pieces. Worst of all, she had to endure the deep agony of watching her only and beloved Son be crucified and abandoned. All of these experiences were a kind of deepening abandonment for her, a participation in her Son's abandonment on the cross. She could do all of this only through the grace of Christ bestowed by the Father through the Holy Spirit, which had preserved her free of sin from the beginning. Because of this total sinlessness, she could respond to her abandonment by abandoning herself to the Father's will. She completely gave away her heart to God.

Mary shows us, however, that the one who gives his or her heart away to God does not *lose heart*: "For whoever would save his life will lose it; and whoever loses his life for my sake, he will save it" (Lk 9: 24). Joining her great and Immaculate Heart to the infinitely capacious Sacred Heart of Jesus, she shows us what love can produce in the docility and Christian maturity of spiritual childhood: she becomes the Mother of us all.

Those of us who come after Mary are given the great gift of Holy Mother Church, whose maternal role is inseparable from Mary's universal motherhood. To live out the Father's wise and loving will in our lives, we are given magisterial guidance and sacramental grace by the Church. A docile yet courageous obedience to our Father, who speaks through our Mother the Church, is necessary for us to pursue holiness, to live out our vocation to do everyday works of supernatural love in a world dying for true love. Graciously embraced ourselves, we Catholic parents confidently allow the channels of the mighty torrent of grace to bear our children along into the heart of God – from baptism to Eucharist to confession to confirmation… and beyond.

Within the sacramental life of Holy Mother Church, and especially with the nourishment of the Eucharist, we fathers and mothers look to God the Father to cultivate the childlike magnanimity of Mary in ourselves and in our children. We pray constantly to the Father, through the intercession of Mary our

Mother, that he pour his graces upon us so that we may be worthy stewards of the precious children he has entrusted to our care. We pray for a gracious advent to be repeated until Love is all in all: Mary prepares our hearts so that grace may take hold of our innermost being, with the Holy Spirit coming from the Father to fructify our families with the Word of God. Thus we too cry out, our hearts great with love, *Magnificat anima mea Dominum*!

"MY SPIRIT REJOICES"

Celebrating Liturgical Seasons in the Home

LISA LICKONA

"My Spirit Rejoices!" Although I did not choose the title for my presentation I cannot think of a more apt and beautiful one – for in my own life I find that sharing the liturgical year with my husband and my seven children is a cause for ever-deepening joy. Not long ago I re-read a book that our Pope Benedict wrote when he was serving the Church as Joseph Cardinal Ratzinger. *A New Song for the Lord* is a beautiful treatise on the meaning of the liturgy. At the beginning of one of the chapters, Ratzinger tells a story that perfectly expresses my own joy. It is the fascinating story of a small group of early Christians who were celebrating Sunday Mass in secret during the persecution of the Emperor Diocletian. The Christians are suddenly discovered by the Roman authorities and sternly questioned about their illegal activities. A transcript of the questioning still exists, and the answers that these men give are an amazing testimony to the power and meaning of the liturgy in the early Church. In the face of the questioning, Emeritus, the owner of the house where the men are gathered, has the question put to him by the proconsul: Why have you done this? Why have you acted in defiance of the caesars? At first Emeritus gives what we might call a "human" answer, one that speaks to the love and fellowship that is shared by those who are united in the eucharistic body of our Lord. Very simply, he states that all those who had gathered in his house were like brothers to him and he wasn't going to kick them out! But this answer does not satisfy the proconsul. Like the dramatic antagonist in a cinematic thriller, he presses Emeritus. We can imagine the tension of the scene as Emeritus faces his questioner. He is facing imprisonment and probably death. As Ratzinger tells it,

> *Once again the proconsul was insistent. And there, in the second response, the real ground and motive came to light. "You had to forbid them entry," the proconsul had said. "I couldn't," answered Emeritus: "Quoniam sine dominico non possumus – for without the Day of the Lord, the mystery of the Lord, we cannot exist."* [1]

At that moment of duress, the truest answer is given, the answer of the heart: *Without the day of our Lord we cannot exist!* What a beautiful and profound answer. We come to be and are held in being by the liturgy. Liturgy is not merely a "thing" to be attended, like a PTA meeting; it is a life-giving event, a moment of genuine communion with God as Father, Son, and Spirit, which re-creates us and gives our existence meaning and purpose. It makes us be who we are.

This profound answer resonates with my own experience. Over the past fifteen years I have spent thousands of hours feeding and dressing and teaching and comforting my children – just like every

---

1. Joseph Cardinal Ratzinger, *A New Song For the Lord: Faith in Christ and Liturgy Today*, trans. Martha Matesich (New York: The Crossroad Publishing Company, 1997), p. 60.

other mother! But this experience of caring for the physical and psychological and educational needs of my children has found its final purpose and meaning in the work I have done to respond to their spiritual needs. Like every other mother, I have also had my difficult moments. I have struggled to keep my sanity in a world that seems to be increasingly hostile to children and the sensibilities that uphold and protect them. Like the early Christians, we face a hostile environment. But also like them, we can find consolation in the Christian community and the beauty of the liturgy. In my life I have come to discover that my motherhood finds its completion in the motherhood of the Church. And my identity as a woman, my identity as a wife and mother, makes the most sense in the loving embrace of my Mother, the Church.

Indeed, my spirit rejoices!

Through our participation in the liturgical life of the Church, we, as mothers and fathers, find the true meaning of our existence. And we can convey to our children the meaning of their existence.

Not long ago, I was helping out as an adult volunteer in the confirmation program at my parish. I was leading a discussion group of twelve bright young ninth- and tenth-graders. We were given the assignment of discussing the different traditions that we observe within the Church. I began to discuss my family's traditions and asked the students to share with me some of the traditions of their own families. Not a single teen came forward. I suggested that, since it was Lent, we could focus on that. Did any of the families do anything special for Lent? One boy raised his hand: "We give up something." "Great," I said, "why do you give up something?" He shrugged.

I left that discussion feeling sad and defeated. These children, who are really the victims of a defective catechesis – and the defective catechesis of their parents! – do not know the basics of Christian tradition. They are uncatechised. But beyond that, they are alienated. They are adrift. For it is through the catechesis that the Church offers us in her own liturgy – the anticipation of

Advent that is rewarded with the coming of the Christ child; the austerity of Lent that ends with the astounding joy of Easter; even the relative calm of Ordinary Time – it is through the living out of these moments that we come to know who we are and why we are! We learn that we are created by a loving God, for him, to the praise of his glory. We learn that through the sin of our own parents and through our own fault we are all broken and needy. We learn of the glorious victory of the resurrected Lord and the final glory that we are all promised. We learn of the beginnings of the Church and the work of Christ that continues on earth until all things are gathered together in him.

How can we carry on without the truths that make sense of our lives? And how can we not bring these truths home to our children? It is these saving truths that we make present to our children as we thoughtfully follow the rhythms of the liturgical year. In this essay I would like to present a starting point for parents who are seeking to "bring home" the liturgy, who would like to teach their children through the creative celebration of the liturgical year in the home. Everything that I present in this essay is something that I have tested on my own children. Collected together, all of these ideas and activities may seem daunting. But even parents who themselves are just beginning to discover the mysteries of our faith can celebrate the liturgical year at home with their children. Take it slow, start simply, share your joy. You will be learning along with your own children, and your joy can become infectious. Theirs can and should infect you also!

What are our goals in celebrating the liturgical year with our children? First among them is that we want to draw our children ever closer to our Triune God, Father, Son, and Holy Spirit. In other words, we are seeking to deepen their faith, hope, and love. We want them to feel that the Catholic Church is their Mother, that the saints are their treasured comrades and friends. We want them to understand Church doctrine and practice, but, even more importantly, we want these saving truths to bear fruit in their lived experience.

Our second goal is closely related to the first: we want to come to this deeper encounter with God in the midst of the family. We want to experience these truths together. Indeed, we want our communion as a family to be an image of the communion of love which God shares in himself. We want therefore to have traditions in our family which contribute to a sense of our unity, our commitment to each other, our shared joy. We want to offer to our children activities and traditions that give them a sense of identity and security and that they will carry with them into their own families.

There are many wonderful resources available for parents who wish to celebrate the liturgical year in the home. Whole books have been written to assist parents in the creative celebration of the liturgical seasons, the principal feast days, and the feasts of the saints. At the conclusion of this essay I provide a list of some of the resources that I have found helpful. Rather than trying to list here all the possible ideas and activities, I would like to present to you, from my own experience, five guiding "principles" for celebrating the liturgical year in the home: (1) find a center; (2) keep a rhythm; (3) keep it simple; (4) follow your heart; (5) listen to your children.

Find a Center

The first thing I want to share with you is something that it took me some years to discover – find a center! By "find a center" I mean, find a central place in your home to teach children what *their* center is. It is no longer in vogue to refer to the Church as feminine, as a "she," but this traditional way of speaking reveals an important truth: the Church is a Mother. That means that she has a womb and we are all children being formed in her womb. Our homes, insofar as they take the character of domestic churches, can become places where we all develop as children of God and especially where our children can grow and develop. [2]

Another important truth comes to mind if we think of the Church as a mother. The Church's motherhood is personified in the Blessed Virgin Mary; we have only to look to her to see what our true center is – for within her womb she bears our Lord and Savior. If we want to draw our children closer to our Lord, we need to put him in a central place in *our* home. In that place we have a crucifix or a picture or an icon. This is where we can gather as a family to pray. In my home, we have an icon of the Sacred Heart in a small shrine over the mantle. When we moved into our home we had it consecrated to the Sacred Heart. We had a big celebration that day and invited our friends and our children's friends.

Wherever your center is, this is the place where you can center your celebration of the liturgical year. You can add pictures of saints, or an image of Mary. You can have candles that you light when you pray. This is the place to keep the family Bible. Some really inventive moms make a side table into a miniature altar and have altar cloths that are the colors of the liturgical season! [3] Another mom has a little altar in her child's room and prays before that every night. You could encourage the children to

---

2. "The Christian family is grafted into the mystery of the Church to such a degree as to become a sharer, in its own way, in the saving mission proper to the Church: by virtue of the sacrament, Christian married couples and parents 'in their state and way of life have their own special gift among the People of God' [*Lumen Gentium*, n. 11]. For this reason they not only *receive* the love of Christ and become a saved community, but they are also called upon to *communicate* Christ's love to their brethren, thus becoming a *saving* community. In this way, while the Christian family is a fruit and sign of the supernatural fecundity of the Church, it stands also as a symbol and participant of the Church's motherhood" (*Familiaris Consortio*, n. 49).

3. Our Father's House has many items that can be used in a family "prayer corner," including book holders for the family Bible, reliquaries, and special tablecloths. They can be found on the web at ourfathershouse.biz.

decorate the altar or draw pictures that make it their own. Perhaps you could have their baptismal candle there. Whatever you do, find your center!

Keep a Rhythm

When we place Jesus at the center of our home, we acknowledge that he is the Lord of our space. When we place him at the center of our family rhythms we acknowledge that he is the Lord of our time! In many ways it is easier to give him the space than the time. We are all very much attached to secular schedules that center on school and work, on extra-curricular activities, and on what is on television. The liturgical year is not the same as the secular year, and deciding as a family to follow the liturgical calendar will require some sacrifices – on everyone's part. This can be the first truth that celebrating the liturgical year will bring home to your children – that we can and should make sacrifices! The natural rhythms of the liturgical year recognize the most basic truth of our faith – that although we are created by and for God, through sin we have fallen far from his grace. This is a counter-cultural truth: commercials must have us believe that deep-down we are really good people and we will be happy only if we are always consuming. We are encouraged to pamper ourselves, to give in to the Christmas goodies that appear in October, to feel entitled to those chocolate eggs in the checkout aisle weeks before Easter. But the rhythms of the liturgical year teach us differently – they are the rhythms of fast and feast, the rhythms of sin and redemption, the rhythms of sorrow and joy. Advent comes before Christmas, Lent before Easter. Even in Ordinary Time, this most basic rhythm is repeated each week: Friday is a day of sacrifice – a mini-Good Friday – and, Sunday, a little Easter, a day of joy and celebration!

So, to start, we can work on ways to acknowledge the true rhythms of feast and fast in our week. Traditionally, many families give up meat on Friday's year-round. In our current culture, just having plain pizza rather than pepperoni can set us apart from our friends. Another counter-cultural move is to try to truly celebrate Sunday as a day of rest, relaxation, and family time. Sunday is a good day to reach out to others in need, especially to the old and sick in our families. [4]

In our family we love to share Sunday brunch after Mass and religious education classes. Our traditional topic of conversation is "what was your favorite part of today's Mass?" This is a topic that everyone, young and old, can contribute to, each according to their level of understanding. The young children's comments can help you as a parent understand what is important to them. So many times they will remark on "what color Father was wearing." School-age children can break out their *MagnifiKid!* and share a part of the readings that they like. [5] And the comments of older children and parents on the homily or the readings are a beautiful occasion for the mysteries of the faith and the meaning of the liturgical year to come alive. One of the complaints of many adults today is that they never heard their own parents talk about the faith, about what it meant to them. We can reverse that trend simply by sharing our faith with our children over the Sunday meal.

As hard as it is to push against the secular rhythms in order to acknowledge the deeper rhythms of the liturgical year, it is eminently worth it. I have celebrated Advent with my children in the way that my own family of origin celebrated Advent – as a season of anticipation and penance. When I was a child, my father would take us four children on a snowy jaunt up the hill from our

---

4. "Sunday is traditionally consecrated by Christian piety to good works and humble service of the sick, the infirm and the elderly. Christians will also sanctify Sunday by devoting time and care to their families and relatives, often difficult to do on other days of the week" (*Catechism of the Catholic Church*, 2186).
5. *MagnifiKid!*, the junior version of Magnificat, is a great resource for Sunday discussion.

rural Pennsylvania home to choose a blue spruce from a large stand of pines on December 22 or 23. We would get the tree up in time for Christmas Eve. The celebration of Christmas would begin that night when my mother read us the account of the Nativity from the Gospel of Matthew. No longer having the luxury of chopping a tree in our backyard, we have flirted with getting our trees up when the getting is good – three or four weeks before Christmas. But this has always felt wrong. In Advent I am trying to teach my children about the longing of the world for the Savior, the anticipation of his coming. And so I have insisted that we travel out to the cut-your-own farm only a few days before Christmas.

This past year was no exception. On December 23, we prepared at 10 A.M. to go out and get the tree. We knew that there would not be anything left at the roadside sales lots, so we planned to check out a farm that we had visited last year. But sudddenly we realized that we didn't remember how to get there. A quick call to friends who had gotten their tree at the same place was unanswered. So we hunkered down to wait for a call back. At around 3 P.M., my eleven-year-old daughter, Kateri, was frantic. We all wanted to see the tree go up and knew that it needed to go up for Christmas Eve to be at all pleasant. As the minutes ticked away without a call back, Kateri finally lost it. She came storming in. "Mom, why didn't we buy a tree three weeks ago when everyone else did!" Mustering my most matronly tone, I replied, "Kate, Jesus was not born three weeks before Christmas and he is going to honor us for honoring his *real* birthday!" And honor us he did. In a few minutes our friends called, and my husband Mark and Kate were on their way out to get the tree. The one they found turned out to be the most beautiful Christmas tree that we have ever found!

Indeed, Jesus will honor us when we honor him, he will bless our families when we give him the space and time in our lives!

KEEP IT SIMPLE

When we are finding ways to bring the liturgy home, it helps to remember to keep it simple. We keep it simple because children are simple! They are simple in the sense that they delight in simple things that we adults often pass by without much notice. Children are delightfully concrete; they are unfailingly incarnational. They learn by touching, by seeing, by doing. Is it any surprise, therefore, that God has chosen to teach us in the liturgy through signs and symbols, words and actions?[6] We do well to teach our children at home in the same way that God our Father and Holy Mother Church teach us. We teach through colors and signs, through songs and rituals, through touching and doing. One simple activity can take the place of many lectures from mom or dad on the "meaning" of this or that holy day.

One Lent I decided to make pretzels on Ash Wednesday.[7] Pretzels really are simple to make and relatively easy, especially if you have ever made a yeast bread. You simply mix the dough, knead it, and shape it into pretzels. Every child who loves to play with play-doh loves to knead and shape! While you are kneading and shaping, it is the perfect time to discuss with your child what fasting is all about. You can share with them the austerity of Lent in earlier times, when people had to give up all meat and even

---

6. In a passage entitled "Catechesis and Liturgy," the *Catechism of the Catholic Church* explains that catechesis is "intrinsically linked with the whole of liturgical and sacramental activity." In other words, the Mass, the sacraments, the Liturgy of the Hours – these are privileged ways of teaching the people of God about who they are. "Liturgical catechesis aims to initiate people into the mystery of Christ... by proceeding from the visible to the invisible, from the sign to the thing signified, from the 'sacraments' to the 'mysteries'" (CCC 1075).

7. This activity is taken from Evelyn Birge Vitz's *A Continual Feast*. This cookbook is a wonderful resource for recipes for many feasts of the liturgical year. Vitz also provides invaluable commentary on the recipes and on the traditions that surround them.

dairy products – hence the pretzels with their simple ingredients of flour, water, honey, and salt. As you shape the pretzels into the shapes of praying hands, you can discuss the lenten discipline of prayer and how we draw closer to Christ through prayer. And of course, at the end of a short time baking you get to eat the pretzels!

This past Lent began with the birth of my seventh child. It was a hard labor and so recovery was slower than normal. Then, when our little Benedict Anselm Marie was two weeks old, the flu went through the house! Fortunately, the baby did not catch the bug, but it was another two weeks of sickness and recovery for the family. In the midst of our illness, Kateri asked me why we hadn't made pretzels yet – after all, we were four weeks into Lent! Here I was, barely able to open a can of soup – thankfully we had a lot of meals from friends – but she was not going to let me forget our lenten tradition! Someone once said that, with a child, "once is a tradition." Keep it simple – so that you can keep up the traditions that they have come to love.

Another tradition we have as a family is to host a party on All Saints' Day. This is one of our most beloved family traditions! It hardly seems to fit the category "simple," and yet, it is just that – a simple variation on a popular theme – the costume party. And this is no Martha Stewart party – but what it lacks in elegance it more than makes up for in joy! At the Saints' party the children – and the adults who are game – dress up as their favorite saints. Costumes are created out of whatever can be scrounged from the attic. Every family brings a dish to pass around. The primary form of entertainment is sharing what we have learned about our saints; the party is capped off by the litany of the saints led by my husband. This kind of activity brings the faith to life for children – it brings together food, friends, and faith. It is a little foretaste of heaven – which, as we all know, will be the real All Saints' Party!

Follow Your Heart

As worthwhile as the All Saints' party has been for my family, if the idea leaves you cold, it is probably not for yours. I have often planned a certain activity for my children and then discovered in the middle of it that it was very difficult to accomplish because my heart was not in it. Although I love to bake, I am a "craft-challenged" person. One year I endeavored to make a paper flower crown with my daughters to honor Mary with our own May-crowning. I didn't really enjoy what I was doing, so I abandoned it in frustration, feeling that I had let down the children and Mary.

Through many such little trials I have discovered another important principle for liturgical celebration in the home: follow your heart. Share with your children precisely those beautiful traditions that move you. Do the things that you love to do, and your own delight will carry you and your children along. If you love to do crafts, then there are many wonderful things to do together. Make rosaries together or Saint Thérèse beads. If you are drawn to a particular saint, find a way to share that love with your children. Go on a pilgrimage to a special place. We made a Sunday pilgrimage to the Shrine of the Little Flower many times when we lived in Michigan. It is a beautiful church and a wonderful place to wander around. Another thing that I love are our traditional hymns and poetry. One Advent I became taken with the hymn "People Look East." The words are the beautiful poetry of one of my favorite poets, Eleanor Farjeon, who also wrote "Morning Has Broken." The melody is easy to learn. So that Advent, I taught this hymn to the children. We would spend only about three minutes a day singing it right before dinner. It was a great hit! Now my children associate "People Look East" with Advent – we all know it and sing it as the Advent candle is lit. These kinds of traditions are simple, so they are easily remembered by the children. And I love them, so I am highly motivated to keep them up.

Teach your children your favorite hymns, even if they are not being sung at your parish church. Another favorite of mine is "Come, Holy Ghost." Not long after this hymn entered my night-time repertoire – the collection of lullabies that I sing to the little ones when I am putting them to bed – our parish was given a new pastor, who resurrected this hymn at daily Mass in the ten days that preceded Pentecost. When little two-year-old Clare heard it sung at church for the first time, she climbed into my lap and whispered into my ear: "It's *my* song!" She was delighted to have *her* song sung at Mass. When we bring beautiful hymns into our family, our children embrace them as their own. Already at two, Clare felt "at home" at Mass.

Another thing that we have done as a family that is very dear to my heart is to introduce the children – even the young ones – to contemplative prayer. I have experienced such joy myself in ador-ation before the Blessed Sacrament and I have wanted to share this with the children. At first, I endeavored to take them to adoration with me, but even when the children were quiet, I found it impos-sible to pray myself! Some parishes have Holy Hours especially for children, but ours does not – and so I continued to wonder about how to introduce the children to contemplative prayer. This past Lent, following a suggestion from the catechetical guide published by the Sisters of Mary, Mother of the Eucharist, I insti-tuted a time in the day when, as a family, we would pray silently for five minutes. We gathered around our center – the Sacred Heart icon – and I explained in very simple terms the difference between mental prayer and vocal prayer. I encouraged them to talk to Jesus and tell him what is in their heart. So, we spent five minutes in prayer. At the end, we prayed the morning psalm from MAGNIFICAT. This took only five minutes a day! And yet these five minutes were a genuinely centering time for our family. At around the time that we started praying together like this, my six-year-old twins both decided to draw pictures of Christ based on the icons that we have on our mantle. Such attentiveness to the face of Christ – this is the fruit of their contemplation!

LISTEN TO YOUR CHILDREN

This final principle is in some ways the most important one: listen to your children! If we are going to feed our children spiritually, we need to become receptive to their spiritual needs, to recognize where they are in their spiritual lives, and to try to meet them there. Let me give you a good example. Part of celebrating the liturgical year is observing the feasts of the saints, celebrating the lives of these exemplary men and women and getting to know them as friends and guides in the spiritual life. Children can learn about the saints in ways that are appropriate for their developmental stage. Preschoolers love picture books – and there are more and more great books on the saints. But they can also benefit from the "touchability" of pictures and statues. When my two oldest girls were little, we made regular visits to the Fatima shrine outside our parish church – my daughters loved to touch the statues of Jacinta, Francisco, and Lucia, to pat the little lambs, to kiss the feet of Mary. I never coached them on this! I would simply tell them the story of the apparitions and emphasize the piety of the child-saints who "loved Mary so much."

School-age children can learn about the lives of the saints in other ways. Gather your children around you and read to them a short account of a saint's life. Then ask them to re-tell the story through drawing or writing. A blank notebook is a wonderful resource here.[8] Have the child decorate it as their own unique

---

8. Very nice, inexpensive, hardback blank books can be purchased from Emmanuel Books, at emannuelbooks.com, 800-871-5598.

"Saint's Book."⁹ Every time you celebrate a special feast day, have the child illustrate a new page. Young children – particularly four to seven years of age – love to draw pictures of what they have learned. Their pictures will often amaze and inspire you! Older children can be encouraged to write a sentence or a paragraph recalling some important fact or event from the life of the saint. You can even encourage the children to write their own prayers to the saint. After a year of such activities – and remember, you don't do every saint, just a handful through the year – the child has made a lovely book to keep.

My twins draw pictures all the time. They love to participate in the Stations of the Cross at our parish, but they do not yet read at the level at which the stations book is written. This past Lent I suggested that we make "Stations of the Cross" books. This activity was a perfect match for where they are developmentally! With very little help from me – I provided the blank books, the colored pencils, and a Bible that had depictions of each station – they illustrated their own books of stations. They then brought these personal books with them to church and looked at their own pictures as a meditation for each station.

At the other end of the spectrum in our family is my fourteen-year-old daughter, Monica. Monica recently outgrew *MagnifiKid!*, and I have noticed a decided deepening in her spiritual life. She is more attentive at Mass. As she matures, her relationship with God is maturing. I decided to get her her own subscription to MAGNIFICAT. This was a perfect fit! She was so thrilled with it – it seemed so "grown up" to her. She prays with MAGNIFICAT every day. And she has become an even more reliable family resource as

9. The idea for the "Saints Book" comes from Laura Berquist, a homeschooling mother and experienced educator who wrote the book *Designing Your Own Classical Curriculum*. Anyone can benefit from the observations that she makes about children's development and what is appropriate for different children at different stages. Berquist also has instructions for making a lovely "Bible Book" for children.

she shares what she has read in MAGNIFICAT with the younger children.

CONCLUSION

In many ways, Monica's deepening faith is the crowning of the past fifteen years of my life. I can see in her the fruit of my many attempts to bring the faith to life for my children in the home. I think that it is important for every parent to recognize that the effort they put into making the liturgical year come alive for their children will be richly repaid. In the liturgy – through Mass, the sacraments, and the recitation of the Liturgy of the Hours – we enter into an encounter with the risen Lord. We are drawn into his presence and we experience his love. Every effort to share the beauty and power of this experience with our children will be returned to us in the faith of our children and, we hope, our grand-children. Just when we wonder how we can continue to move forward in our spiritual lives, the faith of our children will revive us, filling our hearts anew with faith, hope, and love.

This past Holy Saturday, Megan, our eight-year-old neighbor, came over to play. Megan is a sweet girl, but like so many chil-dren today, she is "unchurched." After the playtime, my eight-year-old son Maximilian walked her home. As Max escorted her out the door I heard him say to her, "It is too bad that you aren't Catholic, because tomorrow is Easter and we get to go to Holy Mass, which is very beautiful."

Nothing can warm a mother's heart like hearing her eight-year-old son call the Mass "beautiful." This is what I have sought to share with my children – something that to me is amazingly beautiful, the source of my life. How amazing that, with God's grace, it is also the source of theirs.

Selected Resources

A Continual Feast by Evelyn Birge Vitz, Ignatius Press, 1985.

Catholic Traditions in Crafts by Ann Ball, Our Sunday Visitor Publishing, 1997.

Designing Your Own Classical Curriculum by Laura Berquist, Ignatius Press, 1998.

Marian Devotions in the Domestic Church by Catherine and Peter Fournier, Ignatius Press, 2007.

Remain In Me: Faith Formation Curriculum by Carol Kennedy and Sister John Dominic Rasmussen, O.P., Spiritus Sanctus Publications, 2001.

Saints and Feast Days. Lives of the Saints: With a Calendar and Ways to Celebrate by the Sisters of Notre Dame of Chardon, Ohio, Loyola Press, 1985.

The Religious Potential of the Child by Sofia Cavaletti, Liturgy Training Publications, 1992.

Conclusion: Renewal Through the New Commandment

Peter John Cameron, O.P.

At the Last Supper, Jesus pronounces the new commandment: "I give you a new commandment: love one another. As I have loved you, so you also should love one another" (Jn 13: 34). At first hearing, this command may strike us as hopelessly daunting. How in the world can I possibly love others as Jesus loves, especially those who mistreat me, despise me, or deceive me? Isn't this asking too much? But as we reflect on this commandment, we realize that the Lord is not so much imposing an obligation on us as he is revealing a new reality that has come to be through his life, death, and resurrection.

The New Commandment Reveals Us to Ourselves

The Lord Jesus is manifesting to us that we *can* love one another even as he has loved us. His transformative love blesses us with a new ability because it endows us with *new being* – a sharing in his own life: "Christ enables us to *live in him* all that he himself lived, and *he lives it in us*" (*Catechism of the Catholic Church* [CCC] 521). Saint Basil the Great makes the observation that, in receiving God's commandment of love, we immediately, from the first moment of our existence, possess the ability to love. It is not a coincidence that Christ issues this commandment at the very moment that he gives us his body, blood, soul, and divinity in the Holy Eucharist. In fact, there is benefit that accrues to ourselves when we love our neighbor, since the "encounter with the Eucharistic Lord... acquire[s] its realism and depth in... service to others" (*Deus caritas est* 16, 18).

What is more, with the utterance of this commandment, love becomes more than a "feeling"; "love is not merely a sentiment" (*Deus caritas est* 18), for Gospel charity stands as *the judgment* by which we face all of reality. Our communion with Christ shows us that being charitable to our neighbor is the most reasonable thing we can do.

The *agape* of Jesus Christ, which Pope Benedict XVI refers to as the self-giving love of one who looks exclusively for the good of the other, recreates us so that we become in fact the "new creation" proclaimed by Saint Paul (see 2 Cor 5: 17). Christ gives us his new commandment to imbue us with the awareness of our new identity in him. When temptation to self-doubt threatens, the new commandment ensures that our vocation is not an illusion – we are called and empowered to love others in a way that exceeds even our limitations (see CCC 52).

The reason we can accede to the new commandment with total certainty is that, as Saint John reminds us, "In this is love: not that we have loved God, but that he loved us and sent his Son as expiation for our sins" (1 Jn 4: 10). We love others, not as a slavish response to some moralistic "ought," but rather in order to be true to the divine love that embraces us. As Pope Benedict XVI writes in his encyclical on love, *Deus caritas est*, "God does not demand of us a feeling which we ourselves are incapable of producing. He loves us, he makes us see and experience his love, and since he has 'loved us first,' love can also blossom as a response within us" (17).

SAINT PAUL'S HYMN TO CHARITY

In Saint Paul's classic Hymn to Charity (1 Cor 13: 1-13), the Apostle testifies to the miracle of the love of God that he can "see and experience." Saint Paul knows what Saint John knows – that God is Love. He can with unerring conviction set forth what constitutes love inasmuch as these properties are true of God himself. God's love for Paul has restored and perfected that image of God who is Paul. Using a compelling Pauline geometry, the Apostle makes the claim that love is patient and that love is kind because Love has made *Paul* patient and kind. Love is not jealous, not pompous, not inflated, not rude, not self-seeking, not quick-tempered, and neither is Paul any more! Ever since Paul met this Love personally on the road to Damascus, all these vices in him have been purged and purified. Paul gives incontestable witness that love rejoices with the truth, hopes all things, endures all things, and never fails, because these facts can be verified in his own feeble flesh. Love has made Paul to be something he never could have become on his own. Paul proclaims the astonishing love that has blossomed within him with this declaration: "If I have not love, I am nothing." As he extends that love to others, Paul increasingly becomes what love has made him to be.

Paul must have meditated often on the love that managed to transfigure him right down to the minutiae of his personality, for such meditation returned him effectively to the event that permanently converted him. His meditation was translated into concrete charitable action that in turn rekindled Paul's original encounter with Christ on the road to Damascus. Perhaps that was why Saint Thomas Aquinas was so attentive to the fact that Saint Paul, in introducing his great hymn, calls charity a "road": "I shall show you a still more excellent way" (1 Cor 12: 31; in Greek *hodos*, the root of "method"). "For here we are called wayfarers because we are journeying towards God. On this road progress is made by charity" (*Summa theologiae* IIa IIae q. 24, a. 4).

As Pope Benedict XVI understands it, "Love of neighbor is a path that leads to the encounter with God… Only my readiness to encounter my neighbor and to show him love makes me sensitive to God as well. Only if I serve my neighbor can my eyes be opened to what God does for me and how much he loves me" (*Deus caritas est* 16, 18).

Loving with Christ's Love

The love with which we love our neighbor is not our own natural and defective love but the love of Jesus himself. When we permit Jesus to love us, his love becomes our own with which to love others. This makes it possible for us to love even those whom we do not prefer or whom we find objectionable. In commenting on the new commandment in her autobiography, Saint Thérèse of Lisieux writes: "It is a question of loving one's neighbor as *he, Jesus, has loved him*, and will love him to the consummation of the ages… I would never be able to love my sisters [the other nuns in the Carmel] as you love them unless you, O my Jesus, *loved them in me*. It is because you wanted to give me this grace that you made your *new* commandment. Oh! how I love this new commandment since it gives me the assurance that your will is *to love in me* all those you command me to love!"

Pope Benedict XVI expresses the same truth in these words: "I love even the person whom I do not like or even know. This can only take place on the basis of an intimate encounter with God, an encounter which has become a communion of will, even affecting my feelings. Then I learn to look on this other person not simply with my eyes and my feelings, but from the perspective of Jesus Christ. His friend is my friend. Going beyond exterior appearances, I perceive in others an interior desire for a sign of love, of concern. This I can offer them… I can give them the look of love which they crave" (*Deus caritas est* 18).

LOVE LOVES TO LOVE

Monsignor Romano Guardini once sagely pointed out that in the experience of a great love, everything that happens becomes an event in the ambit of that love. A clear example of this is a story I once heard a priest tell about a teenage boy who was in love with a teenage girl. The parents of the boy did not approve of the two dating, and they forbade their son ever to see the girl again. But secretly the young people continued to meet. One night at the dinner table, the boy volunteered to wash the dinner dishes (something he never did!). With that, the boy's father bellowed, "YOU HAVE BEEN SEEING THAT GIRL!" How did he know? Because the father recognized that the only thing which could move his son to do willingly what he hated to do was love. That action of offering to do the dishes betrayed the experience of the great love in which the teenager was living.

But if such loving actions seem to occur almost automatically when we live within the experience of a great love, why does the Lord have to command us to love one another? Because we tend to grow forgetful, negligent, or lax toward God's love for us. We get deluded. "If anyone says, 'I love God,' but hates his brother, he is a liar; for whoever does not love a brother whom he has seen cannot love God whom he has not seen" (1 Jn 4: 20). Our desire to love our neighbor is the measure of how ardently we live in the truth of God's love for us. The psychologist Rollo May makes the point that the true antithesis of love is not hate but despairing indifference, the feeling that nothing is important. How often does that feeling get the better of us?

CHARITY IS FRIENDSHIP

Saint Thomas Aquinas teaches that charity is not simply "love" (like our love of chocolate or baseball or going to the beach). Rather, charity is *friendship*, which loves both the friend to whom we will good and the good we will to him. This does not mean that the new commandment enjoins us to become "best friends" with every person in the world, but it does compel us to look upon our neighbor with a will that professes, "I want you to exist! It is good that you exist!"

"What we need over and above sheer existence," says the Thomist philosopher Josef Pieper, "is to be loved by another person. Being created by God actually does not suffice, it would seem; the fact of creation needs continuation and perfection by the creative power of human love." [1] Christ's new commandment, delivered the night that Jesus himself calls us his friends, is a consummate act of mercy, for through it the Lord answers our inexorable need for a friend. He makes us his friends in mercy so that we can be merciful friends to others.

And what are the distinguishing characteristics of friendship? According to Aristotle: willing the other's good, being glad that the other is alive, taking pleasure in the companionship of the neighbor, having the same preferences, sharing griefs and joys. To the list Saint Thomas Aquinas adds: an effective sharing of goods, pardoning every offense, contemplating and emulating the virtues of the other, offering consolation in sorrow, and sharing the harmony of wills. And all these, Aristotle and Saint Thomas agree, spring from loving the friend as one loves oneself.

Monsignor Luigi Giussani masterfully sums all this up when he speaks of friendship as *every relationship in which the other's need is shared in its ultimate meaning*. What ultimately do we want when we truly love someone? Saint Thomas Aquinas gives

---

1. *Faith, Hope, Love* (San Francisco: Ignatius Press, 1997), p. 174.

the answer: "We wish that our neighbor may be in God" (*Summa theologiae* IIa IIae q. 25, a. 1). And *anyone* who has been loved by Jesus Christ can do that.

OUR LIFE AS OUR VOCATION TO LOVE

The Vatican II decree on the apostolate of the laity entitled *Apostolicam Actuositatem* tenders this challenge to the lay people of the Church: "By the precept of charity, which is the Lord's greatest commandment, all the faithful are impelled to promote the glory of God through the coming of his kingdom and to obtain eternal life for all people… This life of intimate union with Christ in the Church is nourished by spiritual aids which are common to all the faithful, especially active participation in the sacred liturgy. These are to be used by the laity in such a way that while correctly fulfilling their secular duties in the ordinary conditions of life, they do not separate union with Christ from their life but rather performing their work according to God's will they grow in that union. In this way the laity must make progress in holiness in a happy and ready spirit, trying prudently and patiently to overcome difficulties. Neither family concerns nor other secular affairs should be irrelevant to their spiritual life, in keeping with the words of the Apostle, 'Whatever you do in word or work, do all in the name of the Lord Jesus Christ, giving thanks to God the Father through him'" (3, 4). In this way the new commandment truly will be fulfilled.

LIST OF CONTRIBUTORS

DOUGLAS BUSHMAN is director and associate professor for the Institute for Pastoral Theology at Ave Maria University. He gives retreats and conferences on spirituality, the teachings of Pope John Paul II, and other theological topics for priests, deacons, religious, and associations of the lay faithful.

FATHER PETER JOHN CAMERON, O.P., is the editor-in-chief of MAGNIFICAT, and the author of *Jesus, Present Before Me: Meditations for Eucharistic Adoration*.

FATHER THOMAS CARZON, O.M.V., is pastor of Holy Ghost Church in Denver and is a member of the Oblates of the Virgin Mary.

FATHER ROMANUS CESSARIO, O.P., serves as senior editor of MAGNIFICAT, teaches at Saint John's Seminary in Boston, and has given conferences on a variety of topics related to Christian life.

SISTER MARY TIMOTHEA ELLIOTT, R.S.M., currently teaches Sacred Scripture at St. John Vianney Seminary in Denver, CO. She has contributed articles to MAGNIFICAT since the first year of its publication and lectures widely on topics related to Scripture.

ANTHONY ESOLEN is a professor of English at Providence College. He serves as a senior editor for *Touchstone Magazine*, and is the translator of the Modern Library edition of Dante's *Divine Comedy*.

ANGELA AND DAVID FRANKS are the coordinators of the Massachusetts Catholic Conference's marriage initiative, "The Future Depends on Love." Angela teaches theology part-time for the Archdiocese of Boston and distance-learning programs. David teaches theology at Saint John's Seminary.

FATHER PETER GIRARD, O.P., serves as chaplain to Dominican Cloistered Nuns, teaches at Holy Apostles Seminary in Connecticut, and speaks at Catholic events across the world.

SISTER GENEVIEVE GLEN, O.S.B., a Benedictine nun of the contemplative Abbey of St. Walburga, serves as editor for daily offices for MAGNIFICAT. She writes, teaches, and gives retreats on liturgical and biblical spirituality and has published three collections of original hymn texts with accompanying biblical reflections.

FATHER ANDREW HOFER, O.P., taught at Tangaza College of the Catholic University of Eastern Africa before coming to the University of Notre Dame, where he is now a Ph.D. candidate in theology, specializing in the Fathers of the Church. He writes articles for various theological journals in America and Europe and contributes hymns to MAGNIFICAT.

LISA LICKONA is a wife and mother of seven children. Her writings and lectures explore the Church's rich theology of fatherhood, motherhood, and childhood through her own experience.

RALPH MARTIN is the president of Renewal Ministries, which sponsors the weekly television program *The Choices We Face*. He is also the director of Graduate Theology Programs in the New Evangelization at Sacred Heart Major Seminary in the Archdiocese of Detroit. His book *The Fulfillment of All Desire: A Guidebook for the Journey to God Based on the Wisdom of the Saints* more fully develops the insights in his essay in the present volume.

FATHER MICHAEL MORRIS, O.P., is an arts contributor to MAGNIFICAT. He works in the doctoral program for art and religion at the Graduate Theological Union in Berkeley, where he also serves on the faculty of the Dominican School of Philosophy and Theology.

ANN ORLANDO teaches patristics at Saint John's Seminary in Boston. She also teaches Church history and has spoken on topics in Church history at several Boston-area colleges.

MARILYN QUIRK, a wife, mother, and grandmother, was part of the founding of MAGNIFICAT, A MINISTRY TO CATHOLIC WOMEN, as an outreach to Catholic women. She is presently a member of the Steering Committee for the Southern Regional Conference of the Catholic Charismatic Renewal and is on the Leadership Council of the Renewal. She is a nationally known speaker at seminars, conferences, days of renewal, and retreats.

MONSIGNOR JAMES TURRO writes the *Your Word is a Lamp* column for each issue of MAGNIFICAT. He teaches at the Dunwoodie Seminary in New York and at the Cromwell Seminary in Connecticut. Monsignor Turro conducts retreats and Scripture seminars for priests and religious during the summer months.

Composition and typesetting: FACOMPO, LISIEUX
Printed in September 2008
by Transcontinental, Canada
Edition number: MGN 08008

THE TRIUMPH OF RELIGION IN THE ARTS
A *Painter's* Magnificat
MICHAEL MORRIS, O.P.

The Triumph of Religion in the Arts (1840)
Johann Friedrich Overbeck (1789-1869),
Städel Museum, Frankfurt, Germany.

𝒪n 1798, the future of the Catholic Church looked very bleak. Papal fortunes had reached their nadir. Revolutionary forces from France attacked the Papal States, occupied Rome, staged blasphemous neo-pagan liturgies in Saint Peter's Square, took Pope Pius VI prisoner and drove him and his curia into exile. When the sick and paralyzed pope died captive in the south of France the following year, radical pundits predicted that the ancient papacy had finally come to an end. Meanwhile, secularist forces in both Protestant and Catholic countries formulated legislation that limited the rights of the religious orders and outlawed monastic life. Only in the Papal States and the United States could monks and nuns live out their charisms freely.

While a gathering of cardinals managed to elect a successor to the pope in a long and difficult conclave held in Venice in 1800, the fortunes of the papacy seemed little improved. Soon the new pontiff, Pius VII, was himself transported to France and held there as a virtual prisoner by Napoleon. In this era of violent change and uncertainty, few held out hope for the future.

But hope did spring up in various sectors of society, and one of the areas in which it flowered above the scorched earth of revolution, war, secularism, and anti-Catholic bigotry was in the arts. Social distemper had triggered a cultural ferment, and a romantic longing for what was perceived as the halcyon past caused artists to reassess the role and appearance of religion in the fine arts.

In May of 1809, some students, dissatisfied with their training at the Art Academy in Vienna, traveled to Rome with the intention of revitalizing Christian art. They occupied the abandoned monastery of San Isidoro and formed a community of artists inside its walls. The German leaders of this group, Friedrich Overbeck and Franz Pforr, named their commune the Brotherhood of Saint Luke (after the traditional patron saint of artists, who had reputedly fashioned many icons of the Virgin and Christ when not writing his Gospel), and they dedicated themselves to the renewal of religious art through their lifestyle and their labor. A popular book, *Outpourings from the Heart of an Art-Loving Friar*, written in 1797 by a fellow German, Wilhelm Wackenroder, had inspired the quasi-monastic program they adopted inside their new home. In that book, the author posed as a monastic narrator and wistfully recalled earlier, more innocent times when art had found its inspiration in a living religion – the very thing that the oppressive rationalism of the Enlightenment had tried to destroy. The French Revolution had overthrown the old order, caused the Reign of Terror, and advanced a wave of secularization that came to characterize the modern era. The Brotherhood saw this as the bitter fruit of the Enlightenment. The Napoleonic Wars that followed had ravaged the European continent to the point that people dreamily looked back to the Middle Ages in a new and idealized way. As a consequence, the medieval past became a source of inspiration and a symbol to many of cultural revitalization, national pride, and religious unity. In short, many sought to revive elements from the past in order to be better equipped to face the future. The Brotherhood of Saint Luke, with its membership of deeply religious artists, many of them converts to Catholicism, was but one example of this phenomenal atavistic revolt. Because they adopted wide cloaks, long hair, and beards, they came to be nicknamed "The Nazarenes" by the local populace.

In their quest to renew Christian art, the Nazarenes emulated the work of those fifteenth-century artists working prior to Raphael. They opposed on principle the later trends in art that looked to Greco-Roman and High Renaissance classicism for inspiration. Fra Angelico, himself a painter-monk, and Albrecht Dürer, the embodiment of a German national style springing from medieval Nuremberg, were the Brotherhood's heroes. The Nazarenes had an aversion to all things pagan and found post-Raphaelite art – even religious works – more rooted in the flesh than in the spirit. In an effort to "spiritualize" their art, the Nazarenes de-emphasized the dark rich colors, the complex muscularity, and the frenetic action found in so many paintings of the day. Instead, they developed hieratic forms that were flattened in perspective. They deliberately created stiffly posed figures and filled their canvases with clear, bright coloring. Critics of the Brotherhood claimed that they were straining for a precious naïveté. Adherents, however, embraced this new style with the same enthusiasm of discovery that is today extended to Eastern Orthodox icons.

*W*ith the untimely death of Pforr in 1812, the organizing force behind the Nazarenes was lost, but Overbeck lived on as high priest and soul of the movement. In 1840, he completed a painting that embodied all that the Brotherhood had stood for.[1] Its composition he fashioned on Raphael's *Disputa* and *The School of Athens*, frescoes Overbeck had studied on the walls of the Stanza della Signatura in the Vatican. But his was not a slavish imitation of those masterpieces. Instead, Overbeck wanted to create a didactic proposition, a symbol of hope and inspiration, in a time when the Church was buffeted by hostile forces on every side and losing ground in the culture war of advancing secularization. He wanted Catholic art to return to its spiritual roots.

In deciding what to call his work, Overbeck settled on a title that would immediately impress the viewer with the

---

1. This essay is an outgrowth of my classes on iconography and on modern sacred art, and from a short article I wrote titled "The Future is the Past," which appeared in *The National Catholic Register* on September 11, 1994. Since then, with the advance in research made possible by the Internet, my graduate student assistant Erin Zion has provided me with new data that has helped me to decipher the complex iconography in Friedrich Overbeck's Nazarene masterpiece. To her this essay is gratefully dedicated.

meaning of his painterly composition. He called it *The Triumph of Religion in the Arts*. Afterwards, he felt that it could be abbreviated further to *The Magnificat of Art*, because the central figure of the artwork is the Blessed Virgin Mary, whose song of praise resonates in the heavens and excites all the artists in the assembly likewise to give glory to God.[2] The choice of figures to be included in the painting was made solely on the basis of whether the artist's work contributed to the glory of God and the Church. And in Overbeck's mind "the Church" was none other than the Roman Catholic Church with its dogmas and traditions that he as a convert had embraced with uncompromising zeal.

The painting is divided into two zones. The upper zone is a vision of heaven contemplated by the artists below, who inhabit an idealized earthly realm. The connecting agent between heaven and earth is the fountain shooting up a stream of "living water." It was the deliberate intention of the artist to portray the waters of baptism as a jet stream

---

2. An explanatory pamphlet of the painting written by Overbeck was reprinted in Margaret Howitt's two-volume biography of the artist, *Friedrich Overbeck: Sein Leben und Schaffen. Nach seinen Briefen und anderen Documenten des handschriftlichen Nachlasses*, ed. Franz Binder (Freiburg: B. Herder, 1886), vol. 2, pp. 61-72. An English translation of the pamphlet showing a British appreciation of the painting appeared in an earlier publication, *An Account of the Picture of Frederick Overbeck representing Religion Glorified by the Fine Arts; now in Staedel's Art-Institute, at Frankfort-on-the-Maine. Written in German by the Painter Himself, and Translated by John Macray.* (Oxford: John Henry Parker, 1843); henceforth cited as Macray. The large (392 cm. square) painting still resides in the Städel Art Institute.

surging upward toward everlasting life, in sharp contrast to the classical pagan tradition of sacred waters flowing downward from the heights of Mount Parnassus. Two reflecting pools catch the waters of this symbolic fountain. The upper pool reflects the heavens, while the water in the lower pool captures the reflection of visible earthly forms. In this way, Overbeck makes a comment on the genesis of Christian art. It receives its inspiration from heaven and manifests itself on earth. Just as Christ is God made man, so too does Christian art become incarnational as heavenly ideas take material forms that are perceived and enjoyed by the senses. These forms impress themselves upon the body and move the soul upward toward heaven again.

In choosing the Madonna and her *Magnificat* (Lk 1: 46-55) as the key to this complex painting, Overbeck places poetry as the centerpiece for all the arts. Here the Madonna holds a quill pen, signifying her authorship of that masterpiece which scrolls itself around the body of her child, who is the reason for her sublime happiness. The dithyramb of joy with which Mary greeted her cousin Elizabeth after the Annunciation exemplifies the way that the various art forms have given glory to God in the material world for the blessing of the Incarnation. In this sense, Mary is the first Christian artist, and it is she who epitomizes in her song of exultation the response of humanity to this wondrous mystery. Just as an artist in union with the spirit gives part of himself in the creation of art, so too does Mary produce

through her body the ultimate manifestation of God's handiwork, the child Jesus. Her flesh becomes his flesh. Her womb, likened to the ark of the covenant, was the sanctuary before which the child in the womb of Elizabeth leapt for joy, recalling King David as he danced before the sacred presence (2 Sm 6: 14). Now her lap acts as a heavenly throne upon which the baby Jesus sits as he imparts his blessing. Mother and child are framed in an aureole of gold, and winged cherubs sing her song, which reverberates through history in the prayer of the Church.

On either side of Mary in the celestial sphere are four archetypal figures representing the Fine Arts. Kneeling before her holding his harp is King David. He represents Music. Not only did his playing soothe the troubled psyche of King Saul and expel the evil spirits tormenting him (1 Sm

16: 14-23), but the psalms David has been credited with composing have been interpreted by Christians to point toward Jesus as the fulfillment of mankind's hope and desire. Next to him, standing with a model of the brazen sea in his hands, is David's son, King Solomon. He represents Sculpture, for under his command the lavish adornment of the temple took place, and a magnificent sacred space was created for the Most High God. The huge laver that stood in the court of Solomon's temple was adorned with twelve oxen (1 Kgs 7: 13-51). It represented the cosmos and the creation of the world by God in time. It contained enough water for the multitude of ritual baths demanded by Mosaic law, and it prefigured the baptismal font with its "living water"[3] of initiation into a new covenant. The ox, an animal of sacrifice, became a fitting symbol for the priesthood in the Old Testament. This symbol, too, extends into the New Testament. Opposite King David is the kneeling figure of Saint Luke, who represents Painting. It is because Saint Luke stressed the priesthood of Christ in his Gospel that Saint Jerome ascribed to him the figure of the ox, one of the four beasts seen in the vision of Ezekiel and interpreted by Christians to represent the four evangelists. The winged ox acts as an easel for Luke's board as the artist takes his brush and "writes" an icon portrait of the Virgin seated before him. Standing next

---

3. The prophet Jeremiah (Jer 2: 13) refers to God as the source of living water; Christ identifies himself and the Spirit with the same in John 7: 38.

to Luke is the bearded and elderly Saint John, who represents Architecture. Saint Jerome ascribed to John the Evangelist the figure of an eagle, for in Jerome's estimation Christ's Beloved Disciple grew in holiness and wisdom to view from the greatest heights the beauty of celestial truth. It was thought by the ancients that the eagle alone could stare directly into the sun, and John's mystical vision of the new Jerusalem and his detailed description of its construction in the Book of Revelation (21: 9-27) make him an appropriate representative of architecture in Overbeck's masterpiece.

On the upper left-hand side of the painting, behind David and Solomon, an array of other persons drawn from the Old Testament is presented. Overbeck arranged them according to the symbolic manner in which their roles prefigure that of Christ's. Moses, with rays of light emanating from his head, sits beside his brother Aaron, who wears the headdress of the high priest. Noah, whose head slumps downward toward the white dove with an olive branch in its mouth, seems to be in a state of wine-induced relaxation. In Overbeck's composition they represent the divine order of the arts. Moses the Lawgiver had Aaron as his eloquent spokesman, and it was during his brother's tenure as high priest that the intricate aspects of worship began their development. While Noah is credited with having planted the first vineyard yielding the gift of wine that has long been used in cultic activities, the ark that he built and the sanctuary it provided during the Great Flood prefigure the church building itself, whose central aisle, the nave, derives its etymology from the image of a ship. Christ too, rising from sleep, calmed the tumultuous Sea of Galilee when his apostles feared that their boat would collapse and they would drown. Above Noah and dressed in military attire stands Joshua holding a lance in one hand and a shield in the other. Just as Joshua led the Israelites into the Promised Land, so too does Christ lead his people into the kingdom of his eternal Father. The crowned and vested figure talking to Joshua is the priest-king of Salem, Melchisedech. His offering of bread and wine to the victorious Abraham prefigures the Eucharist and the order of priesthood itself. Behind Joshua stand the elderly Jacob and his beloved son Joseph, who holds a bundle of wheat in his arms. Having survived the betrayal of his brethren, Joseph overcame the bonds of slavery and saved his tribe from starvation by offering them food stored up in Egypt. Similarly, Christ offers the faithful salvation through the power of the eucharistic bread from heaven. Further behind them, in distant shades of gray, stands Abraham holding the sacrificial knife. He acts as a type for the eternal Father, willing to give up his first-born son. Beside him, echoing backwards in time and reflecting the archetypal image of the Madonna and child so colorfully depicted in the very center of this painting, huddle Sarah and her infant son Isaac. Lastly, the artist has included Adam and Eve, our first parents, fashioned by the heavenly Sculptor himself in his own image.

If the figures drawn from the Old Testament represent salvific ideas that would take place in the fullness of time, the figures Overbeck has drawn on the right from the New Testament and epochs thereafter find Christ imitated in his saints. The role of Christ as high priest is reflected in the sacrament of holy orders configured in the persons of three saints seated on their cloudy thrones. Behind Saints Luke and John sit the apostles Peter and Paul alongside the proto-martyr Stephen. Overbeck included them to signify the three orders of the clerical state, bishop, priest, and deacon, which have their roots in apostolic times. Peter holds the keys of the kingdom, Paul grasps his sword, and Stephen, wearing the dalmatic and amice of a deacon while sporting a distinctly clerical tonsure, holds the palm of martyrdom in his hand. Christ's office as a teacher is reflected in Overbeck's inclusion above them of three Doctors of the Church. Saint Augustine is seen in profile wearing a miter, Saint Jerome is cloaked in the scarlet red robes and broad hat of a cardinal, while Saint Thomas Aquinas hovers between them. The sufferings of Christ are reflected by the inclusion of two early Christian martyrs, Saint Sebastian and Pope Saint Fabian. The bare-chested Sebastian holds a quiver of arrows in his arm, and Fabian is robed in a cope and papal tiara. The spotless purity of Christ is further reflected in the inclusion of two of the virgin martyrs: Agnes, whose attribute (the white lamb) peers meekly around Sebastian's arrows, and Cecilia, whose dramatic pose is taken directly from a prototype painted by Raphael. This group concludes with Saint Helena, the dowager empress and mother of Constantine. She holds the cross of Christ she is credited with discovering in her expedition to the Holy Land. It was the cross on which the New Adam was sacrificed and it points toward the Old Adam, who concludes the opposite group and whose bones, legend has it, were buried beneath the mound upon which Christ's cross was raised. Overbeck insisted that the two arms of the heavenly sector have many subtle corresponding relations, but he left those connections for the deciphering spectator to make with the satisfaction of discovery. And that discovery is best achieved by knowledge of Christian iconography, a science of sign and symbol that has long informed the basis of sacred art.

The figures in the heavenly sphere of the painting represent the virtues and the prototypes from which the religious impulse and artistic inspiration flow. The assembly beneath them on the earthly plane is composed of artists who have been in varying degrees receptive to that inspiration and have cloaked religion with the highest efforts of their craft. The artists' faces are recognizable for the most part, and Overbeck did not confine himself to representing those whose work predated that of Raphael. He included many Catholic artists whose realism benefited from a scientific study of nature and who departed from the abstract style of those who harkened to penetrate the world of the Spirit. Thus, despite a certain subjectivity that riled critics of the

work, Overbeck's painterly Catholic manifesto becomes truly catholic in posing a liberal attraction of opposite schools of style and making connections in various media where they had not been made before. He wrote, "Christian art is not exclusively confined to one branch, but embraces all; ennobling and sanctifying all, and presenting them as an offering to him who imparted to man the capacity of exercising them."[4]

Nearest to the lower pool of water lean two artists of the Venetian school. They are Giovanni Bellini and Titian, who gaze at the reflection of two boys sitting on the fountain's rim. One of the boys is half-naked and holding a ring of flowers. Above these figures Overbeck placed Carpaccio, Pordenone, and Correggio, all artists noted for their love of rich color, their careful delineation of the nude figure, and their delight in the effects of light, shade, and shadow. On the other side of the fountain spray, sporting a long gray beard and wearing a dark cap, stands Leonardo da Vinci. He points upward and exhorts his disciples to rise to a higher sphere and strive for greater idealism not found in the lower world of harsh reality. Interestingly, Overbeck placed Holbein right next to Leonardo, feeling that his countryman had taken the lower artistic form of portraiture and conse-crated it to higher purposes, as exemplified by his *Meyer Madonna* found in Dresden, a clearly Catholic composition made in the face of an advancing Protestant aesthetic.

Further over, at the far left of the painting, Overbeck painted members of the Tuscan school in a semicircle

---

4. Macray, p. 8

around Dante, who stands in profile, facing the central fountain, with a crown of laurel leaves on his head and posing as if caught in the middle of a poetic oration. Overbeck believed that Dante's *Divine Comedy* was a perfect work of Christian art, embracing the whole spectrum of ideas that would characterize it as a religious masterpiece for all ages. Dante's contemporaries, Giotto, Simon Memmi, and Orgagna, are positioned in front of him. Nearby, cloaked in a white robe that Overbeck used to symbolize the universality of his genius, stands Raphael surrounded by those artists who exercised an influence in the development of his painting: Fra Bartolomeo, Francesco Francia to his right, and Pietro Perugino, Ghirlandaio, and Massacio to his left.

Down below, seated on a fragment of antique sculpture, are the bareheaded Michelangelo and his artistic precursor, Lucas Signorelli. They have their backs to the fountain. Overbeck, who saw in the work of these two artists a radical turn toward a celebration of the fleshly in religious art, portrays Michelangelo as disconnected from the rest of the assembly and lost in his own thought. Signorelli tries to rouse his attention by pointing him back toward Dante, whose exhortations cast a spell over the rest of the Tuscan school.

The attention around Dante that unites nearly all the artists assembled on the left of the fountain contrasts sharply with the division of little groupings of artists portrayed on

the right. Representing artists from both the north and the south of Europe, the groupings harmonize in couplings that Overbeck has devised for symbolic purposes. Lucas von Leyden extends his hand, which is grasped warmly by Mantegna, as Dürer rises conspicuously between them. The friendly connection between printmaker and painter is witnessed by Dürer, the master of both; a German, Martin Schongauer, on the left, and an Italian, Marcantonio Raimondi, on the right, complete this quintuplet. Standing strikingly on the right in his black and white habit is the Dominican painter, Blessed Fra Angelico. He is the epitome of the painter-monk, bridging with equal balance the physical and spiritual aspects of art idolized in Wackenroder's *Outpourings*. He commands the attention of no fewer than seven other figures. Before him stand the Van Eyck brothers, Jan resting his arm on the older Hubert's shoulder. They represent the production of religious art from the world of the layman, whereas the friar represents art springing from the cloister. Angelico's pupil, Gozzoli, stands close by his master, just as Hemlink, the pupil of the Van Eyck brothers, stands close to them. In between is a mysterious bearded man whom Overbeck included as a tribute to the anonymous designer of the Cologne Cathedral. That cathedral rises mournfully unfinished in the background to the right, a victim (as Overbeck points out) of the strife that gripped Germany in the Reformation of the sixteenth century and robbed his native land of many fine works of

religious art and stunted the artistic growth of the sacred.[5]
Two women stand before the cathedral, and Overbeck
suggests that these represent the many women who were
also deeply involved in the liturgical arts and placed their
talents in the service of religion. In front of them stands a
man in pilgrim's gear holding a staff. That is Jan van Scorel,
who was the first Dutch artist to study in Italy and who made
a pilgrimage to the Holy Land before gaining an appointment back in Rome as the keeper of the papal art collection
from his fellow Utrecht native, Pope Hadrian VI. Behind van
Scorel stands another pilgrim, this one from Spain, a nation
curiously underrepresented in this august assembly.

While poet, painters, and printmakers stand on the
terrace around the mystical fountain, Overbeck pushes the
architects and the sculptors into the foreground. Two
figures, pope and emperor, act as foundational pillars to the
lower picture plane. In Overbeck's worldview it is the
Church and the State that support the entire edifice of the
Fine Arts. The pontiff looks upward toward the heavens. His
face is modeled on traditional images of Pope Saint Gregory
the Great. His counterpart looks downward, concerned with
earthly affairs, and his face is modeled on that of
Charlemagne. The pope holds a scroll on which some lines

---

5. Forty years after Overbeck finished his painting, the Cologne Cathedral was
finally completed. In 1880 it was the largest structure in the world.

of Gregorian chant are inscribed. This is Overbeck's homage to the glorious contribution the Church has made to the history of music. The development of Christian architecture, too, is noted below, as young students from various nations (including a Franciscan novice) sit and kneel on the ruins of a pagan temple. They look at the sketch brought to them by a wandering pilgrim (representing the architect of Saint Stephen's Cathedral in Vienna) who gives them a history lesson as he points out to them the detailed plan of a basilica, the earliest form of church architecture inherited from the ancients. Both occidental and oriental influences on Church architecture are recognized by Overbeck, since his pilgrim leans on the shoulders of a turbaned Moor. But the full flower of Christian architecture, in Overbeck's estimation, is to be found in the pointed architecture mastered by the medieval period. He underscores this by introducing the red-cloaked figure of Erwin von Steinbach, the architect of the Strasbourg Cathedral, who holds the sketch of a Gothic edifice in front of the pontiff and a bishop (the latter representing the ecclesial figure usually responsible for cathedral building). The master of the competing classical style, Brunelleschi, somberly surveys the sketch as he stands behind the pope. The head of Bramante, wedged between episcopal miter and papal tiara, engages itself in dialogue with two medieval German architects, one of whom sports a black cap and represents the anonymous builder of the cathedral of Ulm.

Is that a princely Medici patron standing behind the figure of the emperor? Overbeck does not identify the distinguished person, but his coupling of figures from north and south has now become customary in his schema of cultural and religious unity. The left side of the painting's foreground is devoted to sculpture, and Nicola Pisano is seen bending over and pointing out to his students the details of a bas-relief decorating the side of an ancient sarcophagus. The fact that the sarcophagus rests on the decapitated torso of an antique idol and that the bas-relief tells the story of the women on their way to the tomb of the resurrected Christ is a not-so-subtle statement that Christianity may have initially adopted the forms of the pagan ancient world from which it sprang, but it quickly harnessed those forms in the service of the Gospel. Overbeck compares this assimilation to ancient Israel emerging from the cultural bondage of its captors, taking the gold and silver vessels they had brought with them out of Egypt and melting them down in order to consecrate them anew to the service of the true God in his Temple. In the Christian tradition of sculpture, Overbeck places three masters next to the emperor: Lucas della Robbia, Lorenzo Ghiberti, and Paul Vischer, representing spirituality, beauty, and truth respectively. These are elements that Overbeck declares should never be missing in the work of a Christian artist.

Since even in Catholic countries monasticism came under attack in the mid-nineteenth century, Overbeck defiantly places two seated monks in the middle of the painting. They are looking at illuminated manuscripts, an art form that flourished in the quiet retreat of the cloister. The artist reminds his viewers to take a lesson from history and avoid the tumult of the world if the exercise of religious art is to gain new life. Only in solitude and prayerful silence can contemplation be experienced, and only through the fruits of contemplation can one hope to follow the path of the great masters who glorified religion and the Church with their God-given talent.

riedrich Overbeck's pictorial manifesto uses the memory of a glorious past to offer fresh impetus and hope to young artists desirous of renewing the cultural traditions of Christianity in a world grown hostile to it. He enthrones the Virgin Mary as a mentor and a model, so that those seeking guidance and inspiration may not stray far from the very heartbeat of their Savior.

In a visual footnote both discreet and humble, Overbeck painted his own face behind that of Dante's, and he included the portraits of two other Nazarenes to his right (from the left: Peter Cornelius and Philipp Veit). His intended message becomes clear: if one would be numbered among the worthies who have glorified religion in the arts, one must not only cultivate their skill but also rediscover and reverence the underlying Spirit that generates the good, the true, and the beautiful.